Drawing Lessons for Beginners

CUTE ANIMALS

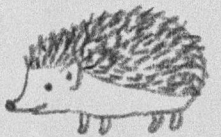

Quarto.com

© 2019 Ai Akikusa / PIE International
English edition © 2021 Quarto Publishing Group USA Inc

English edition first published in 2021 by Quarry Books, an imprint of The Quarto Group,
100 Cummings Center, Suite 265-D, Beverly, MA 01915, USA.
T (978) 282-9590 F (978) 283-2742

Quarry Books titles are also available at discount for retail, wholesale, promotional, and bulk purchase. For details, contact the Special Sales Manager by email at specialsales@quarto.com or by mail at The Quarto Group, Attn: Special Sales Manager, 100 Cummings Center, Suite 265-D, Beverly, MA 01915, USA.

ISBN: 978-0-7603-7220-3

Library of Congress Cataloging-in-Publication Data is available.

PIE International

Originally published in Japan by PIE International
Under the title どうぶつのかたち練習帖 (*Doubutsu no Katachi Rensyu Cyou*)
Japanese ISBN: 978-4-7562-5158-9 C0071

Designed by Mayuko Watanabe (Oshidori)
Edited by Kayako Nezu
Written and illustrated by Ai Akikusa

Drawing Lessons for Beginners

CUTE ANIMALS

Learn to draw animals
Start with basic shapes, then make them cute!

AI AKIKUSA

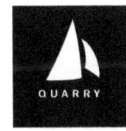

CONTENTS

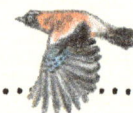

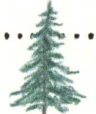

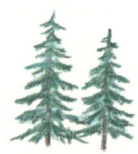

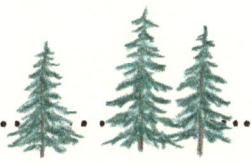

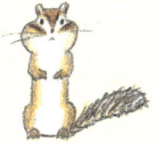

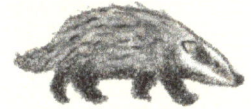

INTRODUCTION

When you look at the shapes of animals, there are bumps and curves in unexpected areas.

Animals are built differently from one another—some can run faster, some can eat more easily, and some can swim better. It can be interesting to draw animals when you look closely at these kinds of characteristics.

I'd like you to enjoy observing the characteristics of these animals rather than copying the examples. Then, you'll eventually notice the unique aspects of each animal.

As you get used to drawing animals, you can try drawing different motions or positions such as running or sleeping, or you can even try drawing the animal upright.

ANIMAL BODIES

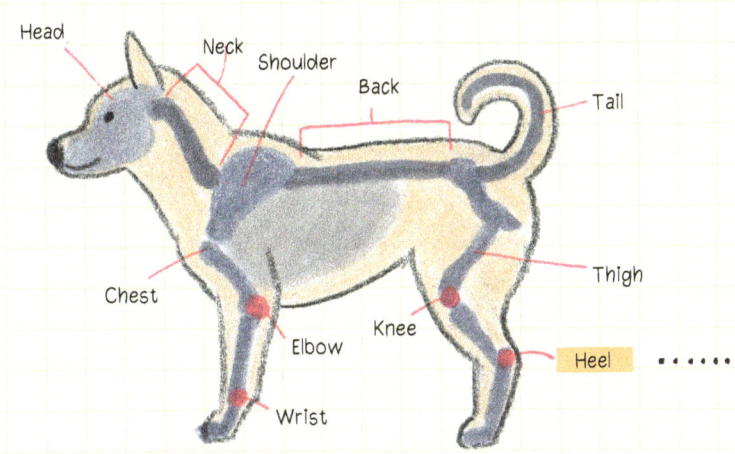

Head
Neck
Shoulder
Back
Tail
Chest
Elbow
Knee
Thigh
Wrist
Heel

Animal heels

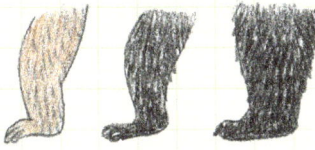

Many animals have paws shaped like they are tiptoeing because their heels do not touch the ground, but there are also some whose heels do touch the ground.

Monkey   Red panda   Bear

Animals whose heels touch the ground can easily stand up on two legs.

There are many kinds of hooves and paws.

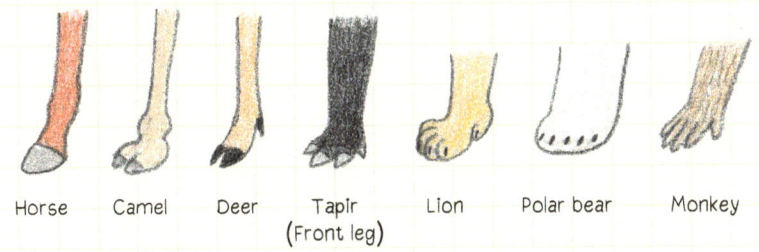

Horse   Camel   Deer   Tapir (Front leg)   Lion   Polar bear   Monkey

ANIMAL FACES

Eye location

Mostly seen in carnivores, forward-facing eyes can help animals locate prey.

Eyes on the sides of animals' heads, which are mostly seen in herbivores, have wider peripheral vision so that the animals can spot predators.

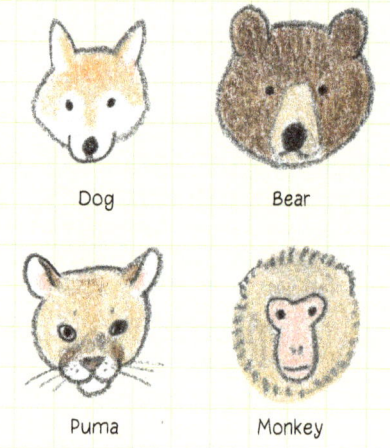

Dog   Bear

Puma   Monkey

Both eyes are located on the front of the face.

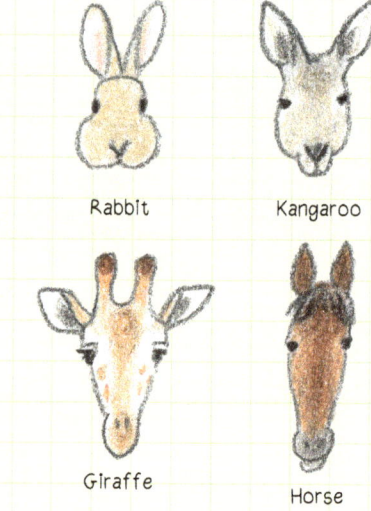

Rabbit   Kangaroo

Giraffe   Horse

Eyes are attached to the sides of the face.

Upper face shapes

Curved faces

Cats' noses don't stick out as much as monkeys' noses.

Otters have flatter noses and heads than the other animals.

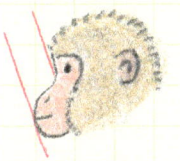
Monkey

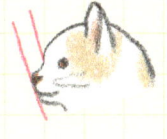
Cat

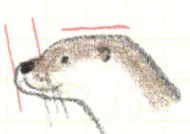
River otter

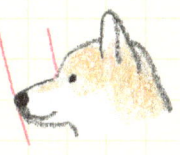
Dog

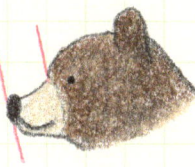
Bear

Straight faces

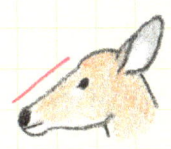
Deer

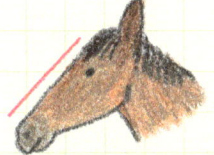
Horse

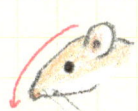
Mouse

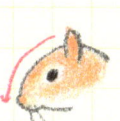
Chipmunk

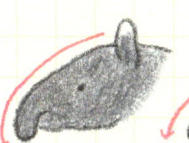
Tapir

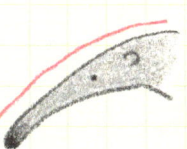
Anteater

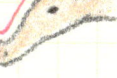
Aardvark

The deer's face is one of the straightest of all these animals.

DRAWING BALANCED BODIES

When you look at the shape of animal bodies, capture the balance of the three sections: head, body, and legs.

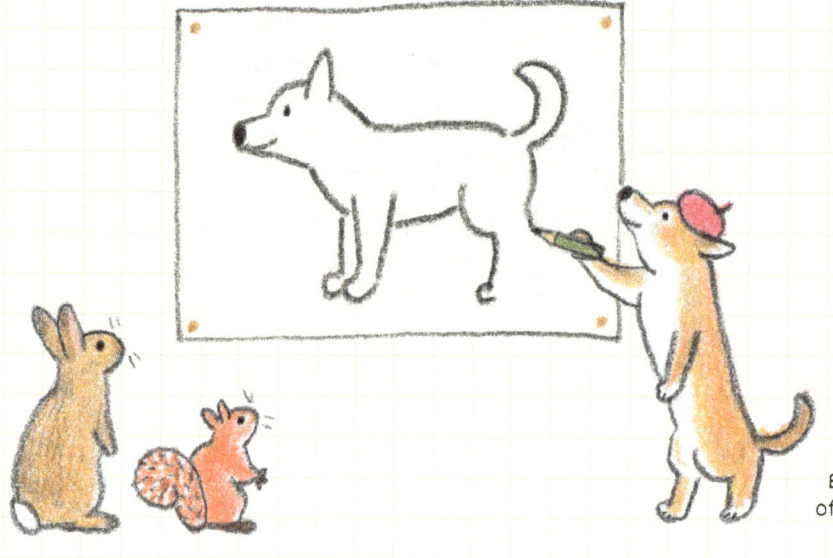

Let's use dogs as an example. Drawing dogs is a great way to learn how to balance body parts because they have various head, body, and leg shapes.

Being able to capture the balance of the three parts in dogs is useful for drawing other animals.

Front view

There are so many different types of dogs. Some have wide bodies,
faces, or shoulders, and others have narrow bodies, faces, or shoulders.

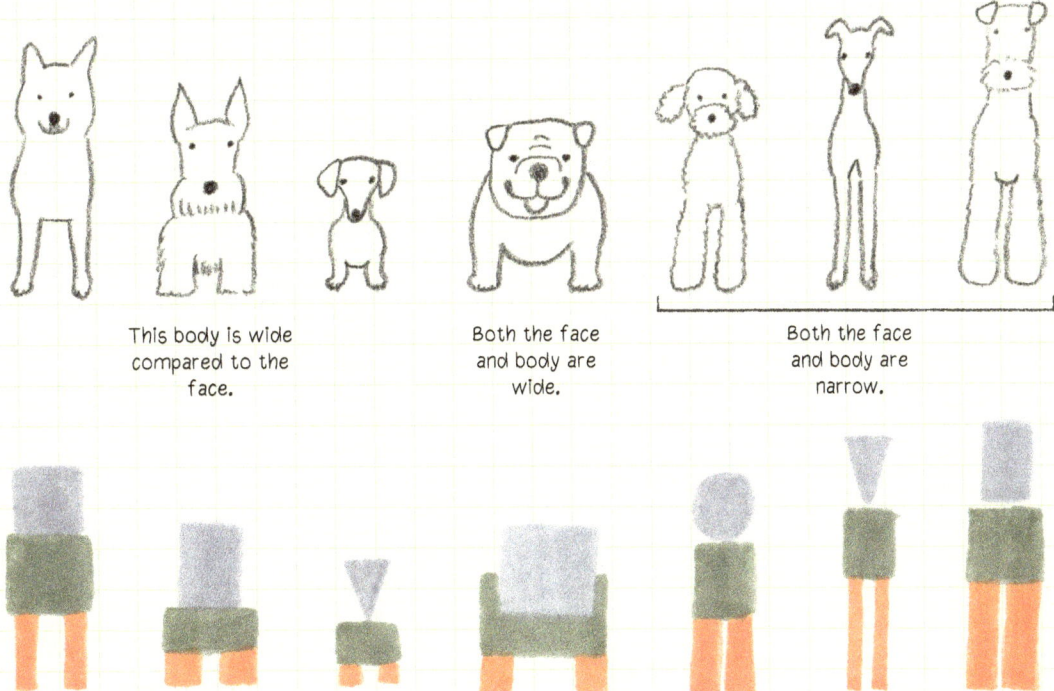

This body is wide
compared to the
face.

Both the face
and body are
wide.

Both the face
and body are
narrow.

From the side

Let's look at balancing of the length of the body and the legs.

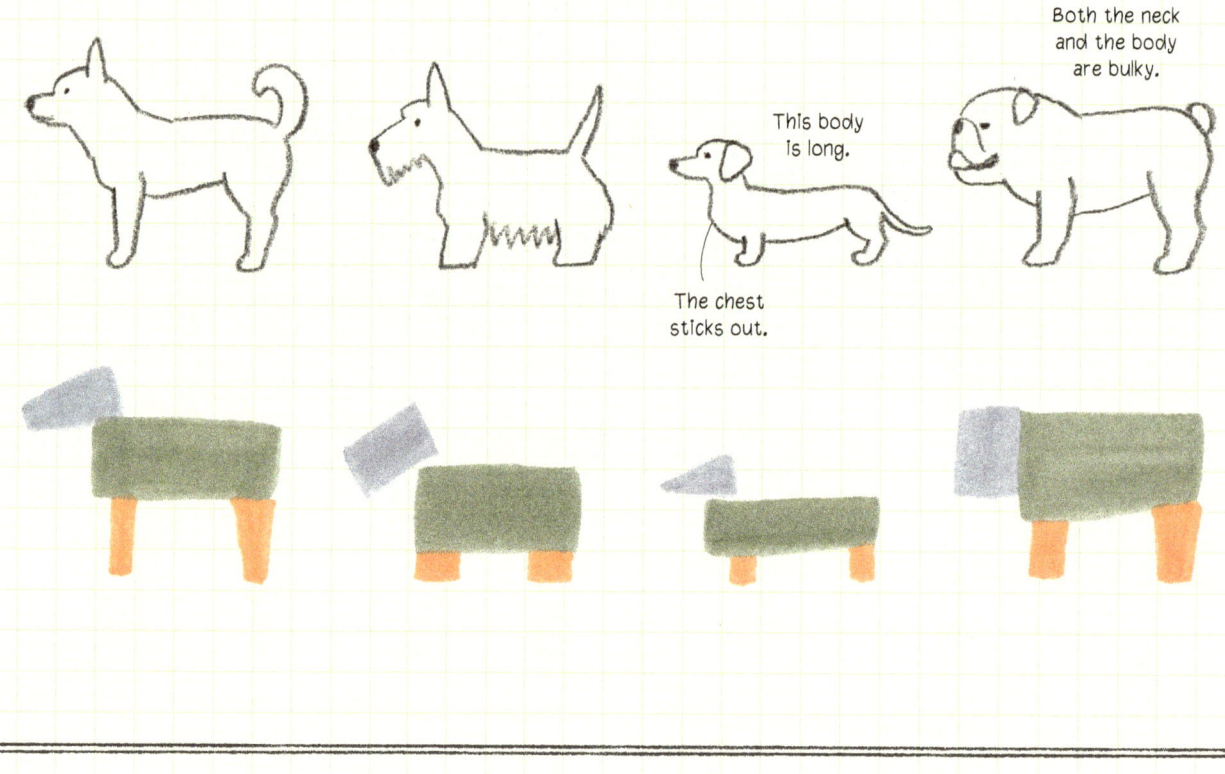

This body is long.

The chest sticks out.

Both the neck and the body are bulky.

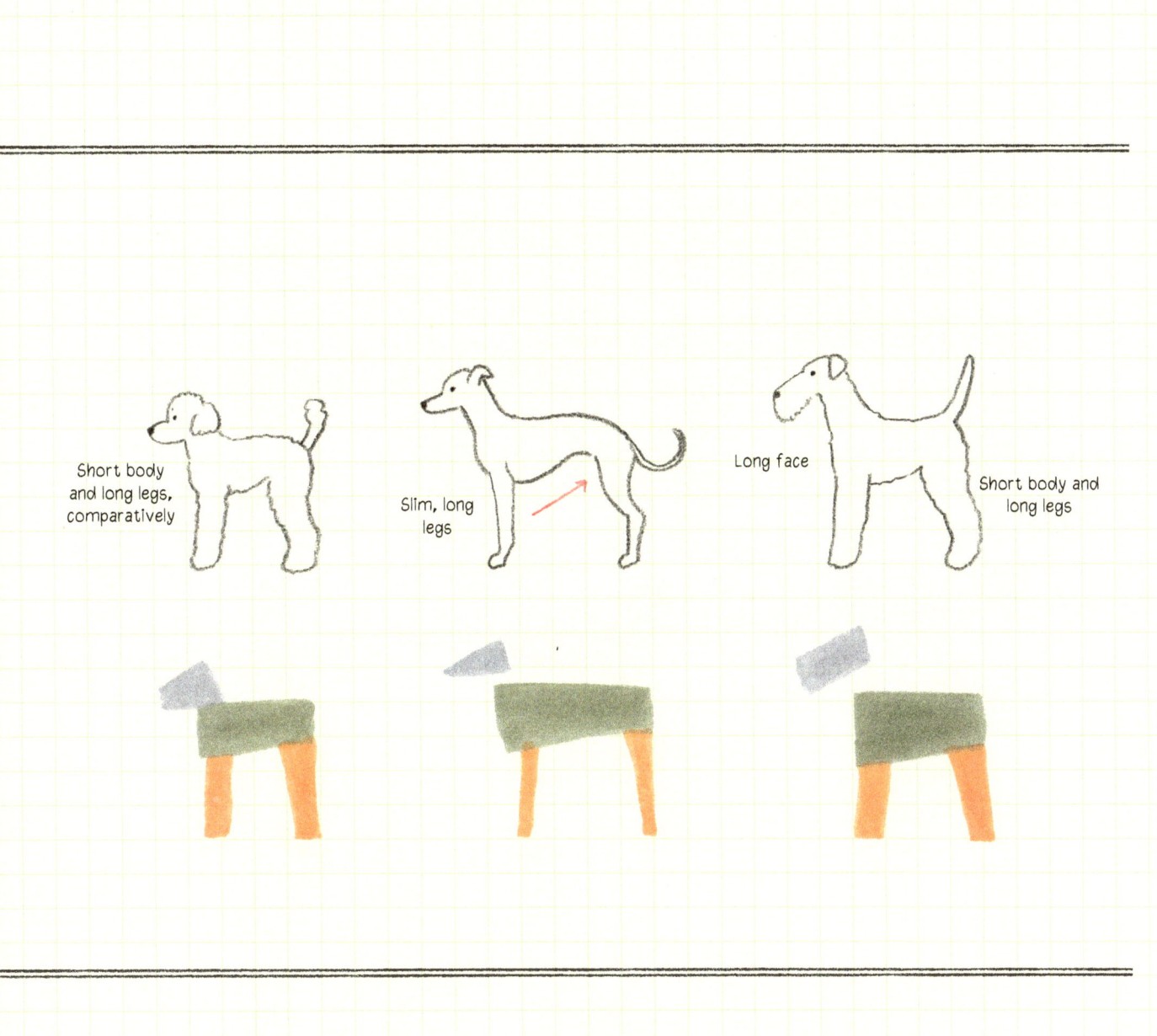

Short body
and long legs,
comparatively

Slim, long
legs

Long face

Short body and
long legs

FACIAL BALANCE

Let's look at general face shapes, the distance between the eyes,
the distance between the eyes and nose, and more.

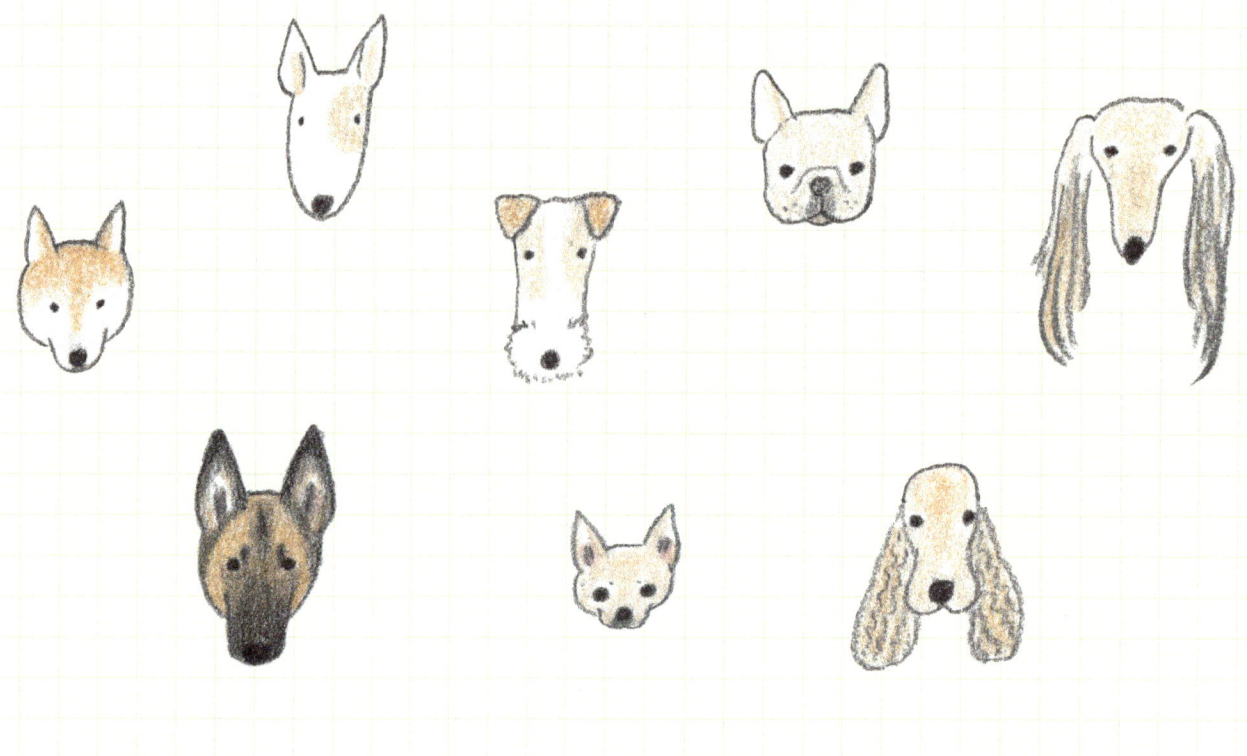

How deep is the curve from the forehead to the nose? How long is the nose?

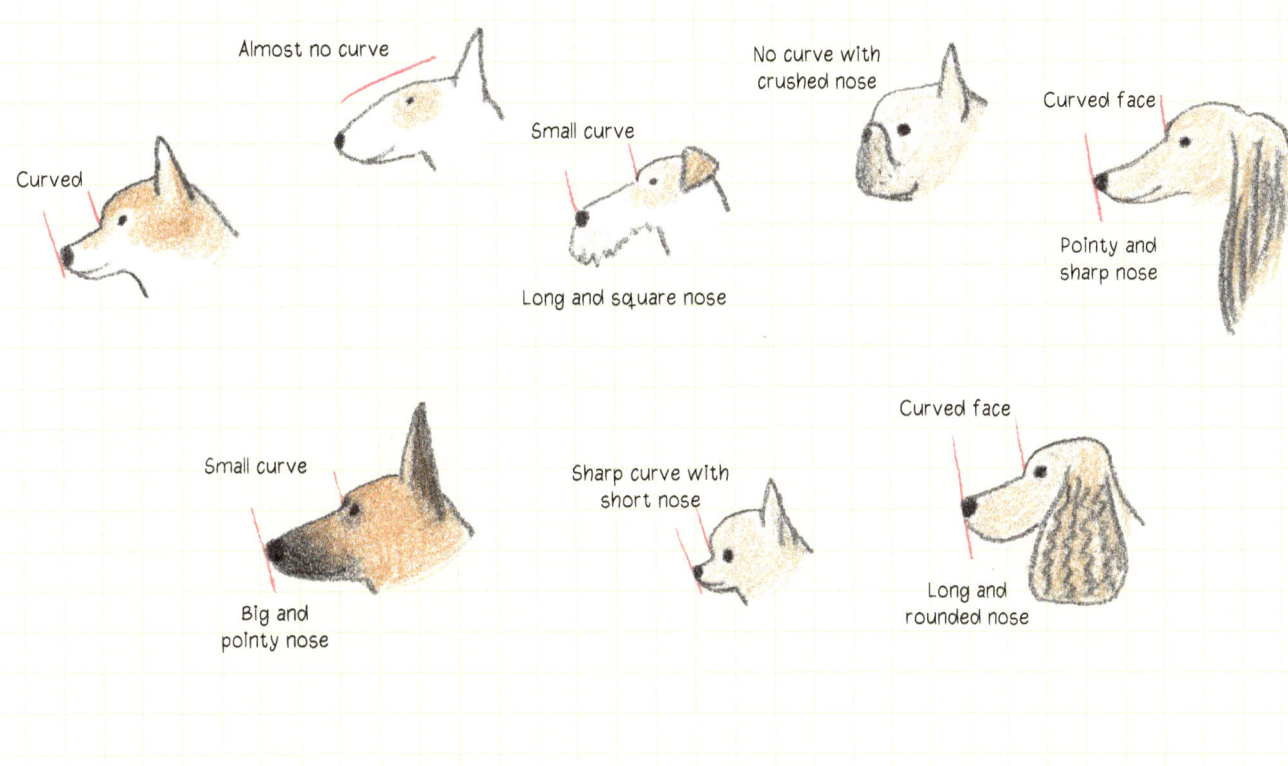

Curved

Almost no curve

Small curve

Long and square nose

No curve with crushed nose

Curved face

Pointy and sharp nose

Small curve

Big and pointy nose

Sharp curve with short nose

Curved face

Long and rounded nose

SHIBA INU

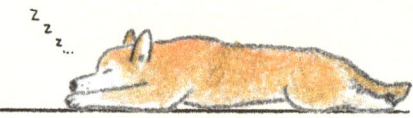

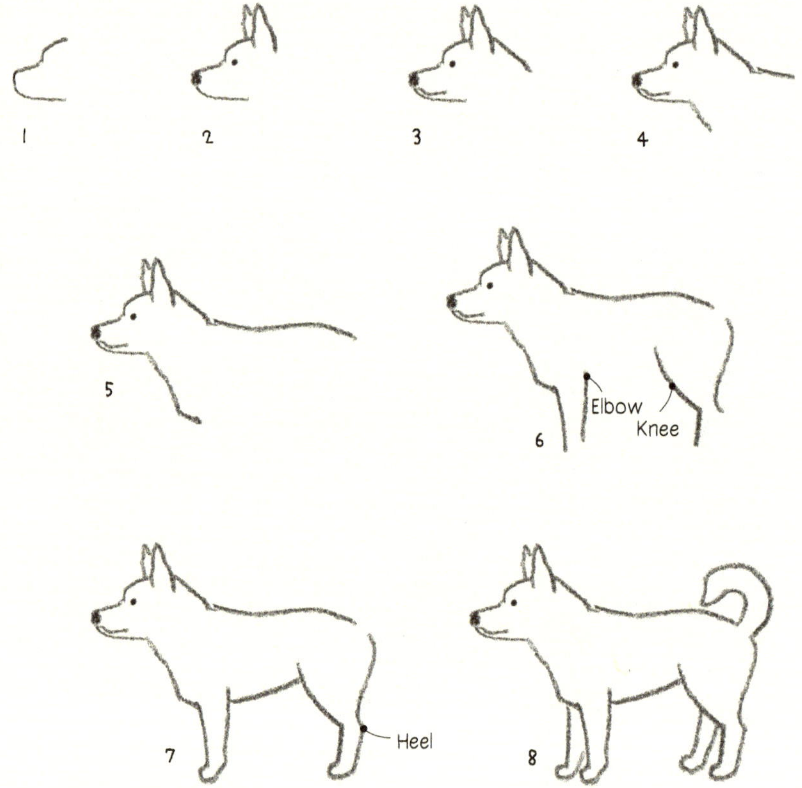

1

2

3

4

5

6   Elbow
     Knee

7   Heel

8

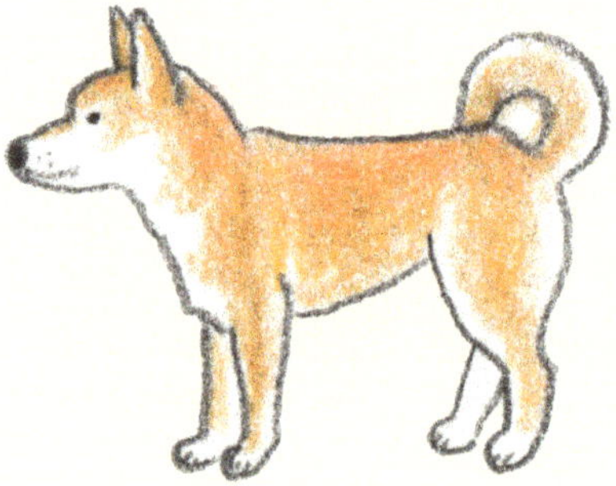

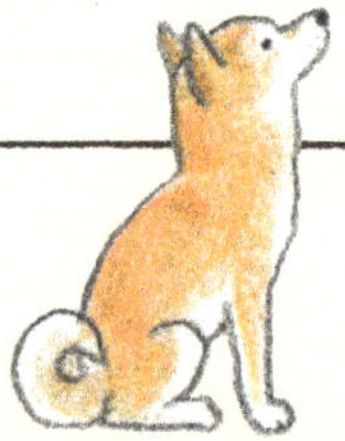

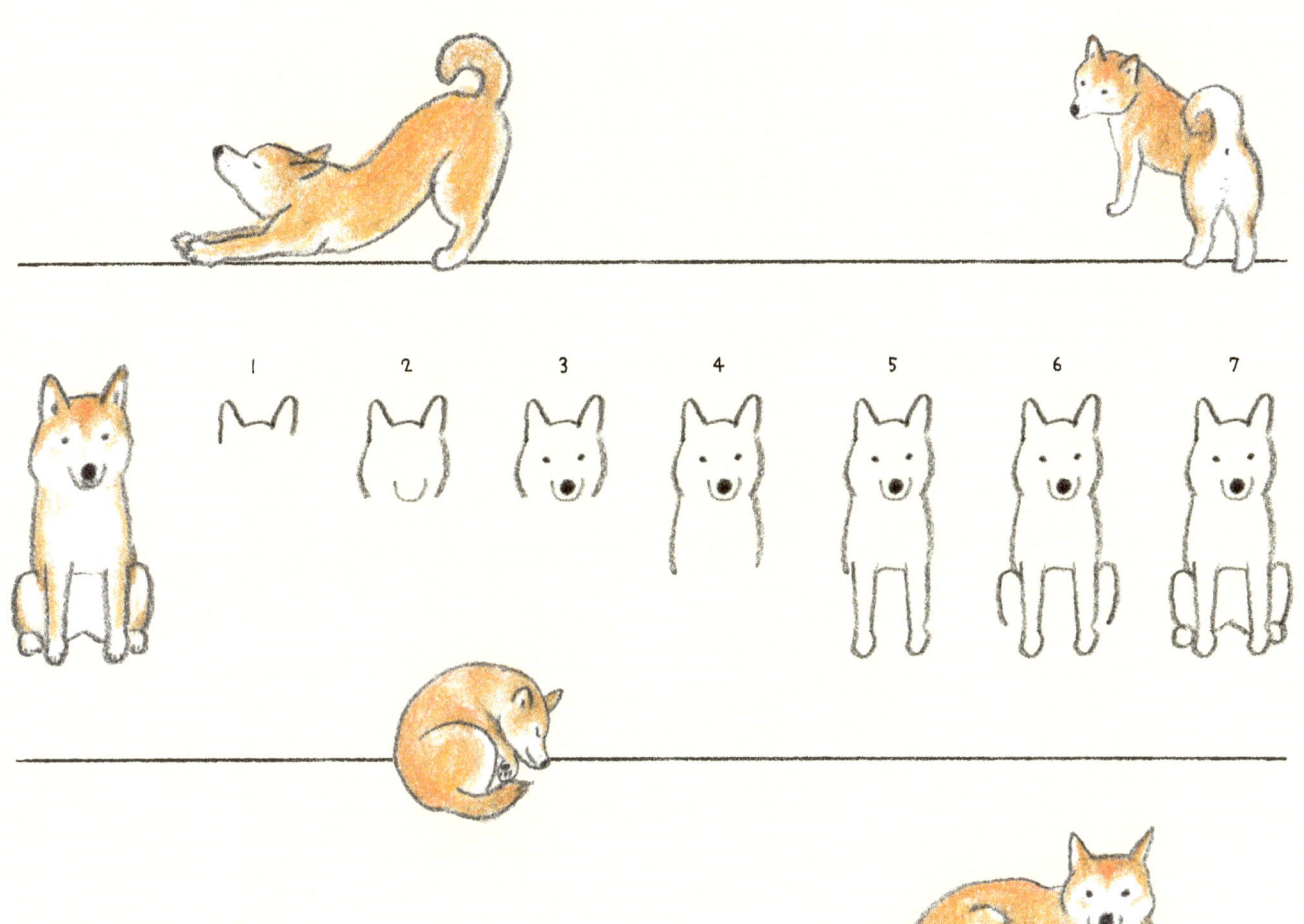

DIFFERENT KINDS OF DOGS

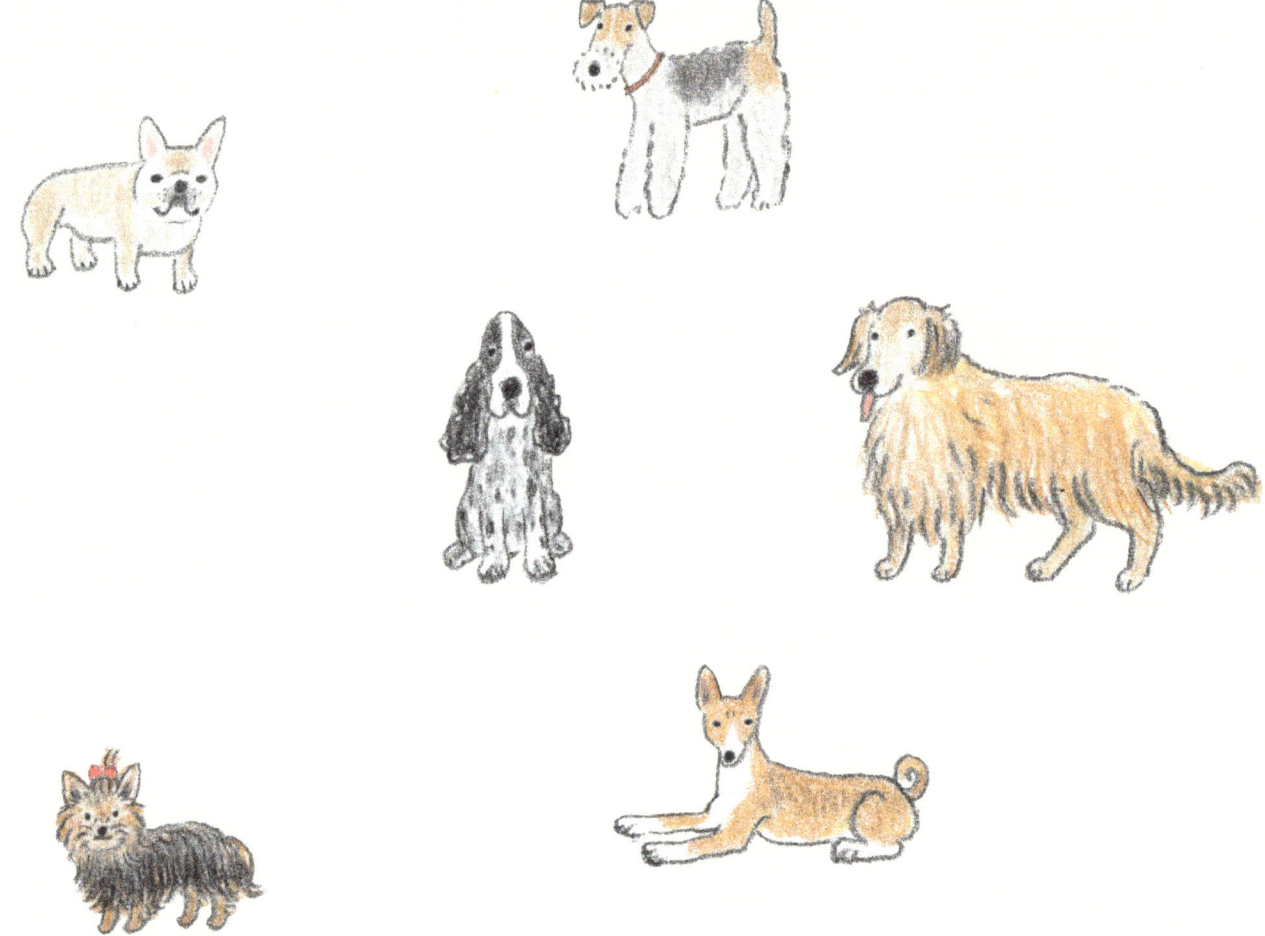

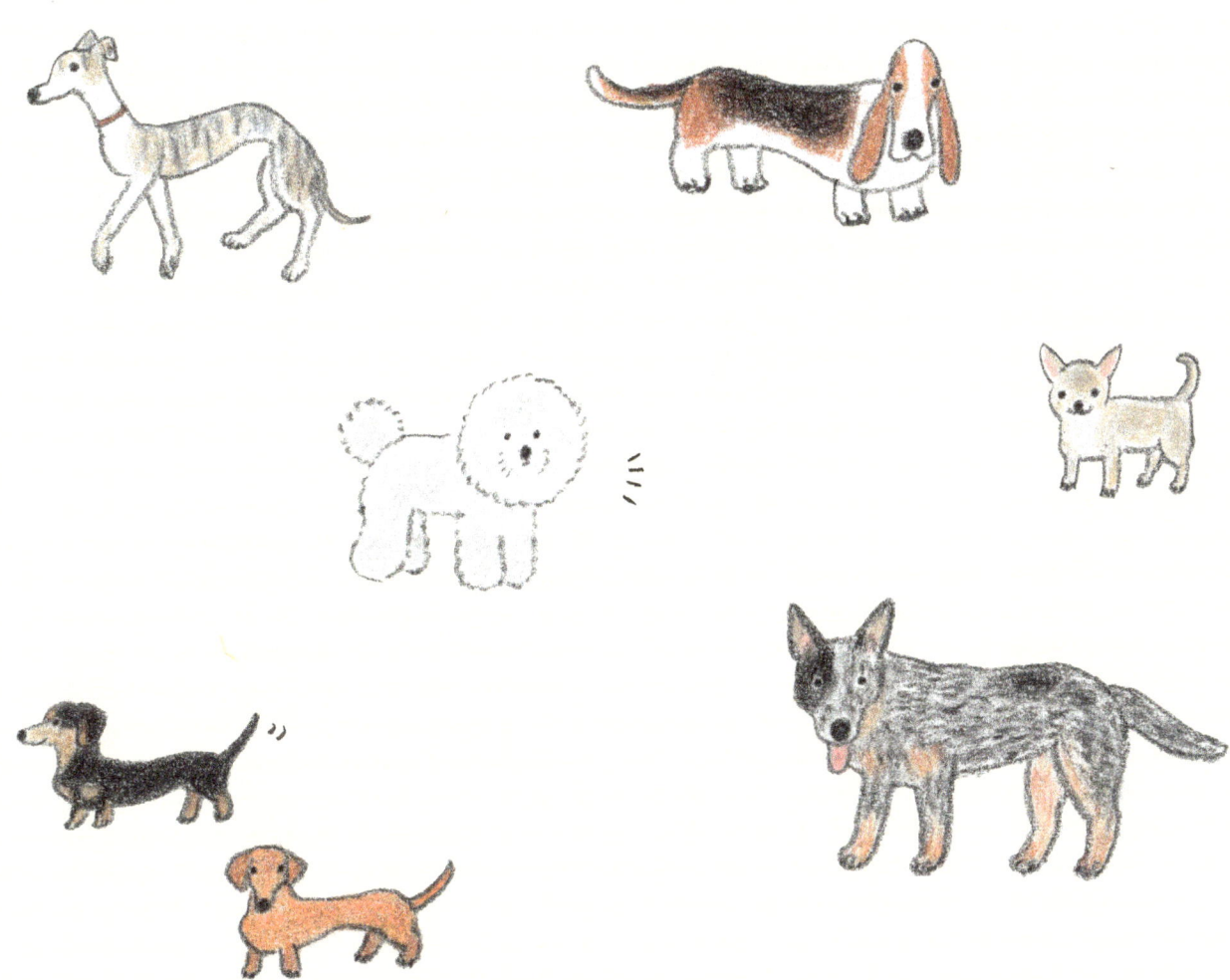

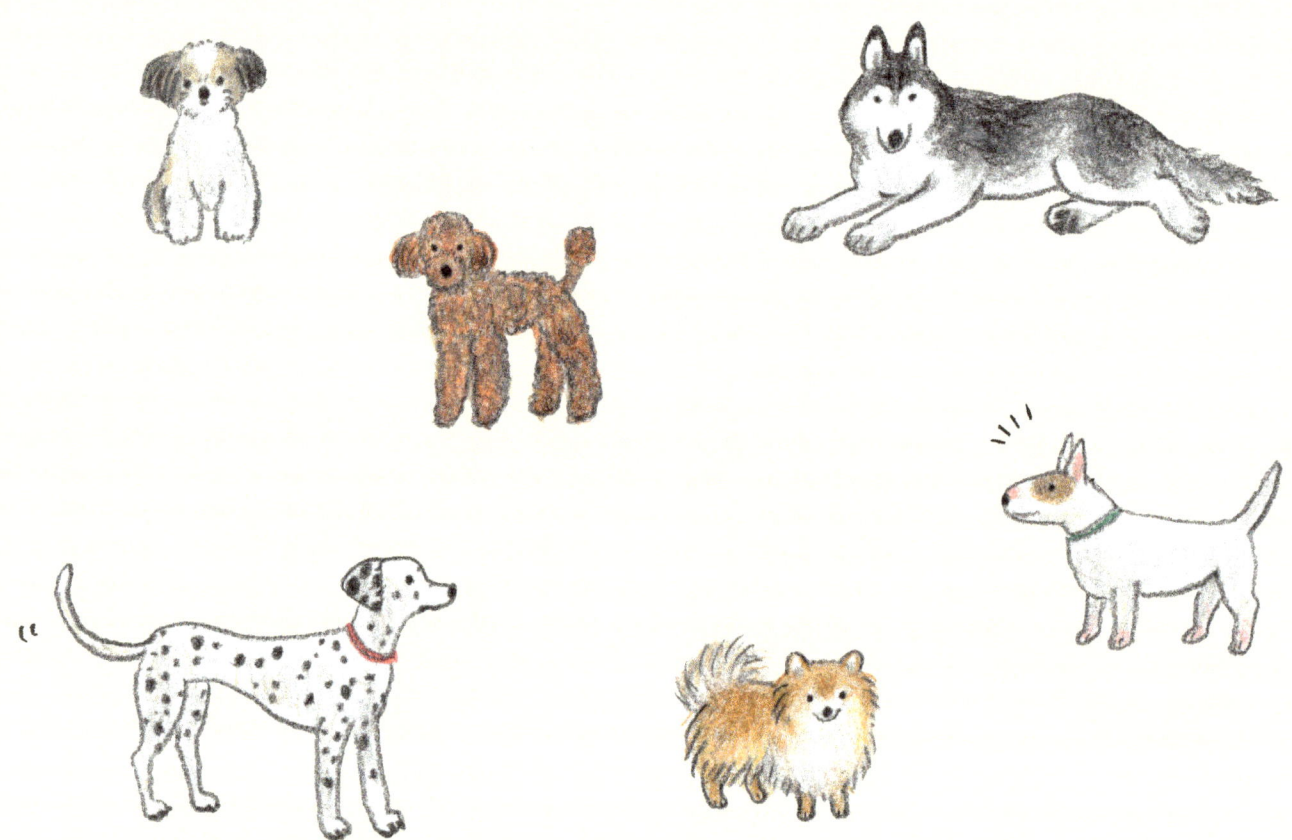

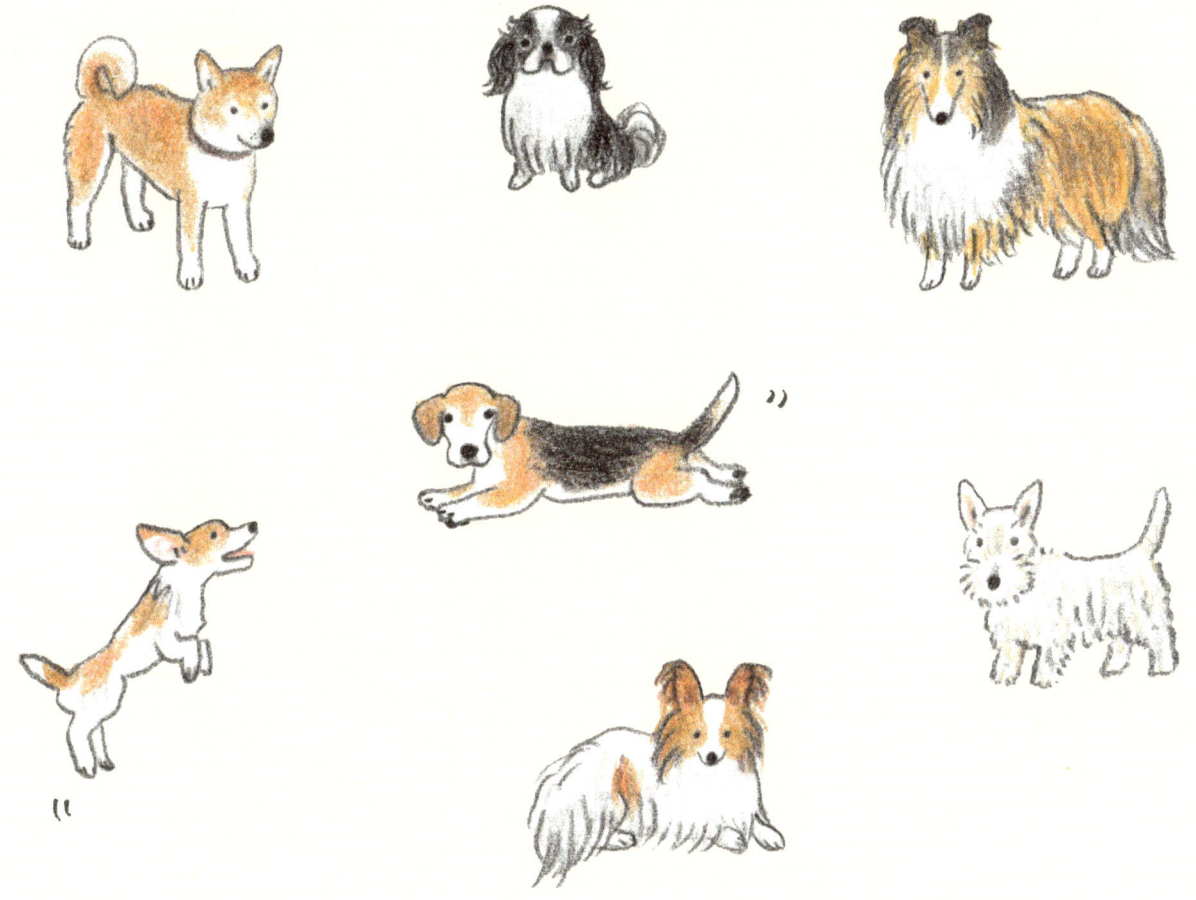

WOLF

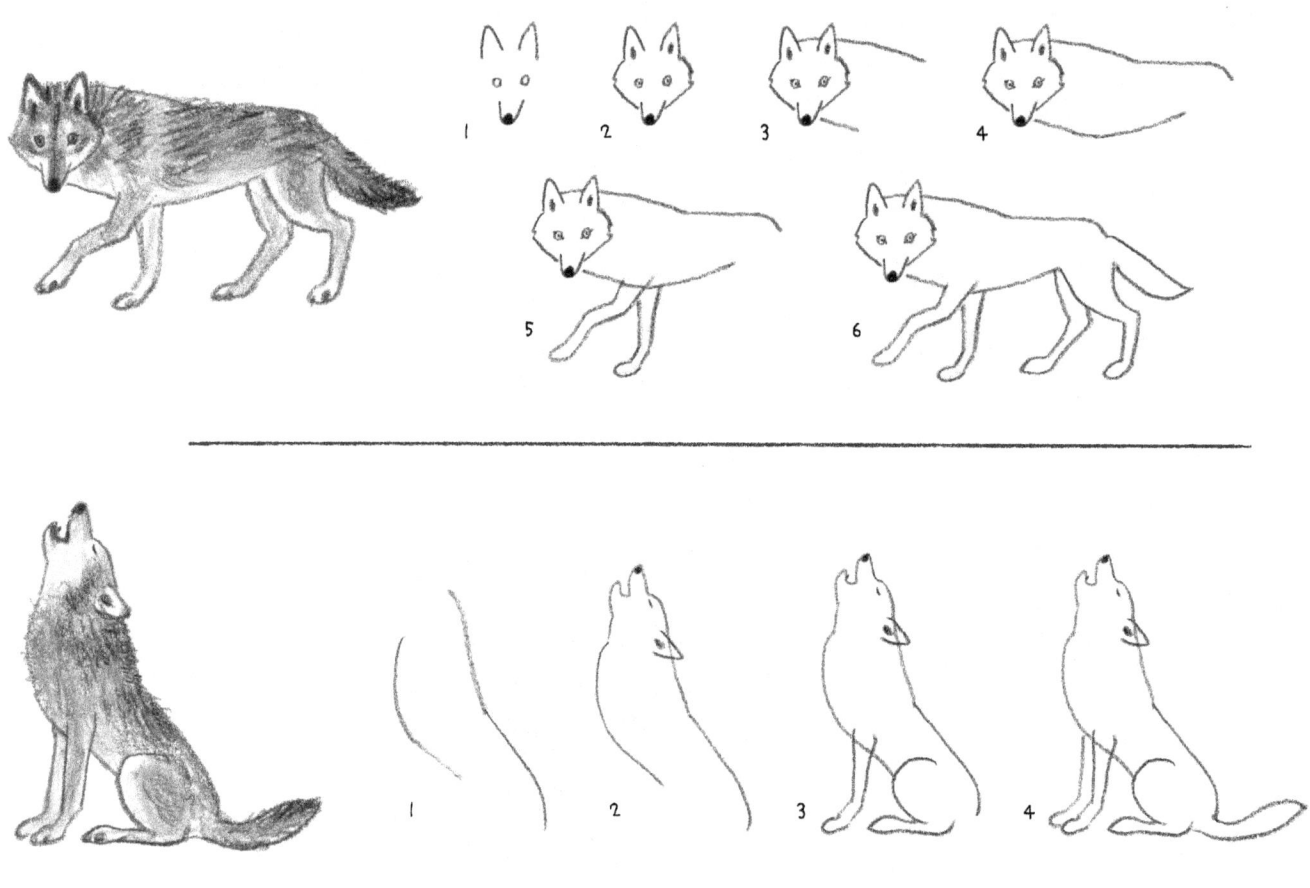

BLUE FOX

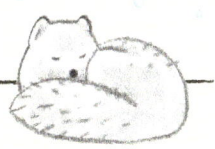

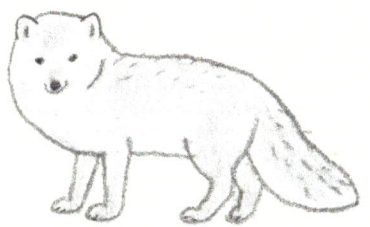

The winter coat is
pure white.

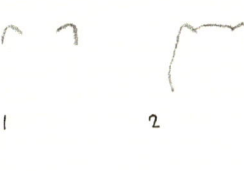

1

2

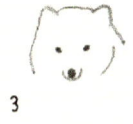

3

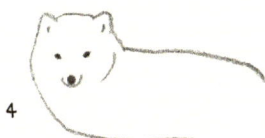

4

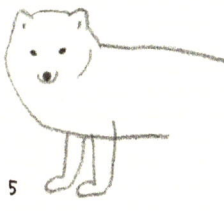

5

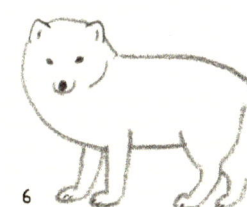

6

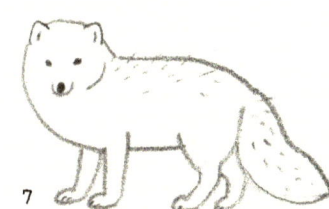

7

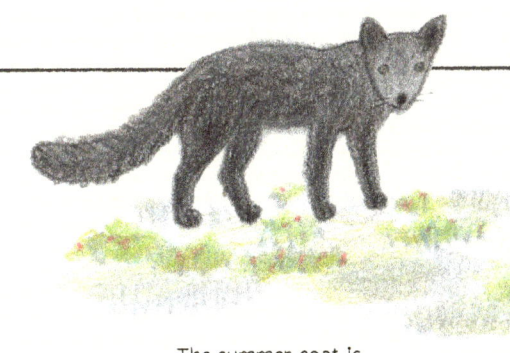

The summer coat is
short and silver.

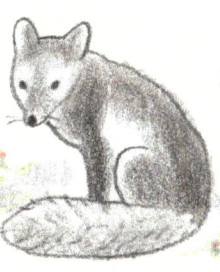

The intermediate coat
is between its summer
and winter coats.

FOX

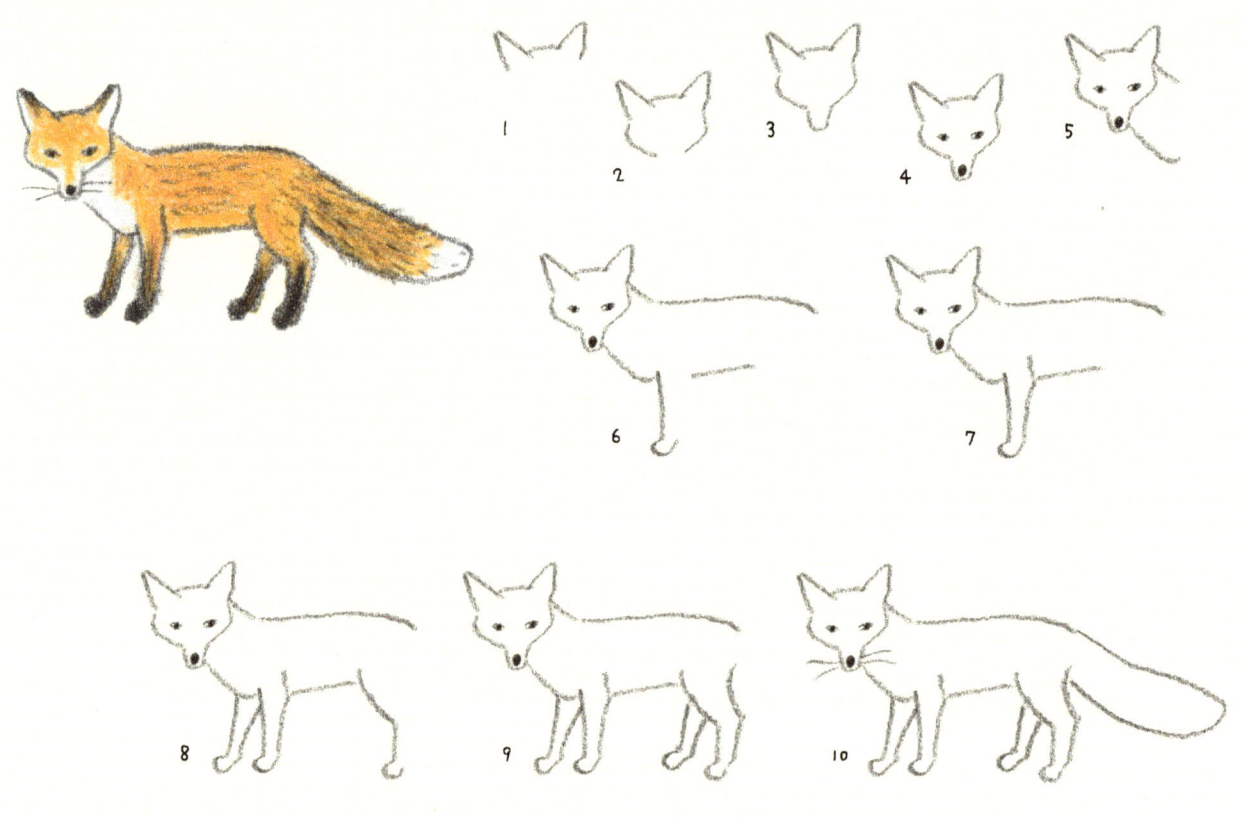

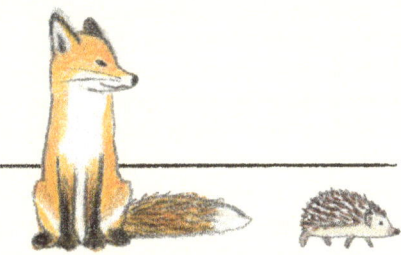

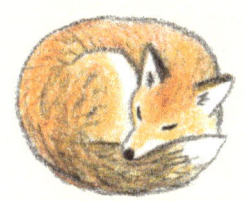

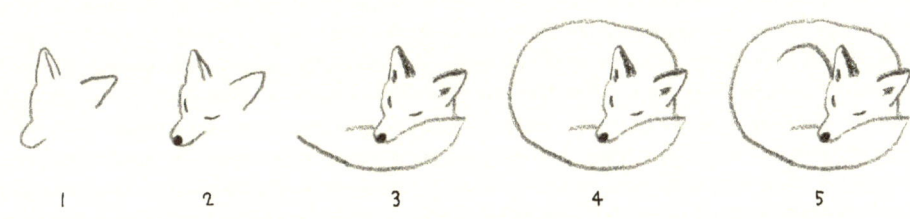

1 2 3 4 5

RACCOON DOG

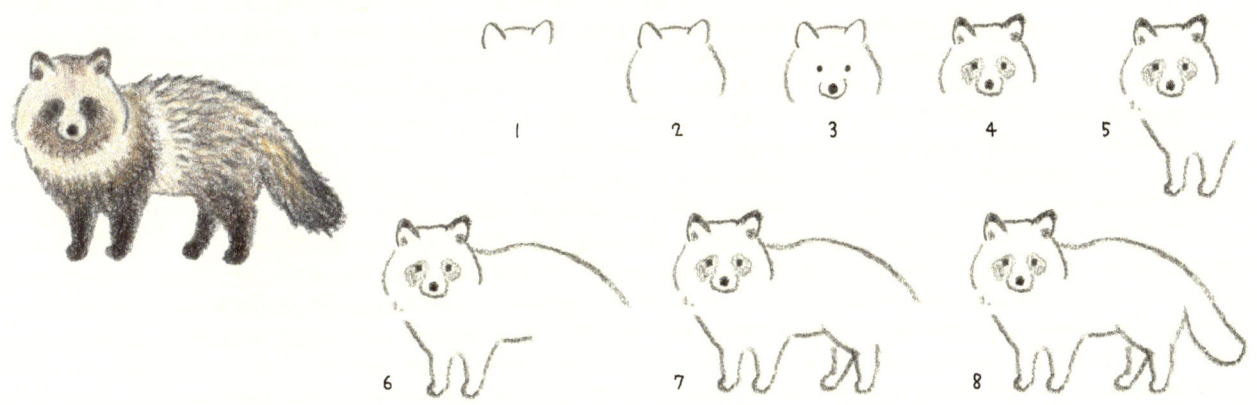

1 2 3 4 5

6 7 8

HEDGEHOG

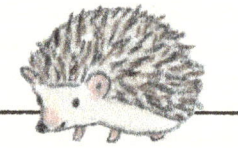

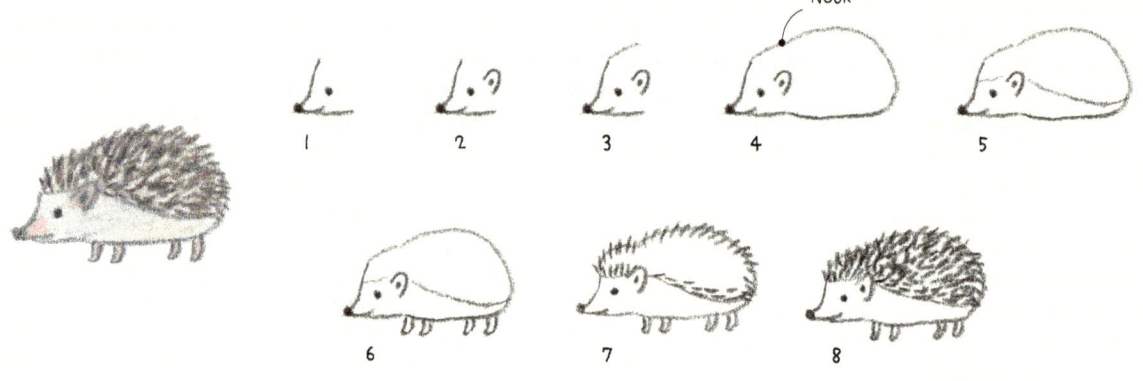

Neck

1 2 3 4 5

6 7 8

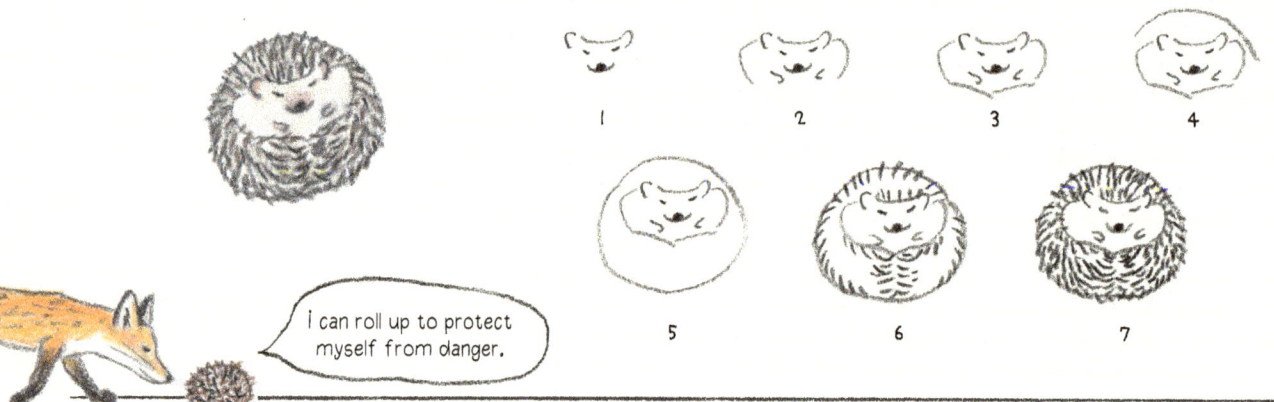

1 2 3 4

5 6 7

I can roll up to protect myself from danger.

FIELD MOUSE

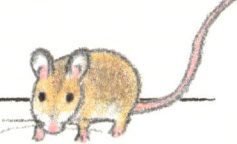

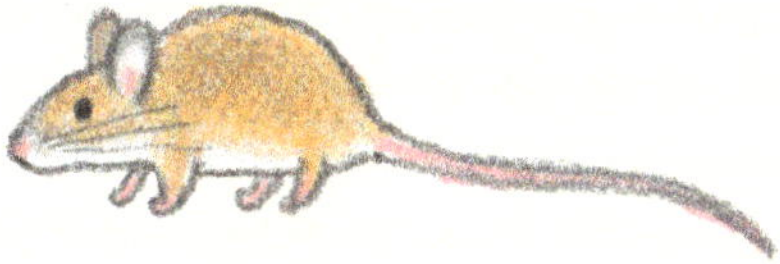

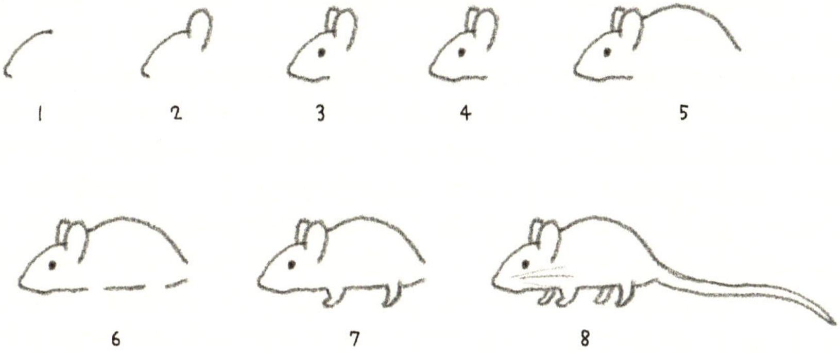

1

2

3

4

5

6

7

8

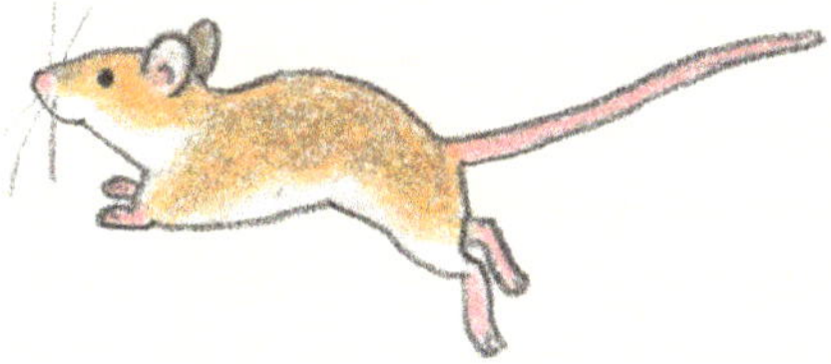

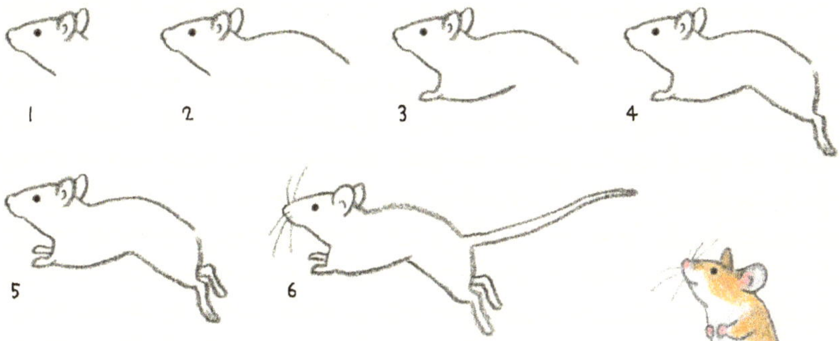

1

2

3

4

5

6

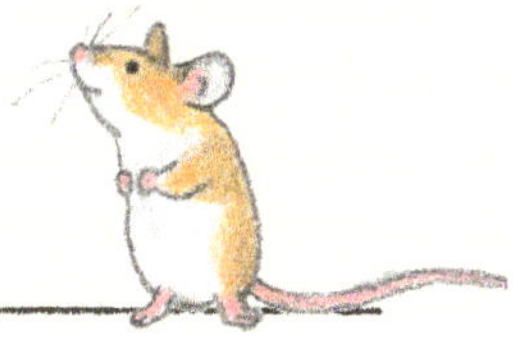

SQUIRREL

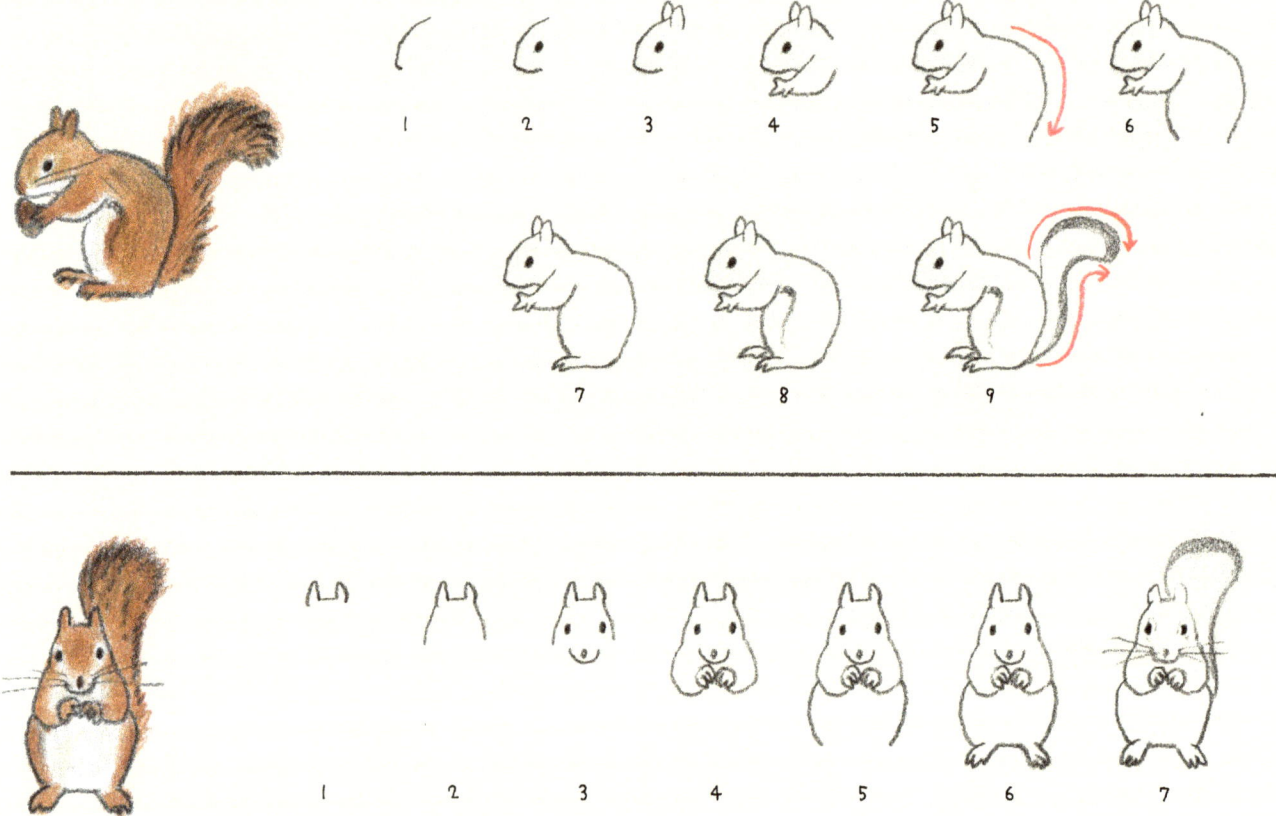

1 2 3 4 5 6

7 8 9

1 2 3 4 5 6 7

CHIPMUNK

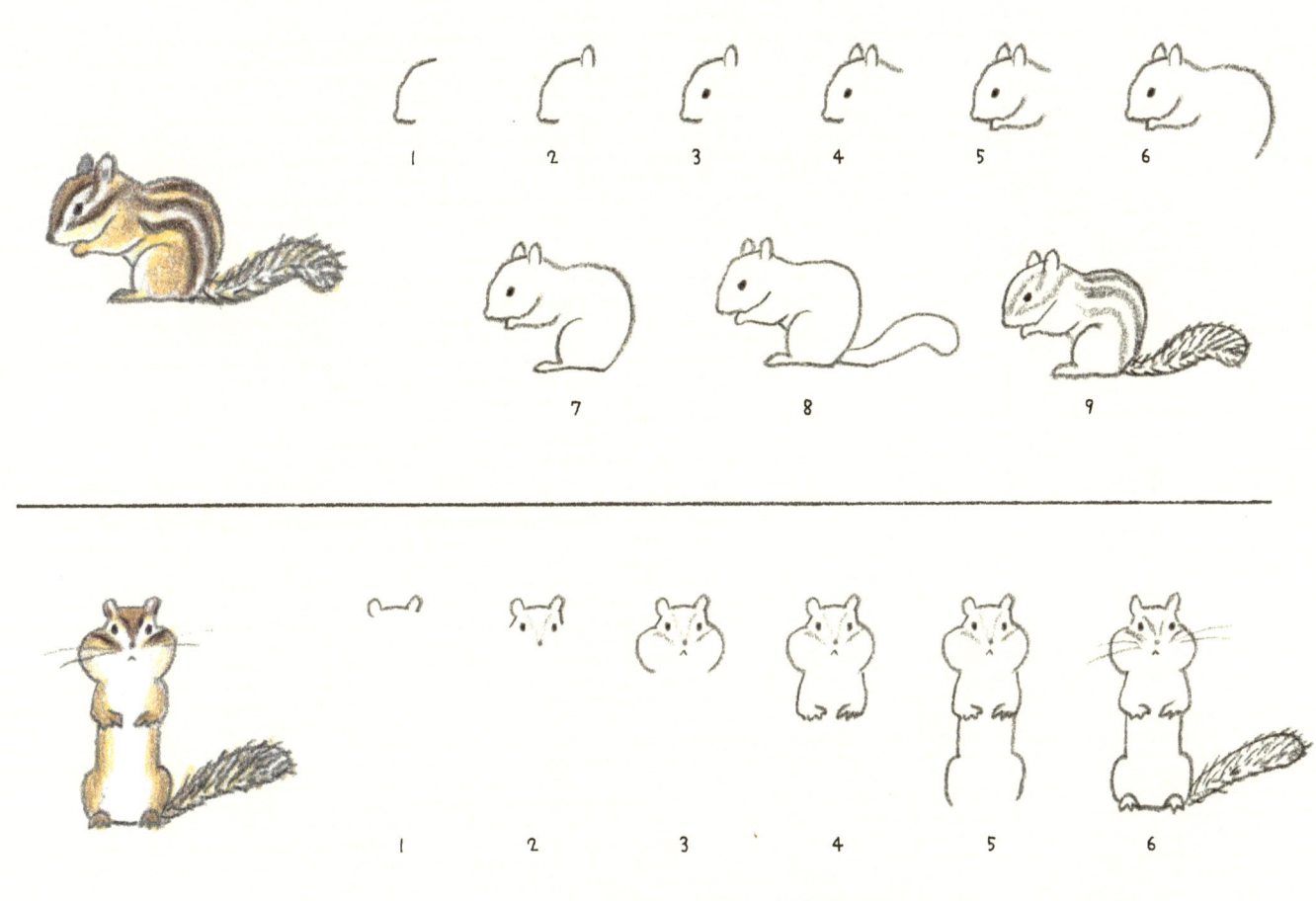

1
2
3
4
5
6

7
8
9

1
2
3
4
5
6

CAPYBARA

Capybaras are the biggest animal in the rodent family.

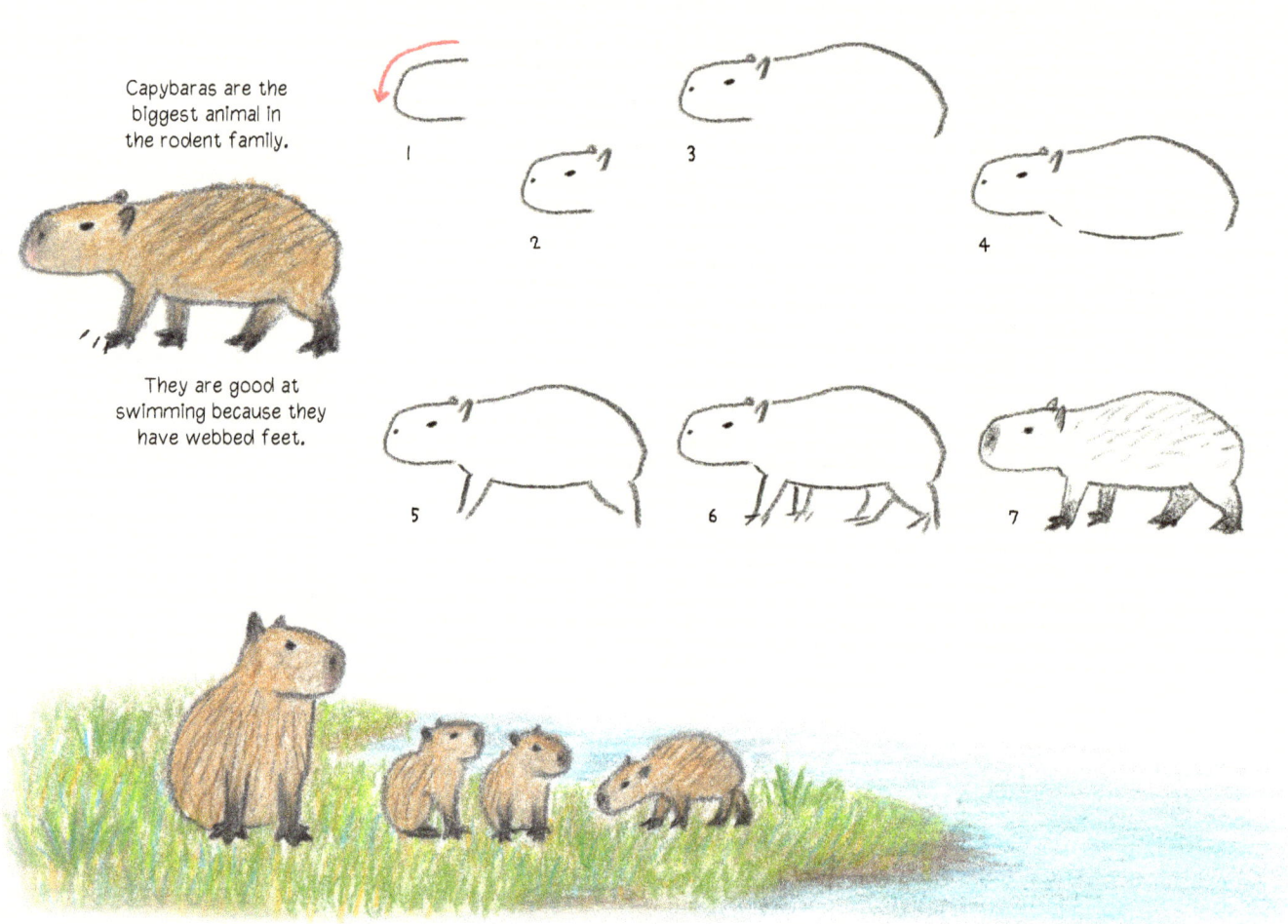

They are good at swimming because they have webbed feet.

1

2

3

4

5

6

7

They live on the waterfront and always stay in herds.

BEAVER

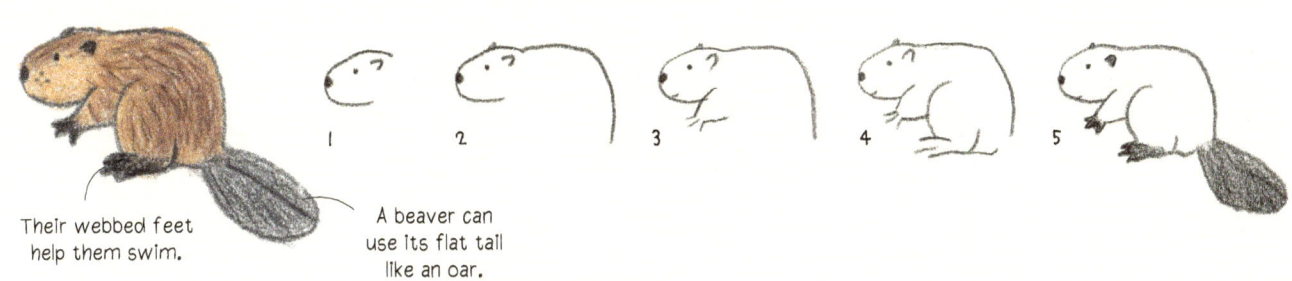

Their webbed feet help them swim.

A beaver can use its flat tail like an oar.

1 2 3 4 5

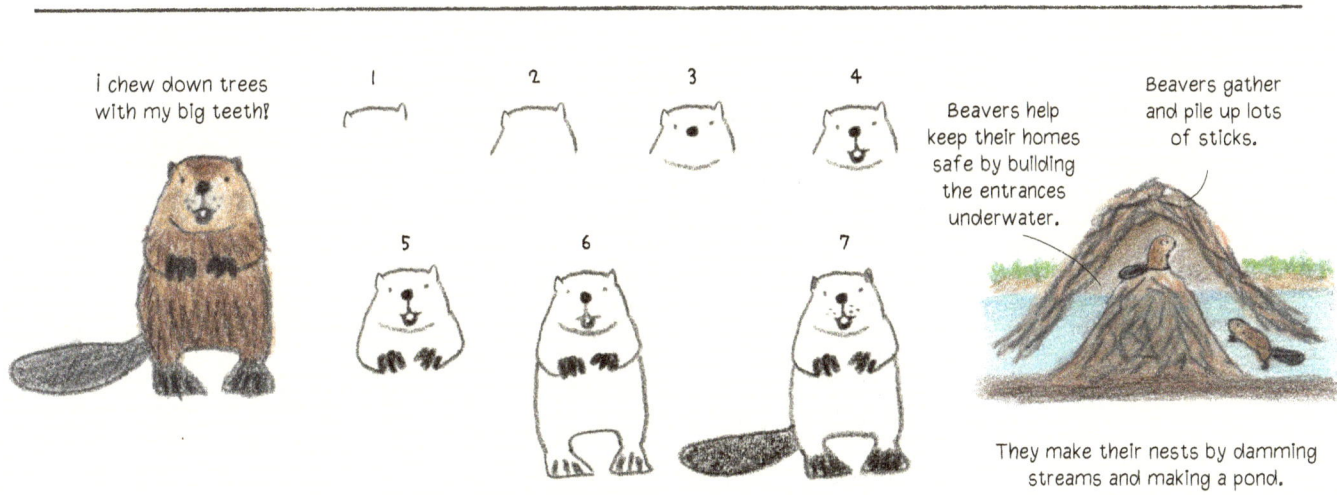

i chew down trees with my big teeth!

1 2 3 4

5 6 7

Beavers help keep their homes safe by building the entrances underwater.

Beavers gather and pile up lots of sticks.

They make their nests by damming streams and making a pond.

FLYING SQUIRREL

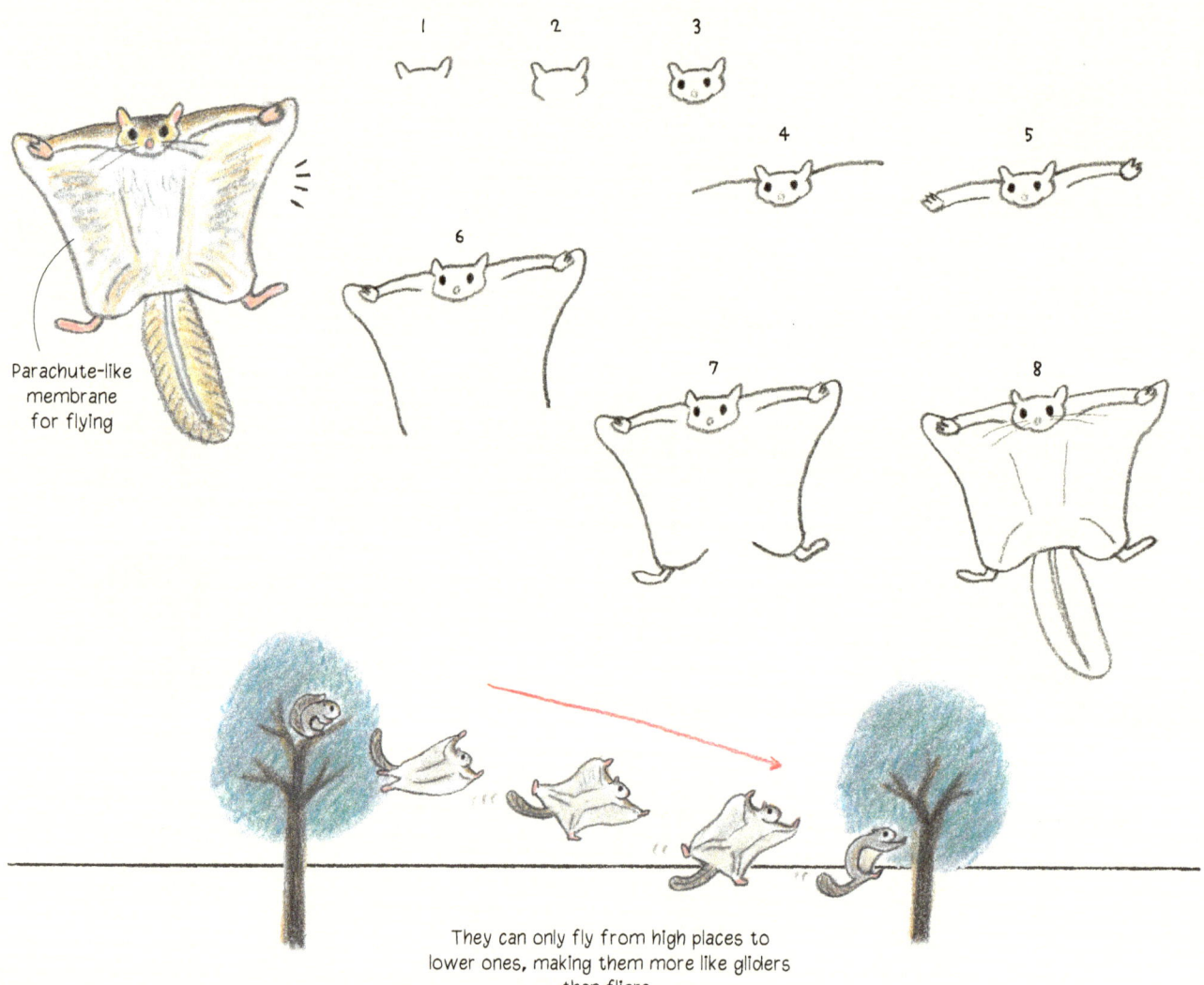

1

2

3

4

5

6

7

8

Parachute-like
membrane
for flying

They can only fly from high places to
lower ones, making them more like gliders
than fliers.

SKUNK

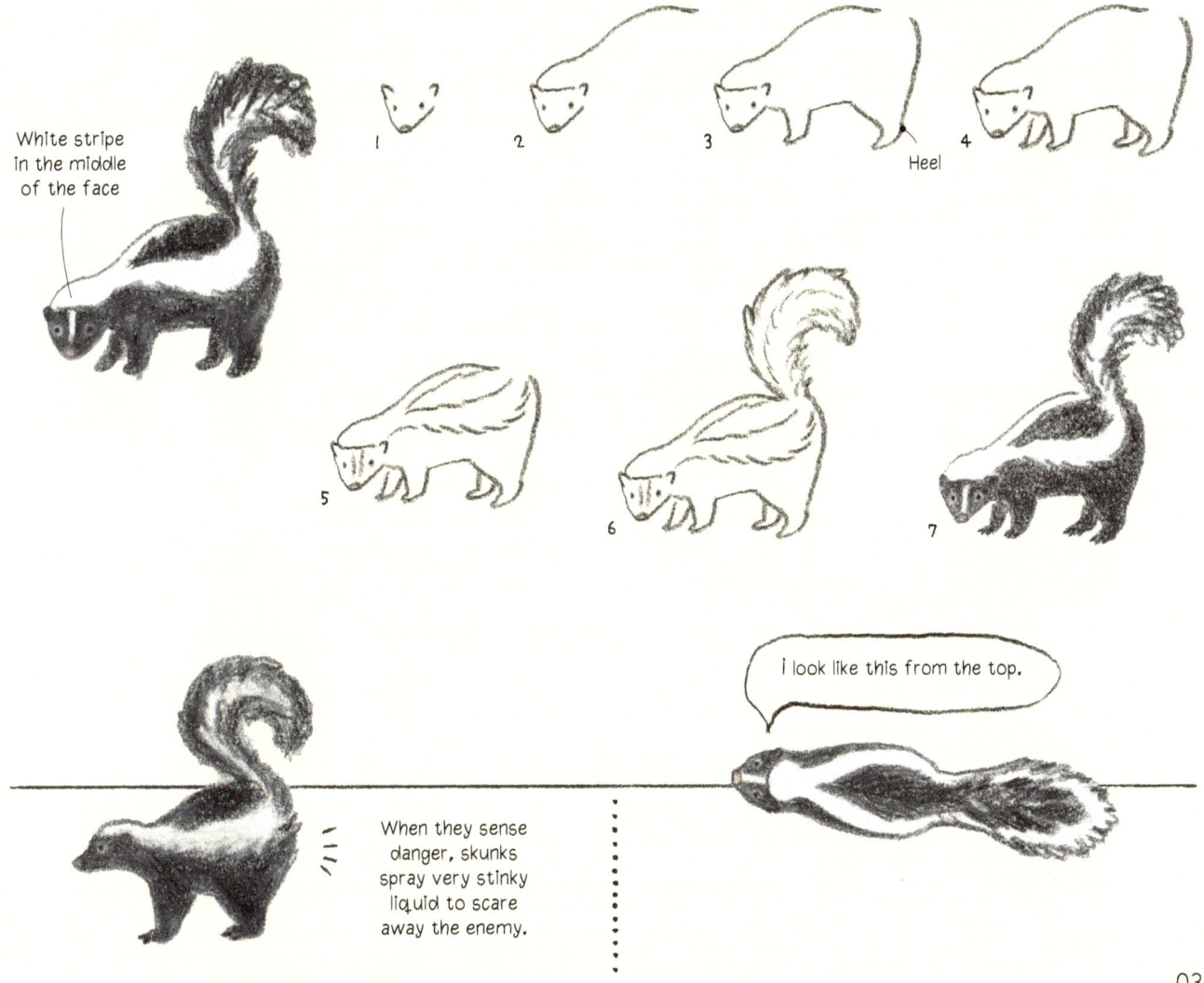

White stripe in the middle of the face

1
2
3
Heel
4
5
6
7

When they sense danger, skunks spray very stinky liquid to scare away the enemy.

I look like this from the top.

RABBIT

Rabbits have long ears that hear sounds well. The big ears have a lot of mobility, so rabbits can hear from many directions.

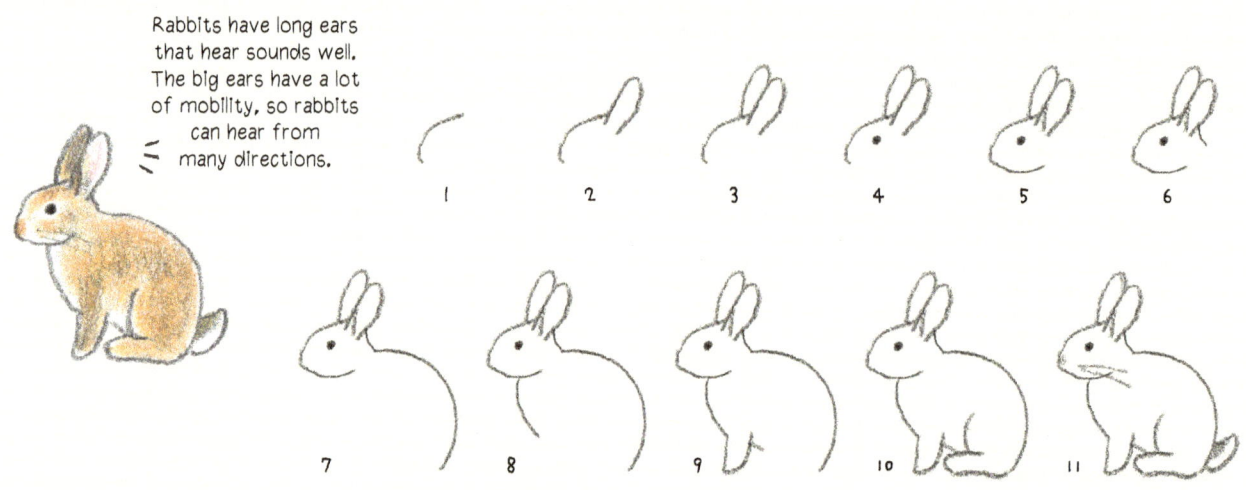

MOLE

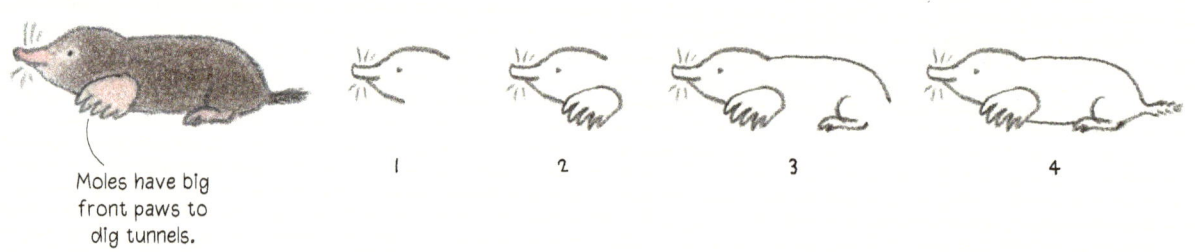

Moles have big front paws to dig tunnels.

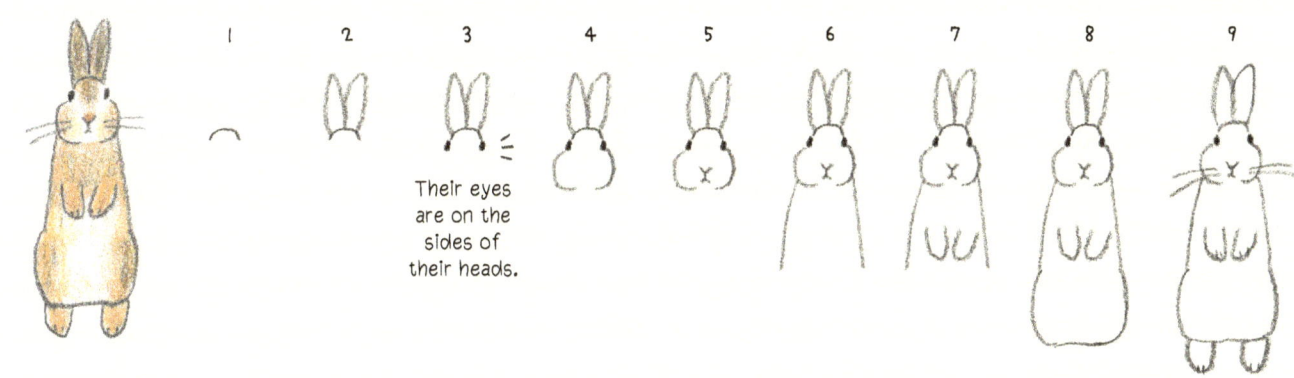

1   2   3   4   5   6   7   8   9

Their eyes
are on the
sides of
their heads.

JAPANESE DORMOUSE

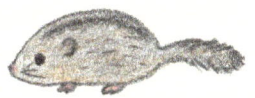

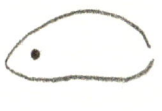

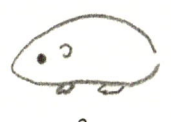

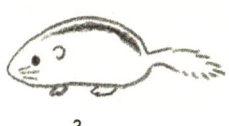

1   2   3

Rabbit Movements and Poses

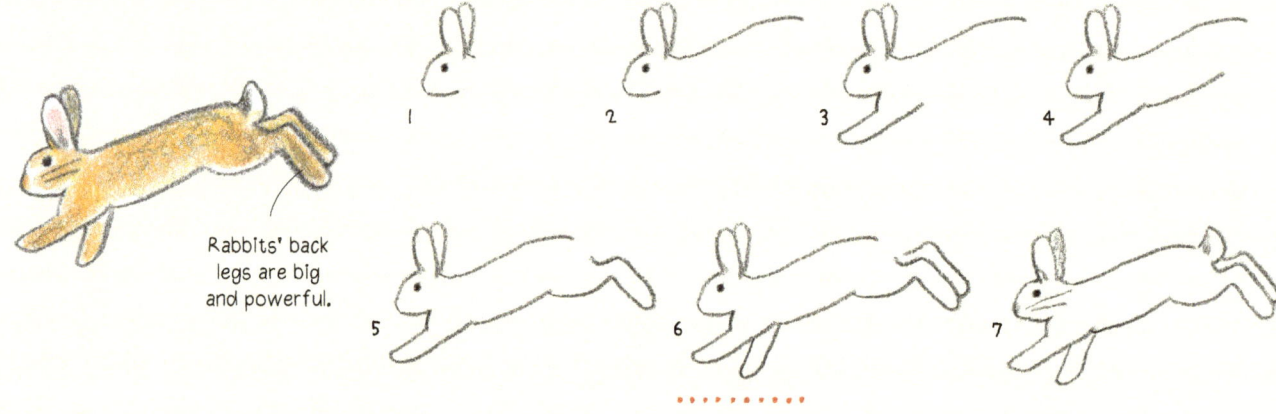

Rabbits' back legs are big and powerful.

1
2
3
4
5
6
7

Front feet	Back feet	Front feet	Back feet	Front feet	Back feet	Front feet	Back feet

Rabbit footprints

Front paws touch the ground one after the other.

Back paws touch the ground side by side.

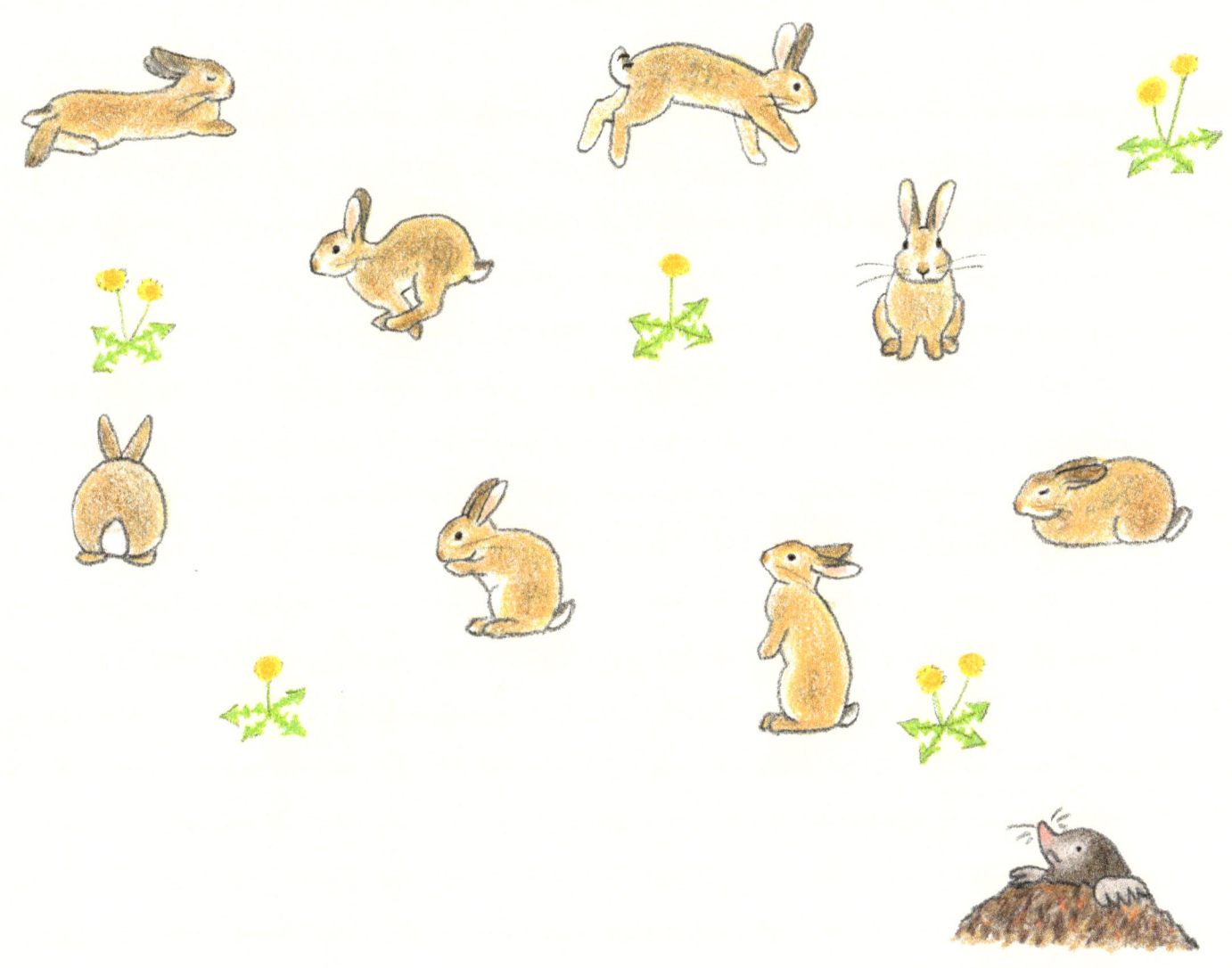

WEASEL

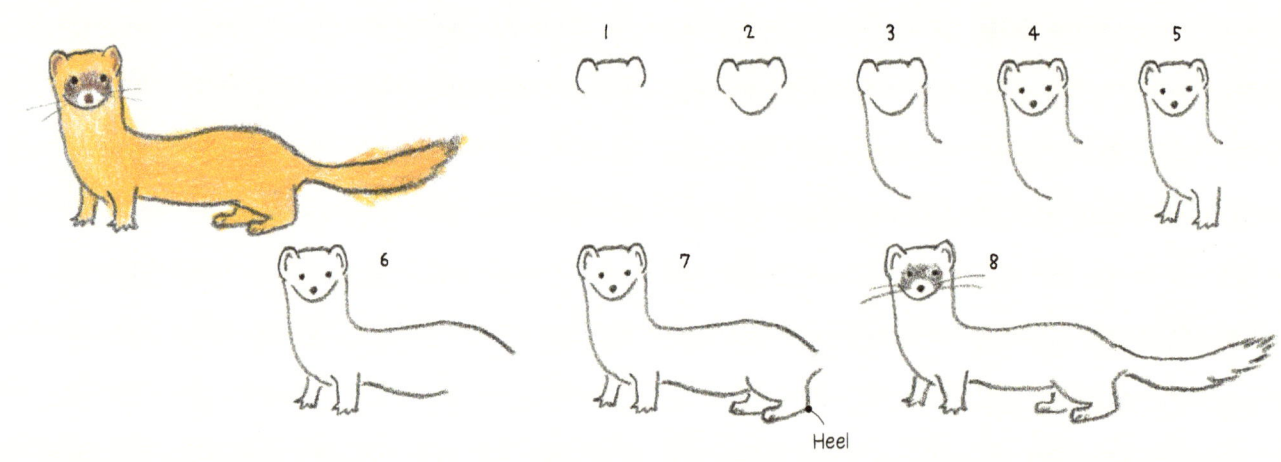

1 2 3 4 5

6 7 8

Heel

STOAT/SHORT-TAILED WEASEL

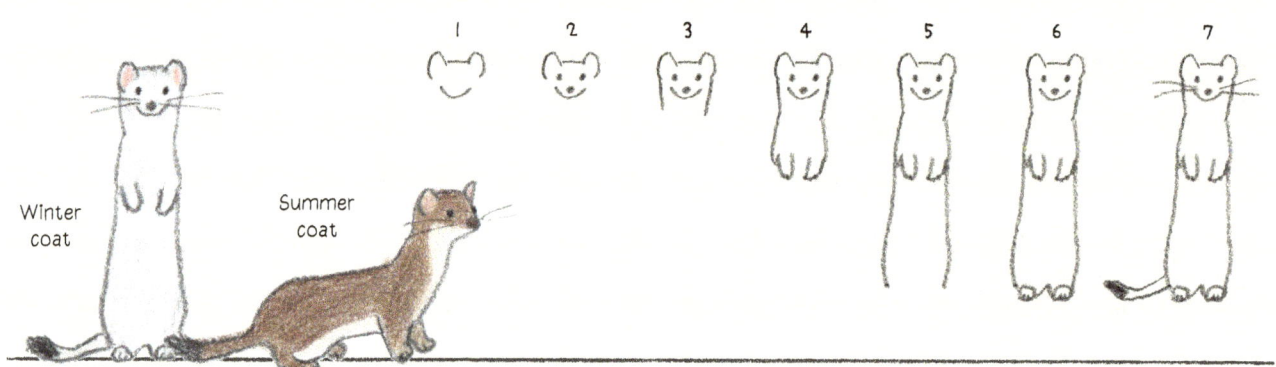

Winter coat

Summer coat

1 2 3 4 5 6 7

BADGER

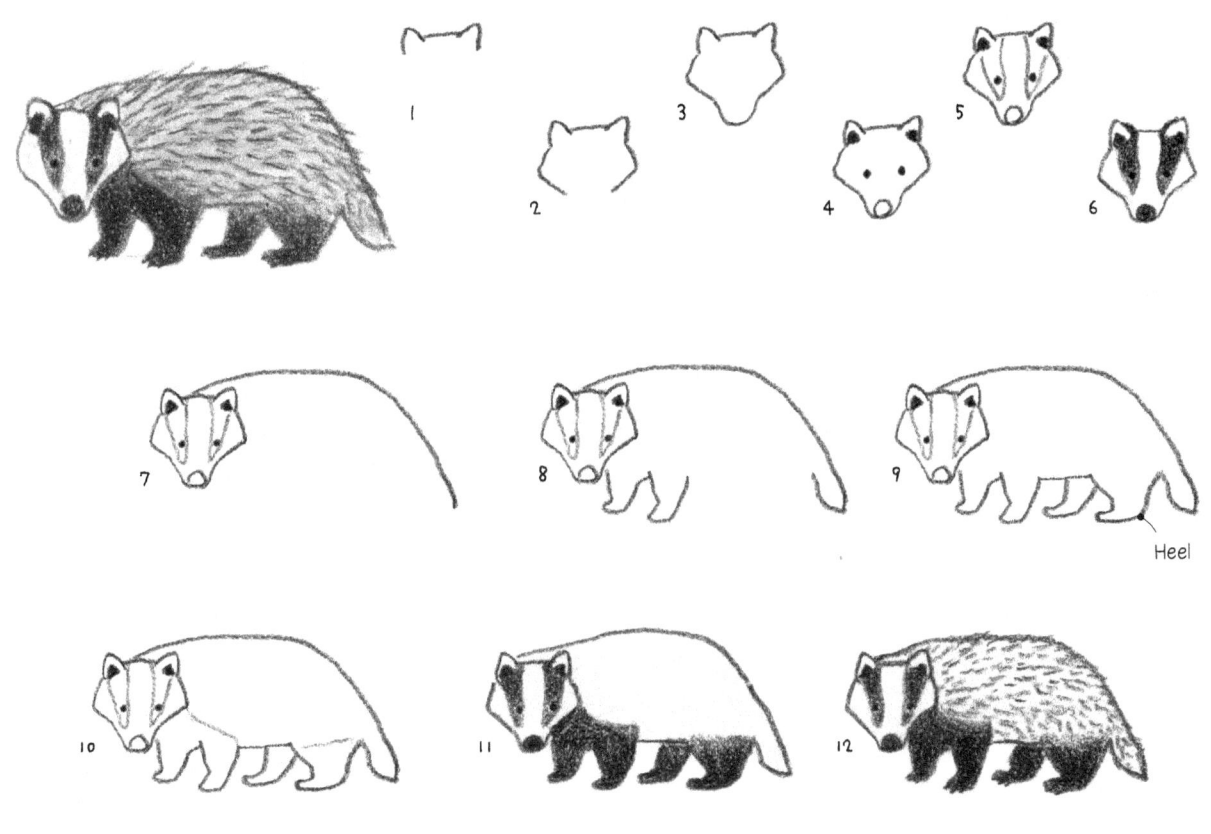

Heel

SEA OTTER

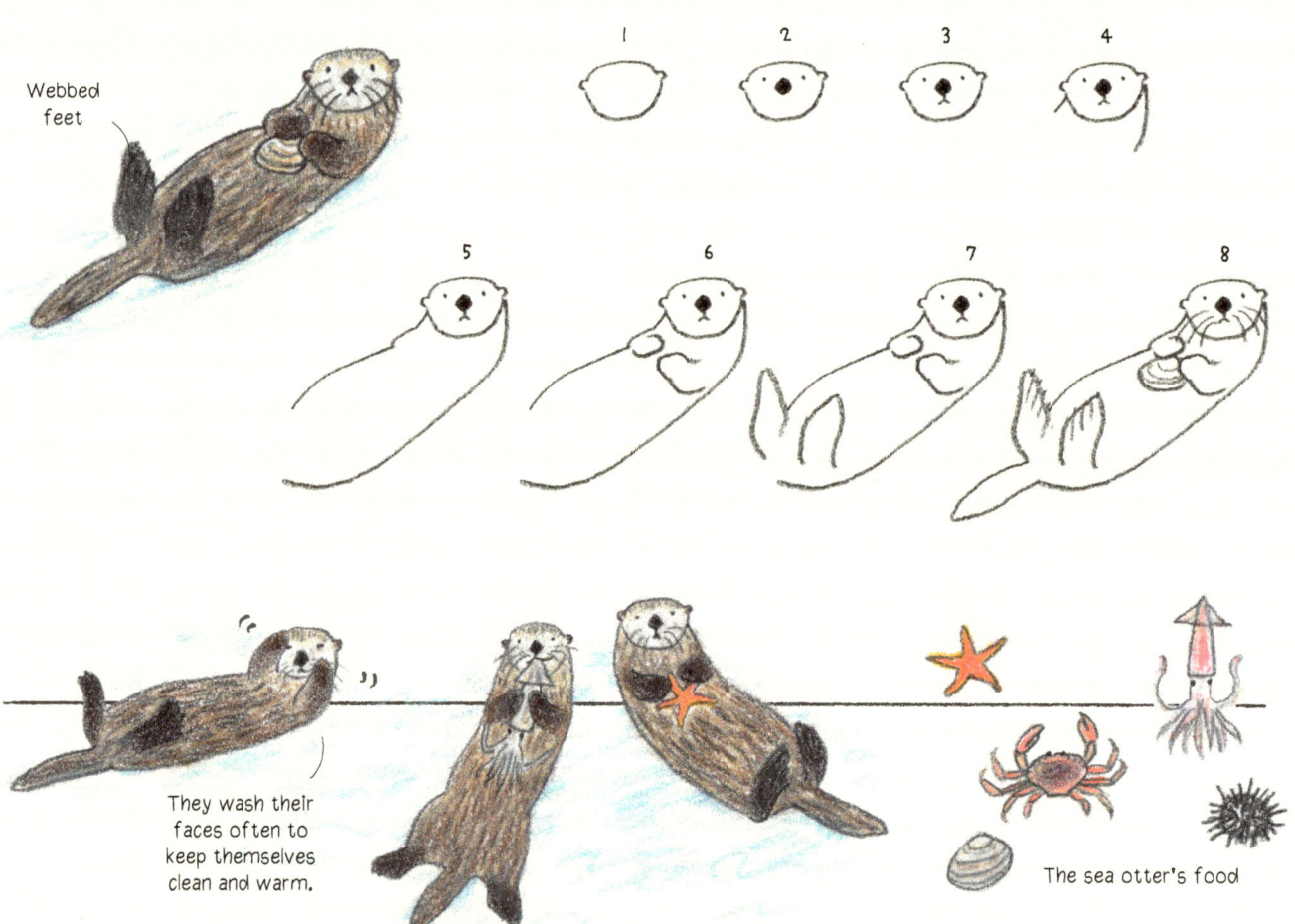

Webbed feet

1 2 3 4

5 6 7 8

They wash their faces often to keep themselves clean and warm.

The sea otter's food

RIVER OTTER

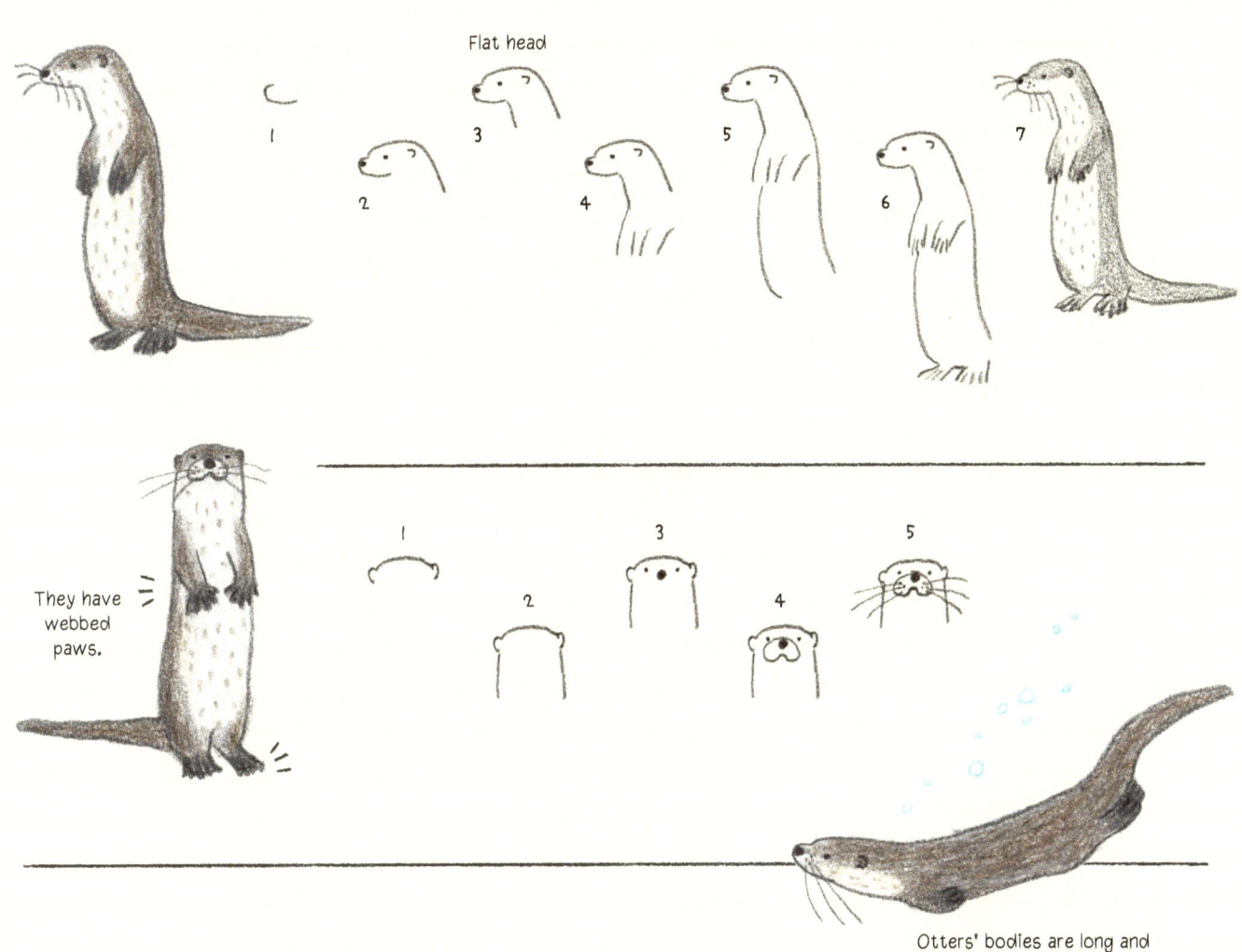

Flat head

1

2

3

4

5

6

7

They have webbed paws.

1

2

3

4

5

Otters' bodies are long and flexible, perfect for swimming.

RACCOON

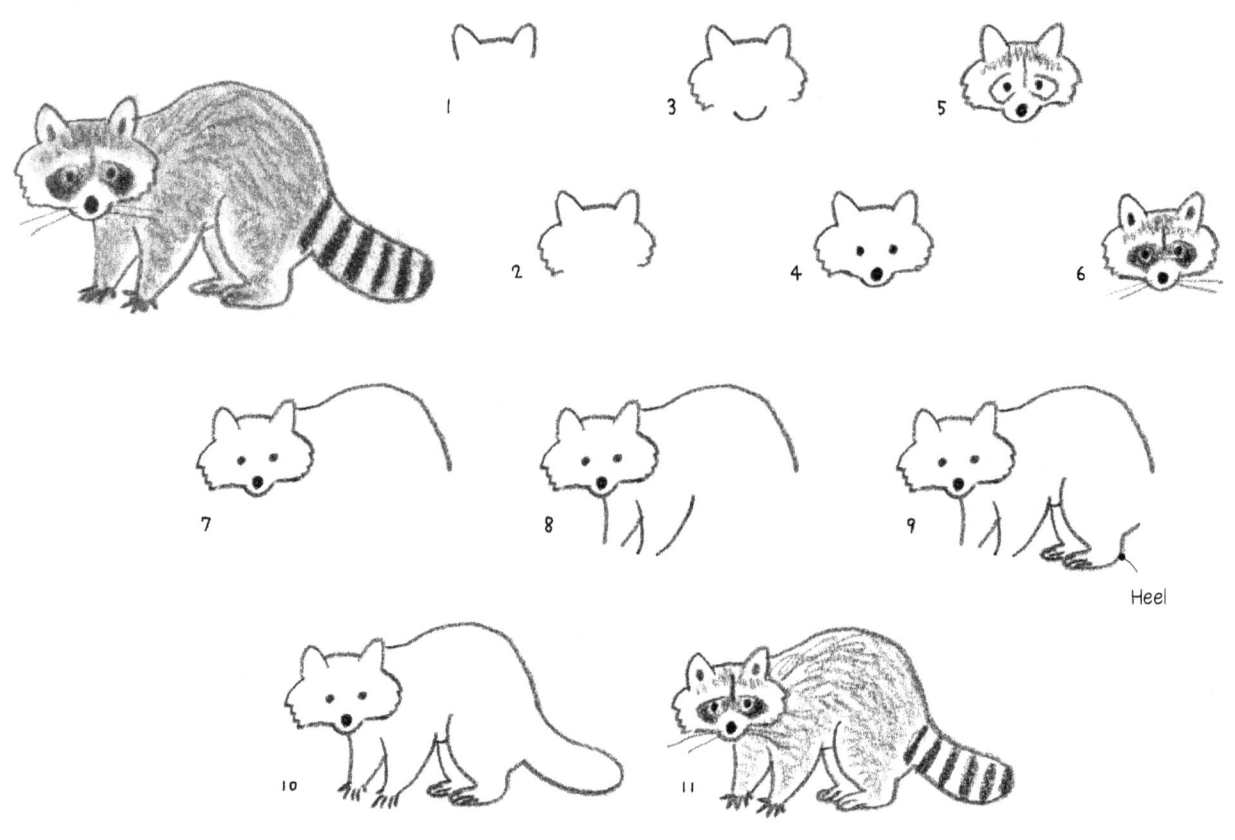

1
2
3
4
5
6
7
8
9
Heel
10
11

RED PANDA

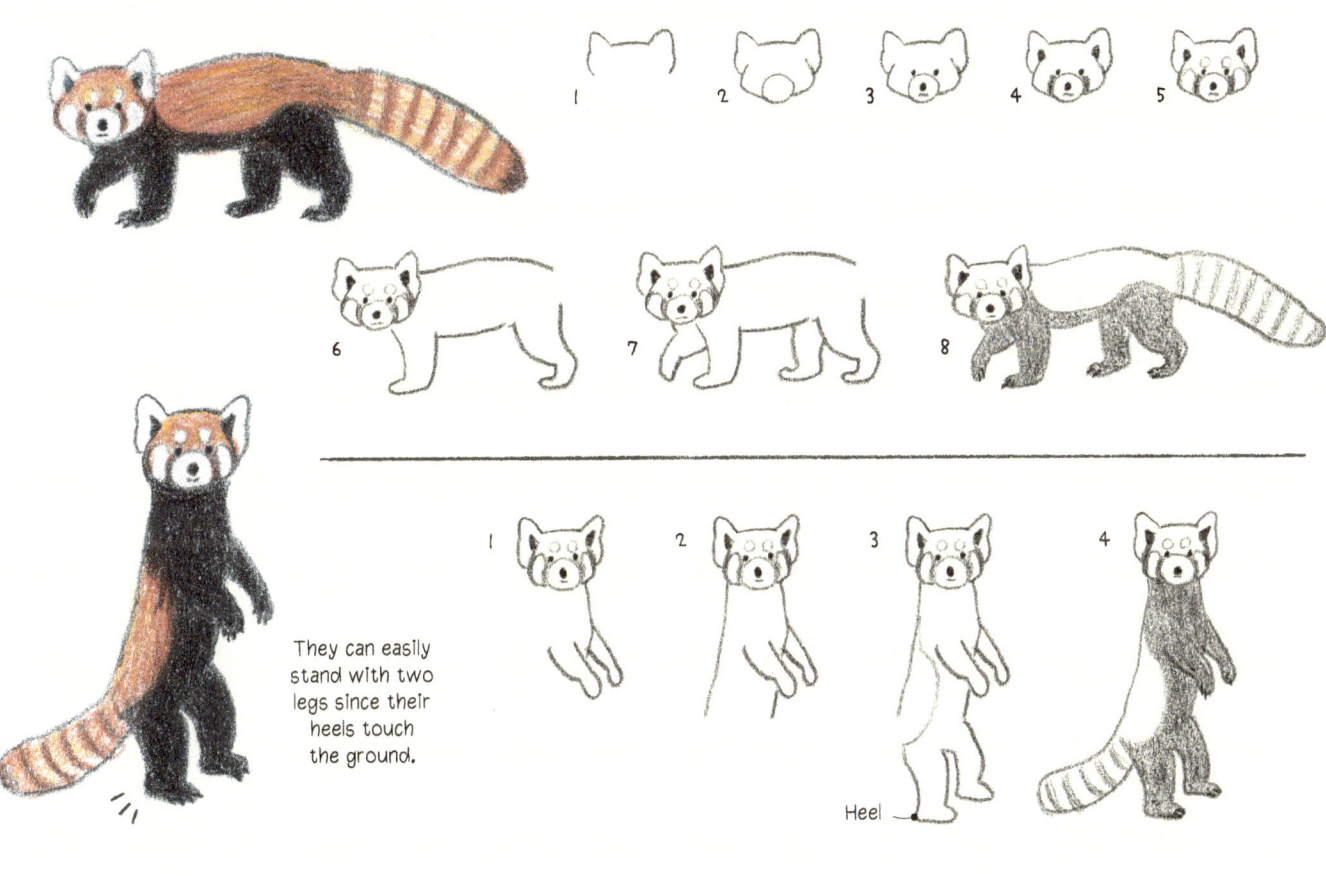

1   2   3   4   5

6   7   8

They can easily
stand with two
legs since their
heels touch
the ground.

1   2   3   4

Heel

BLACK BEAR

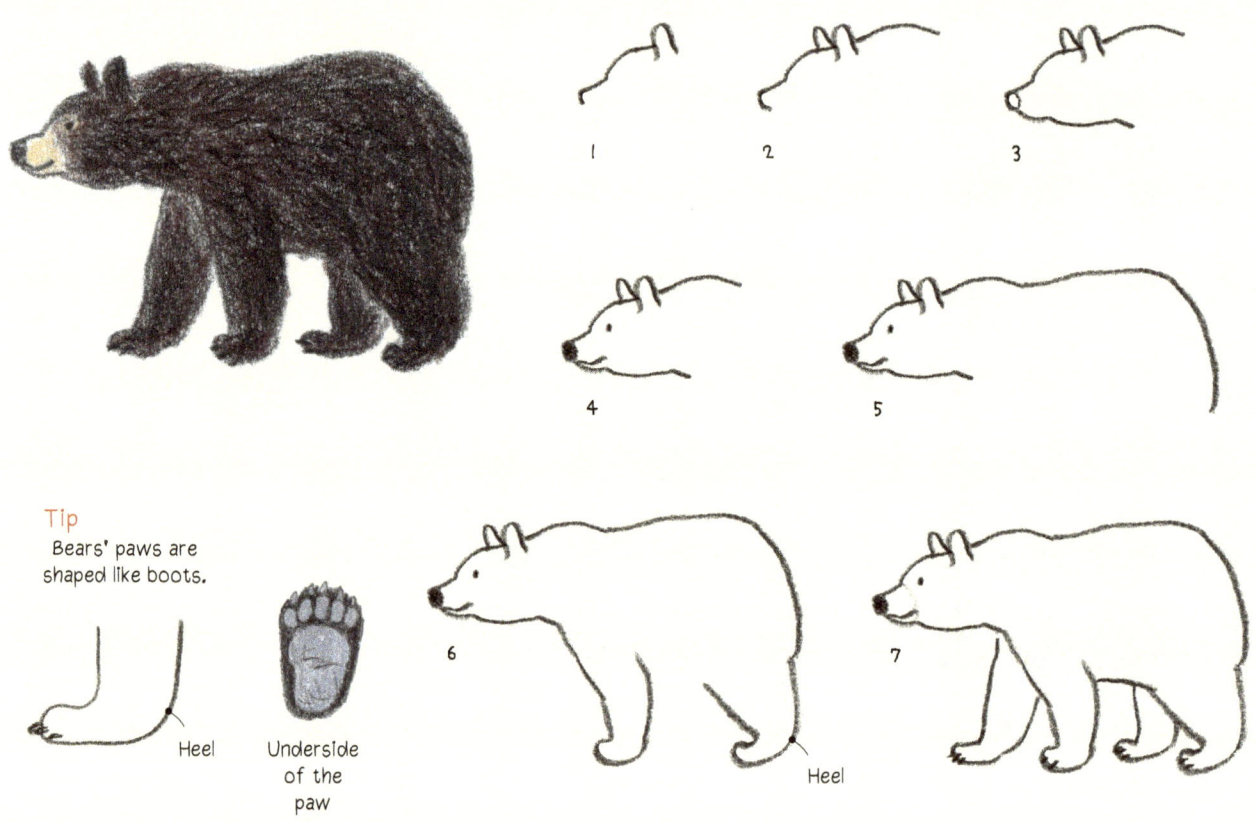

1

2

3

4

5

Tip

Bears' paws are shaped like boots.

Heel

Underside of the paw

6

Heel

7

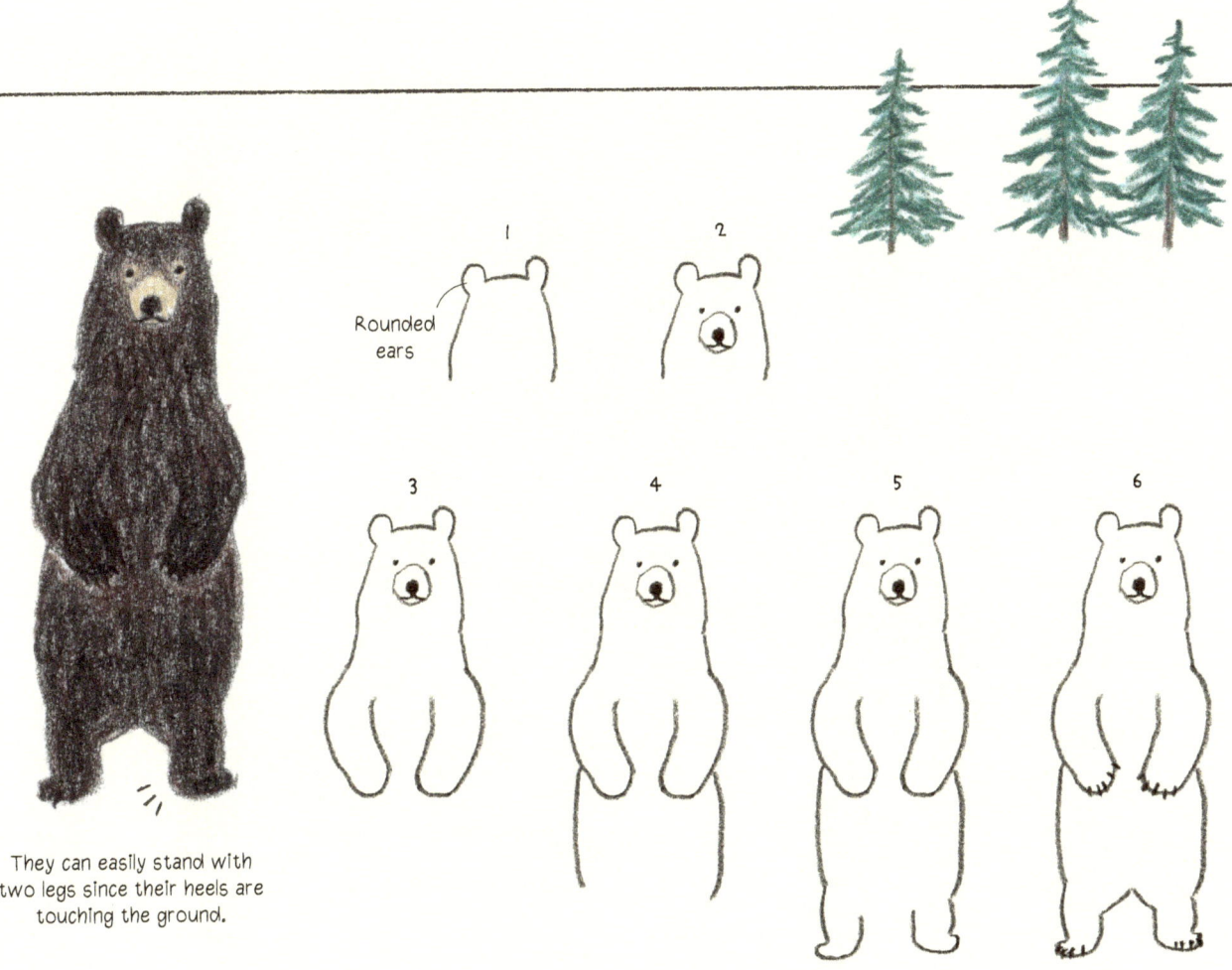

Rounded
ears

1

2

3

4

5

6

They can easily stand with
two legs since their heels are
touching the ground.

POLAR BEAR

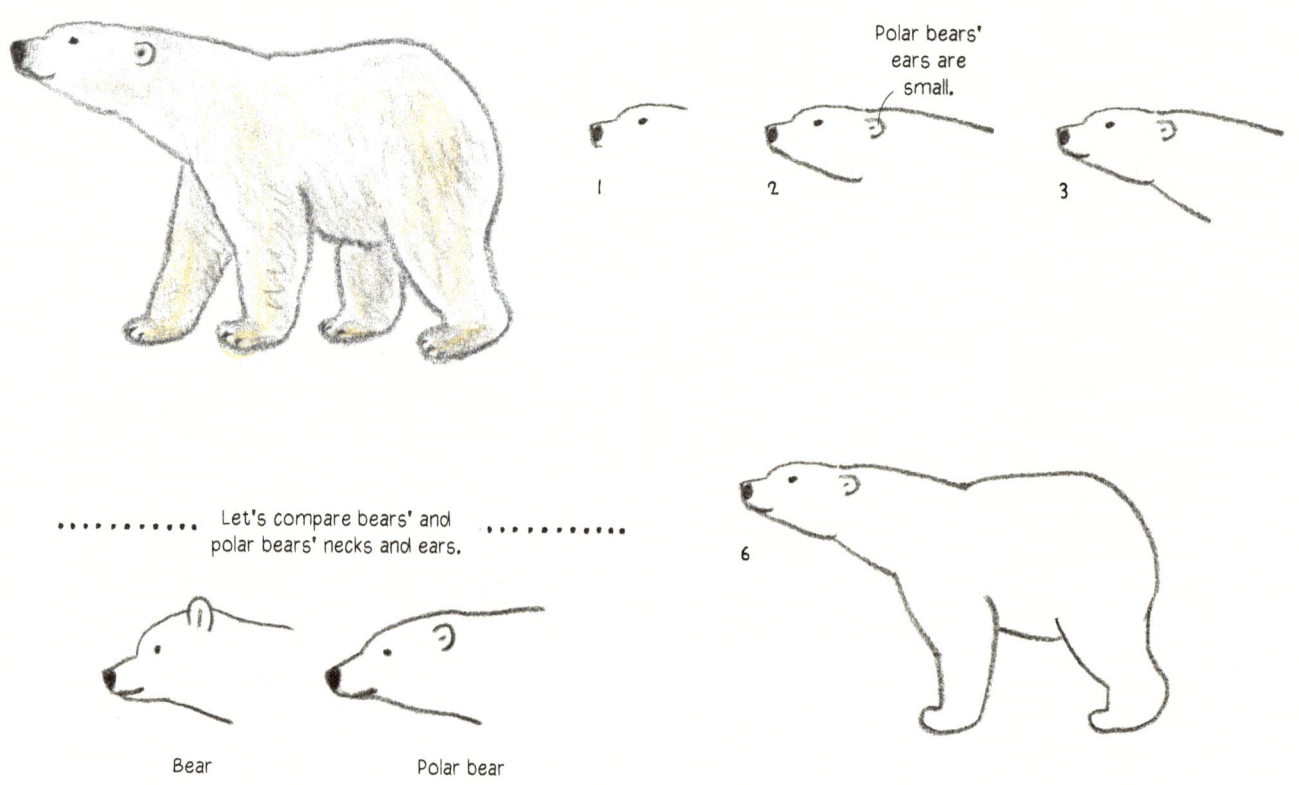

Polar bears' ears are small.

1

2

3

Let's compare bears' and polar bears' necks and ears.

Bear

Polar bear

6

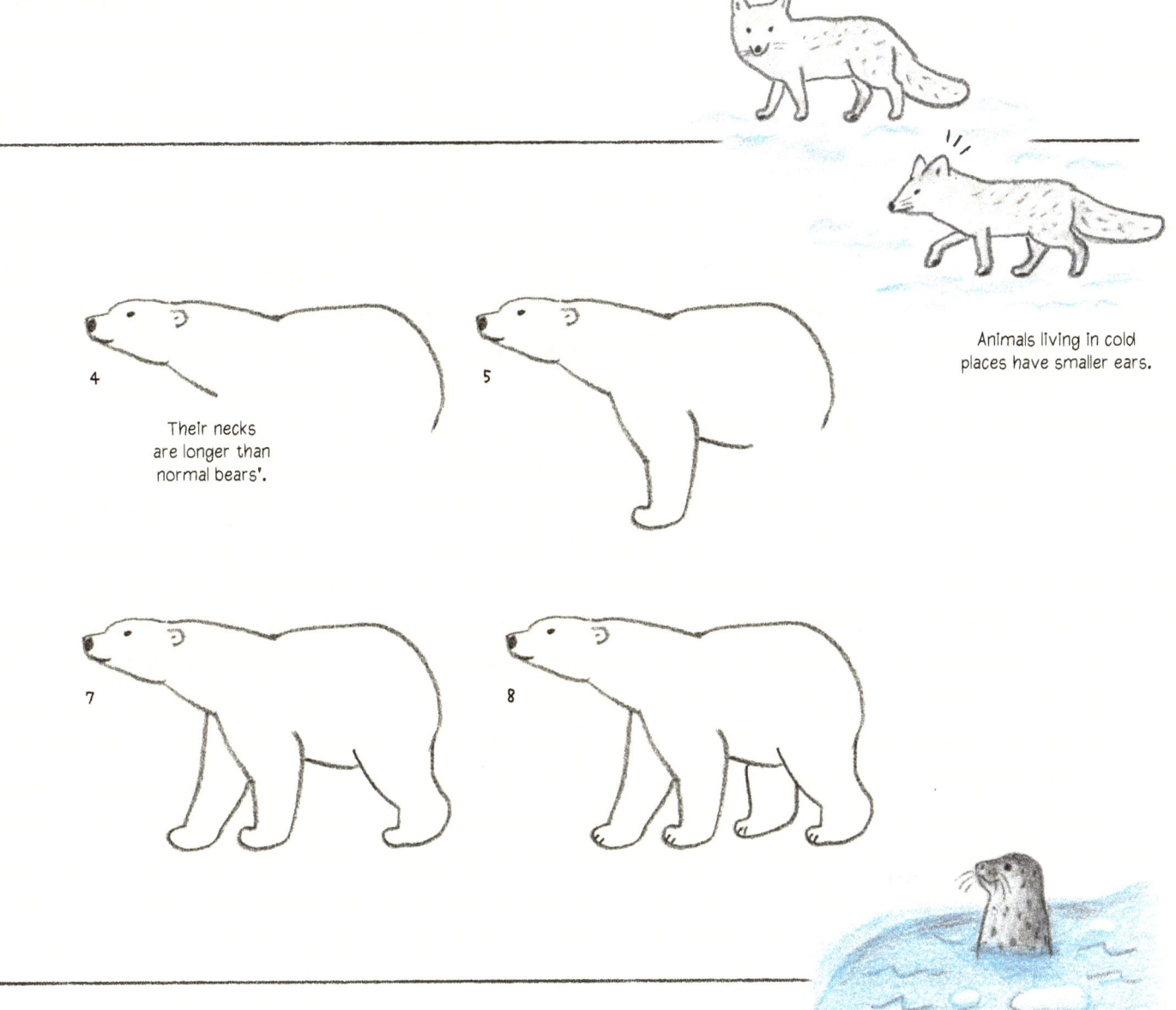

Animals living in cold places have smaller ears.

4

Their necks
are longer than
normal bears'.

5

7

8

Polar bears eat seals.

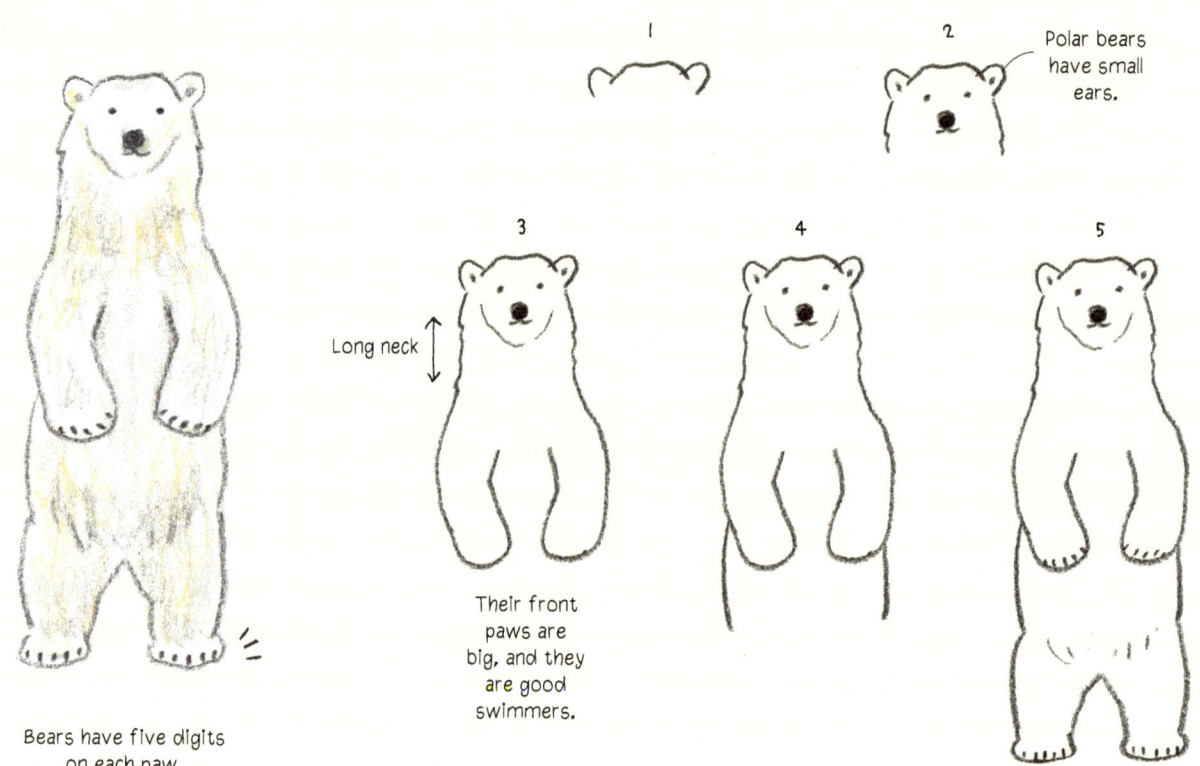

1

2

Polar bears have small ears.

3

Long neck

Their front paws are big, and they are good swimmers.

4

5

Bears have five digits on each paw.

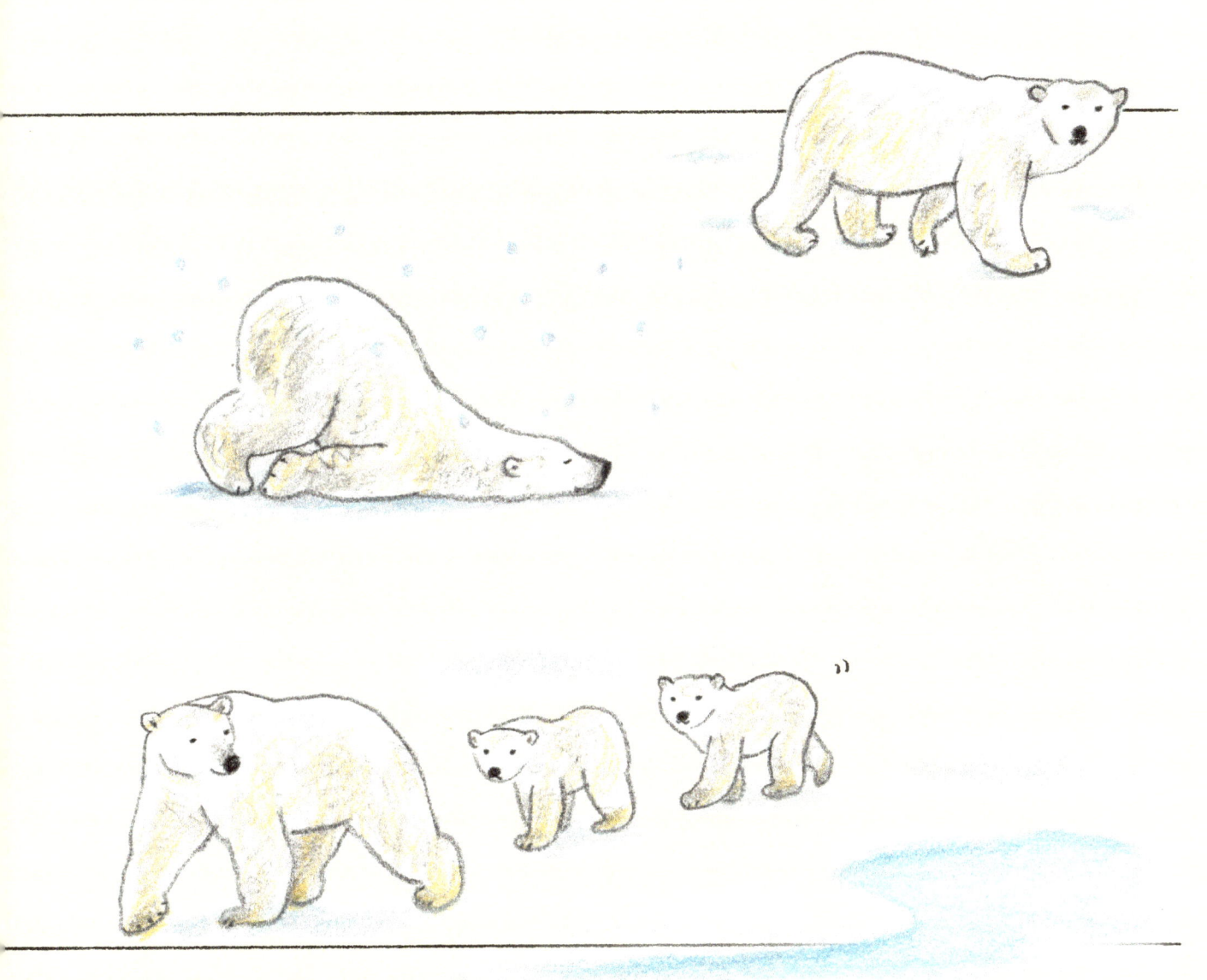

DEER

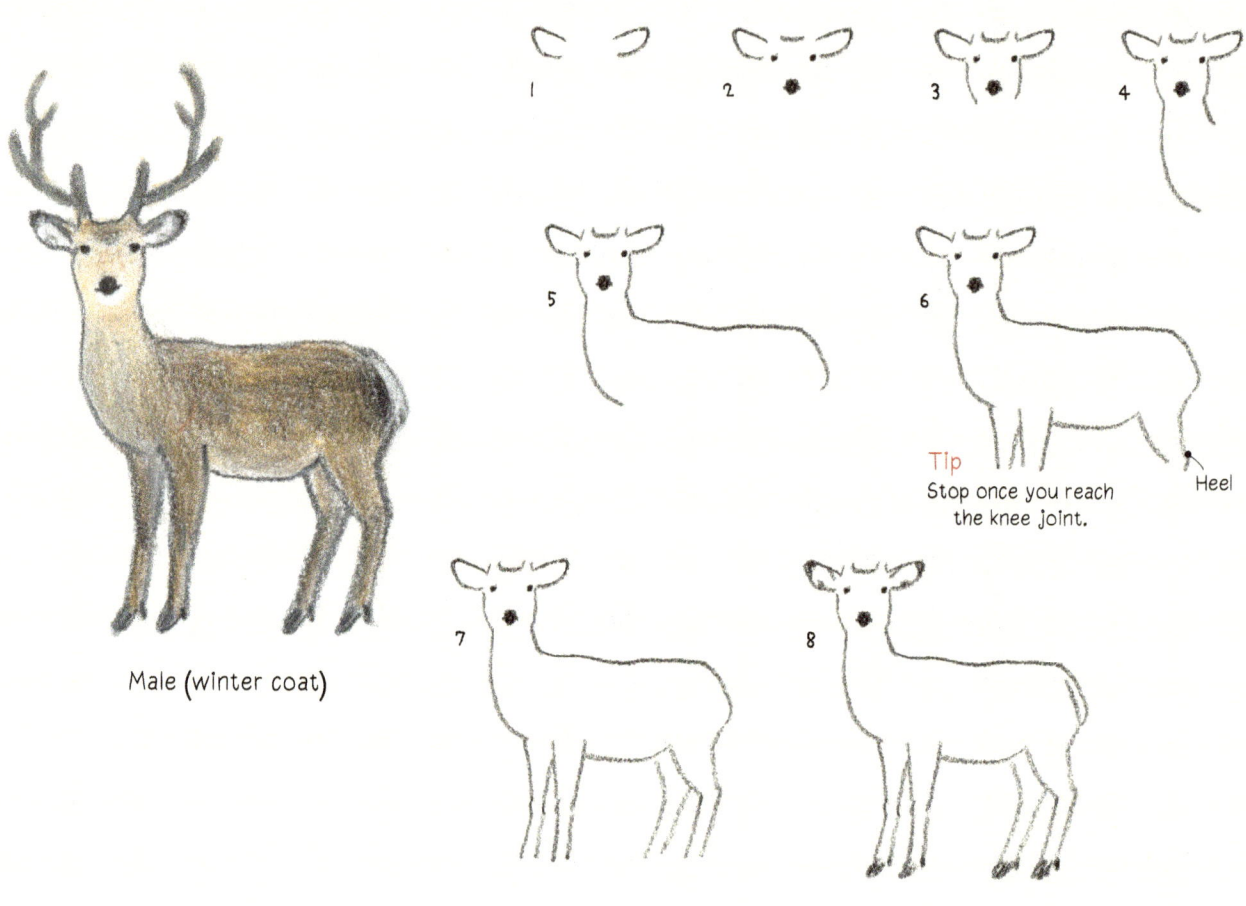

Male (winter coat)

1

2

3

4

5

6

Tip
Stop once you reach
the knee joint.

Heel

7

8

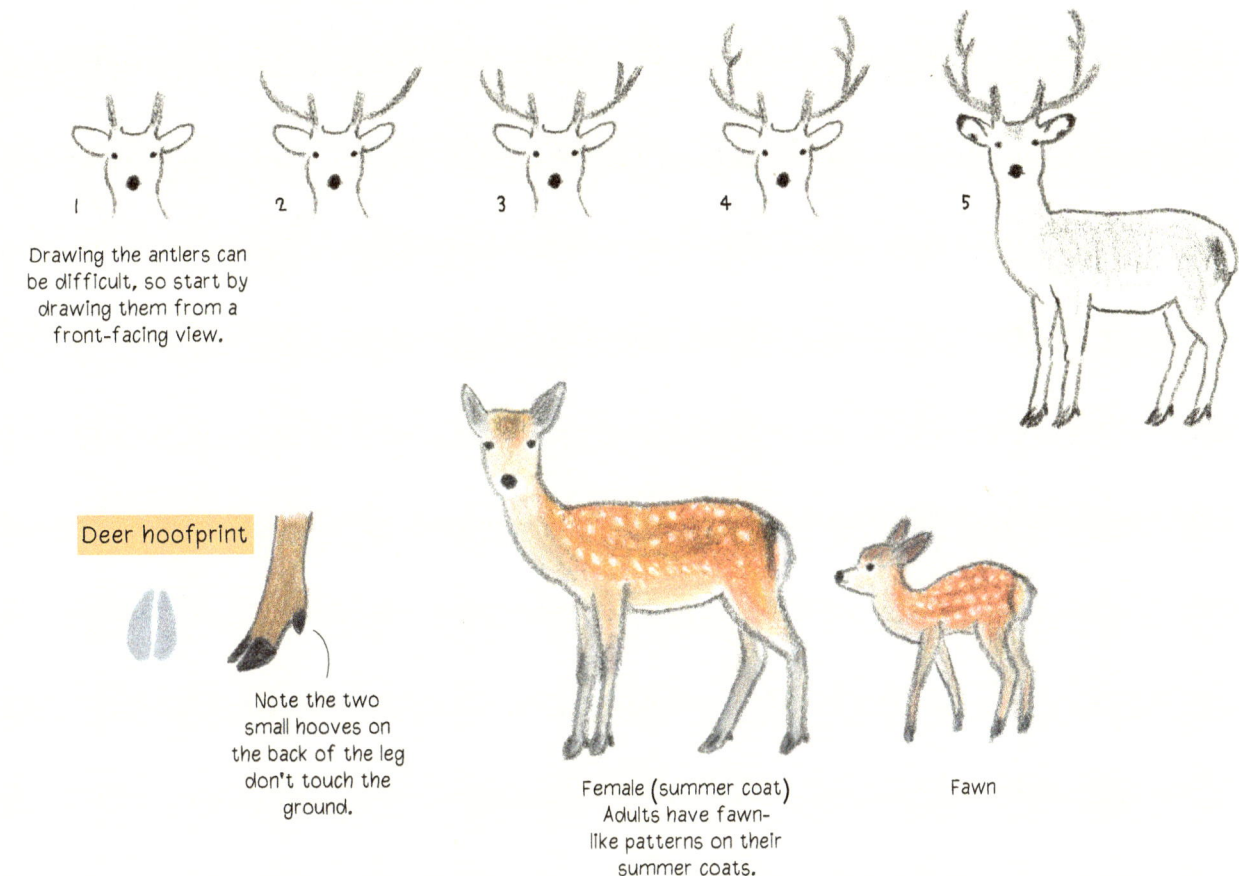

1

2

3

4

5

Drawing the antlers can be difficult, so start by drawing them from a front-facing view.

Deer hoofprint

Note the two small hooves on the back of the leg don't touch the ground.

Female (summer coat)
Adults have fawn-like patterns on their summer coats.

Fawn

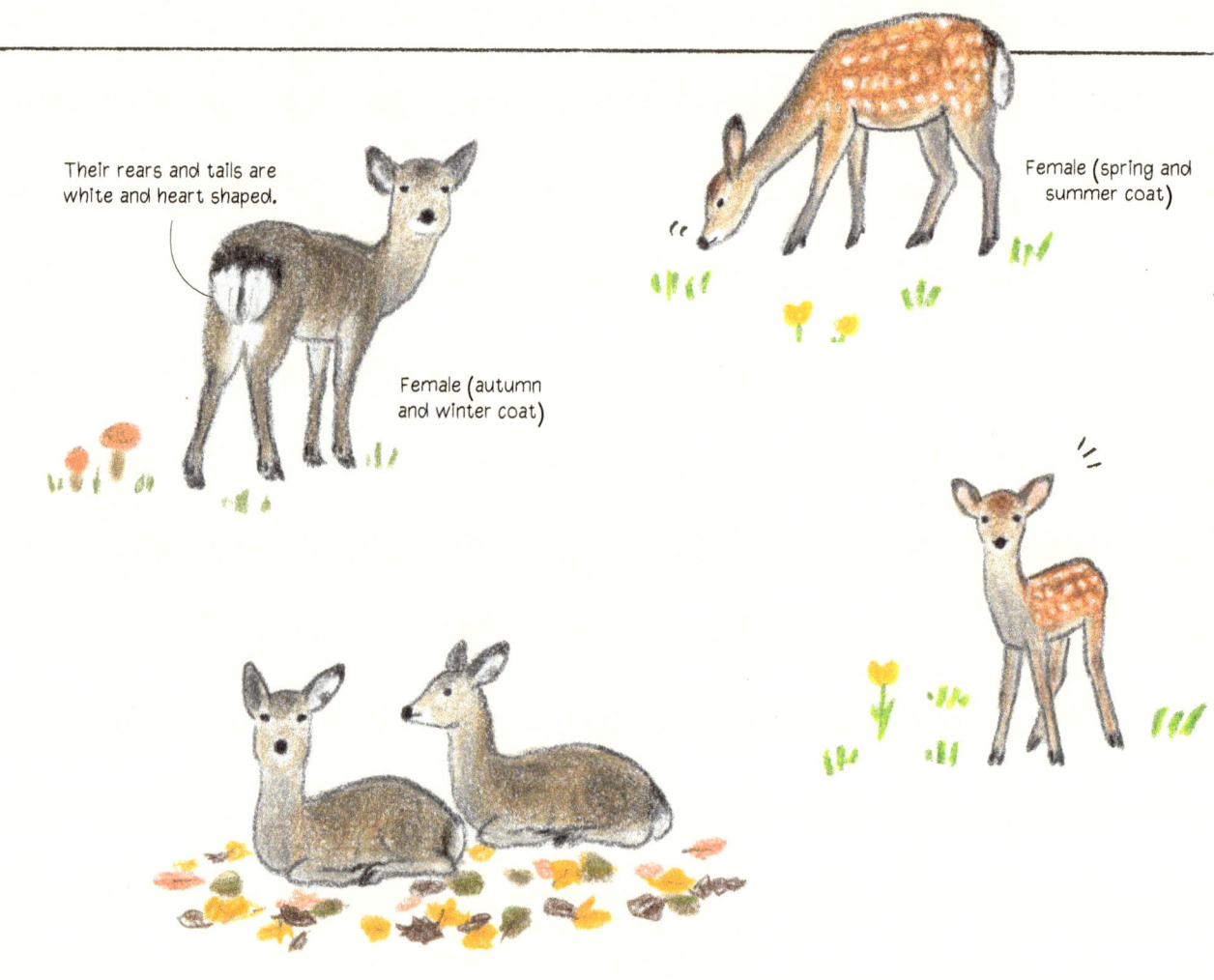

Their rears and tails are white and heart shaped.

Female (autumn and winter coat)

Female (spring and summer coat)

OTHER MEMBERS OF THE DEER FAMILY

Reindeer

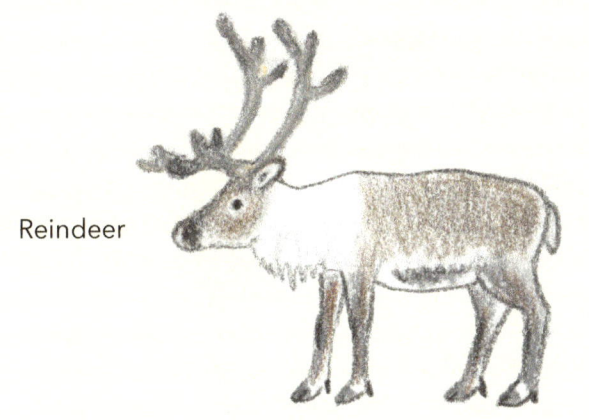

Reindeer hoofprint

Reindeer toes and feet, which keep them from sinking into snow, are bigger and wider than a deer's.

Tip
Divide the horns into two sections, front and back, so that they're easier to draw.

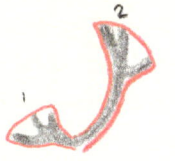
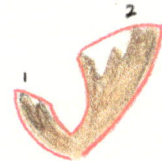

Moose

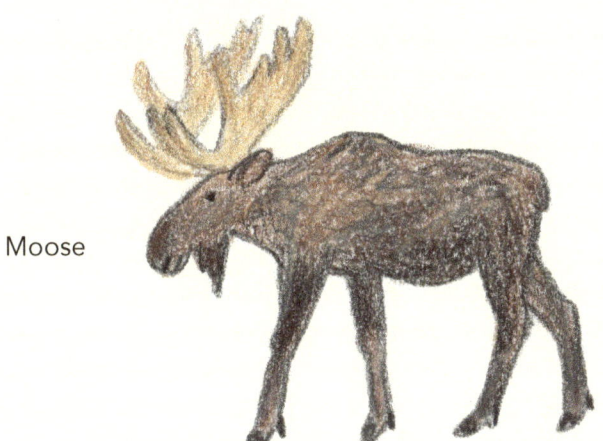

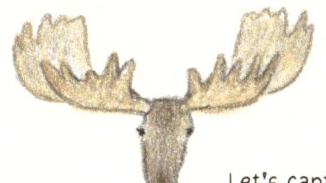

Let's capture their horns from the front.

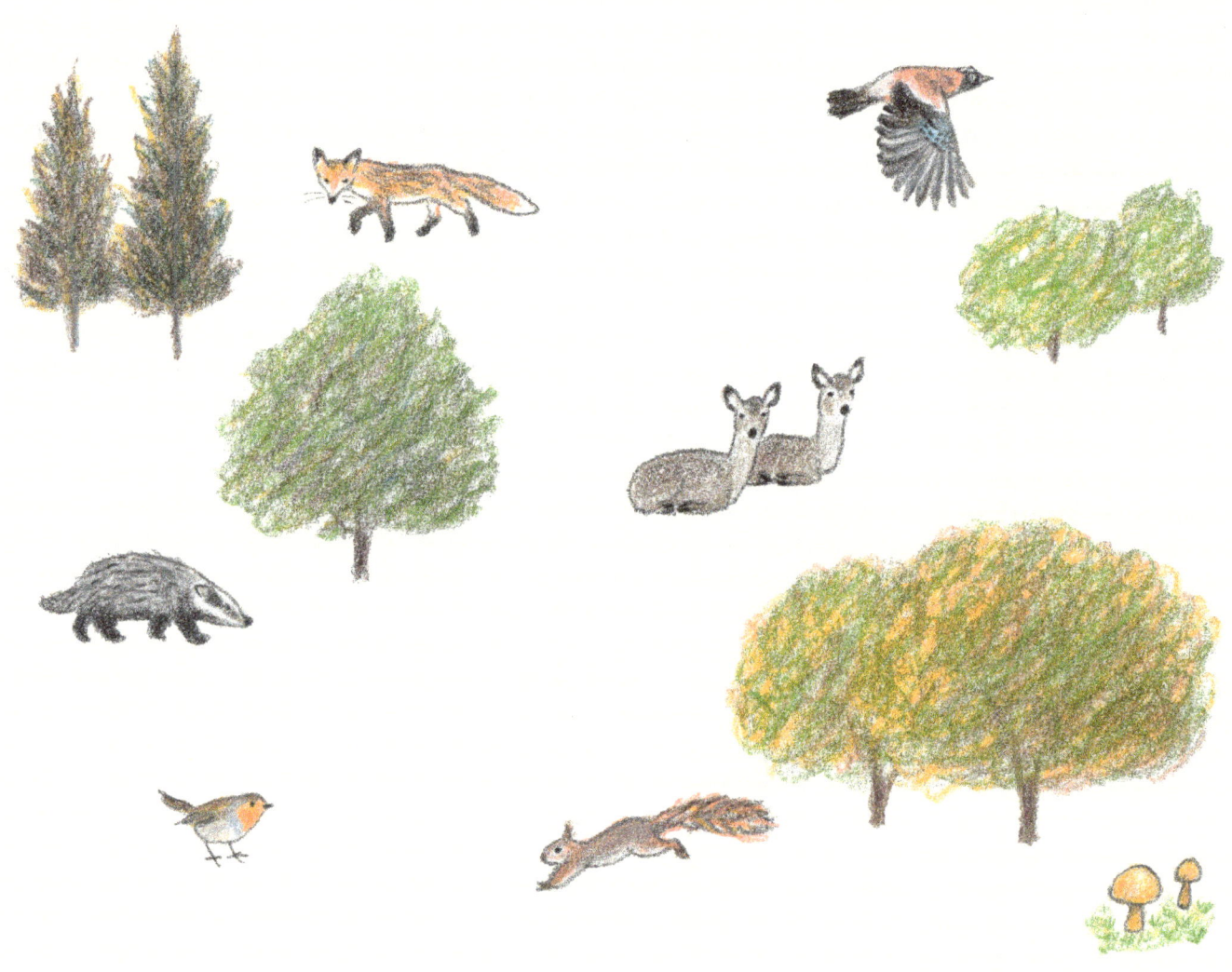

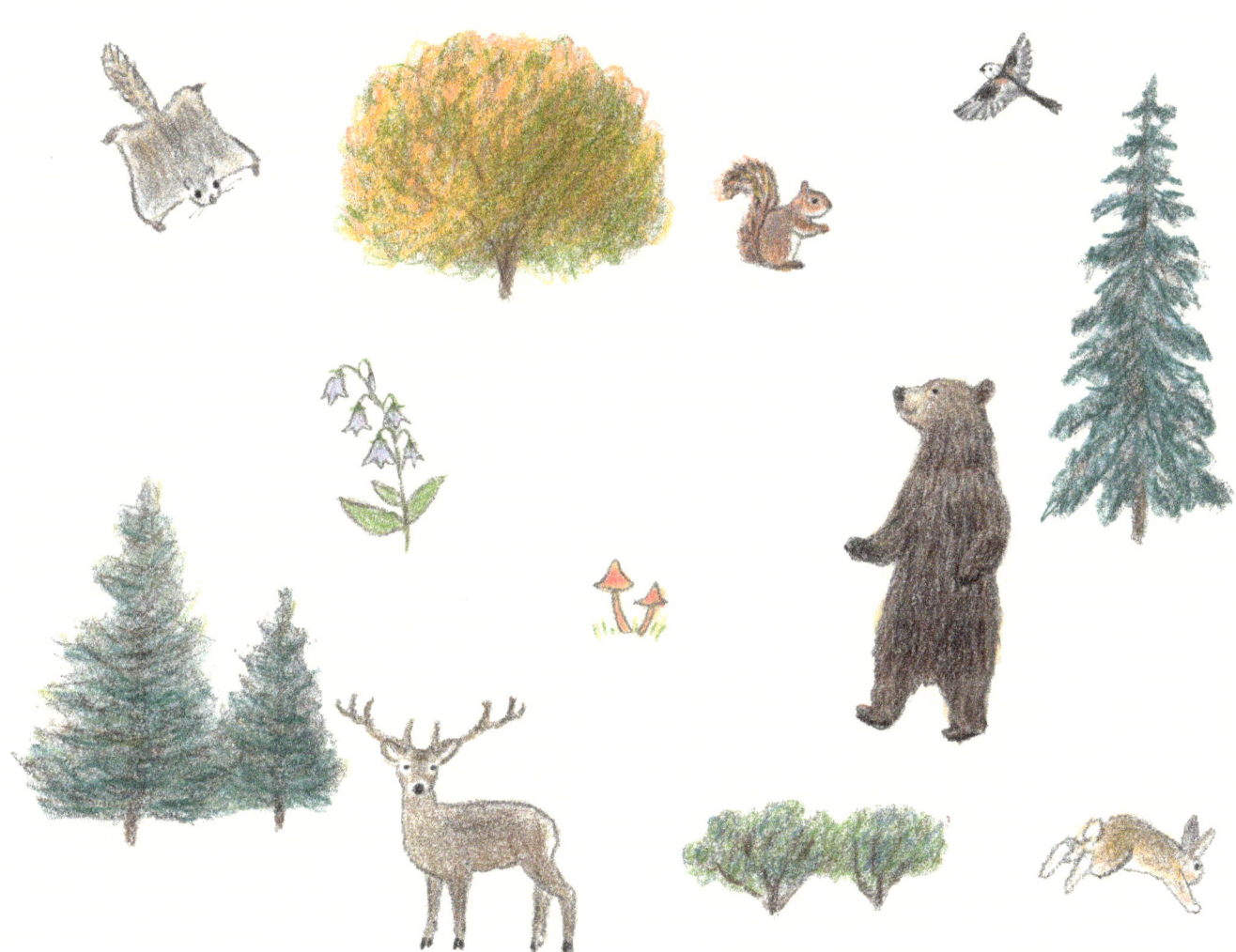

COW

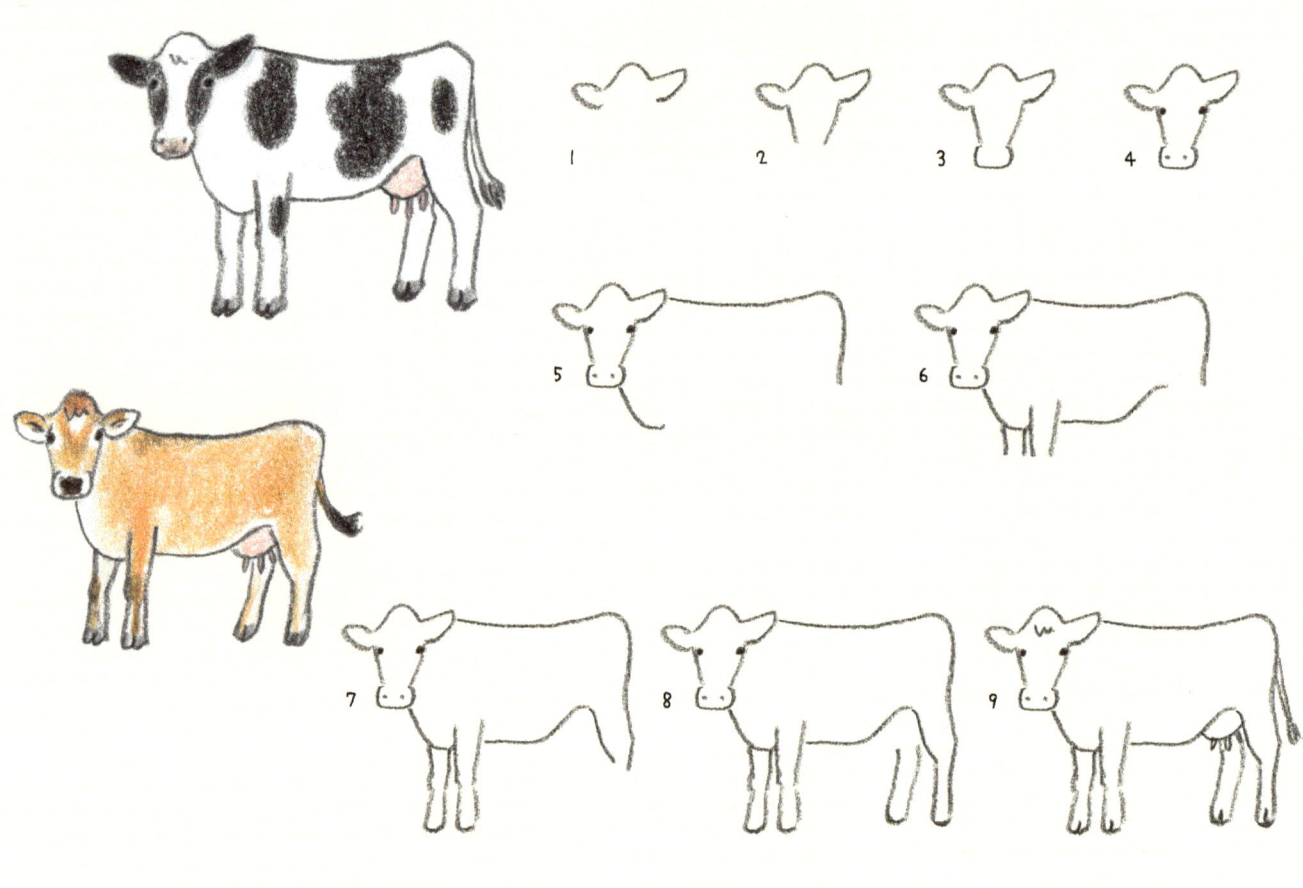

OTHER MEMBERS OF THE COW FAMILY

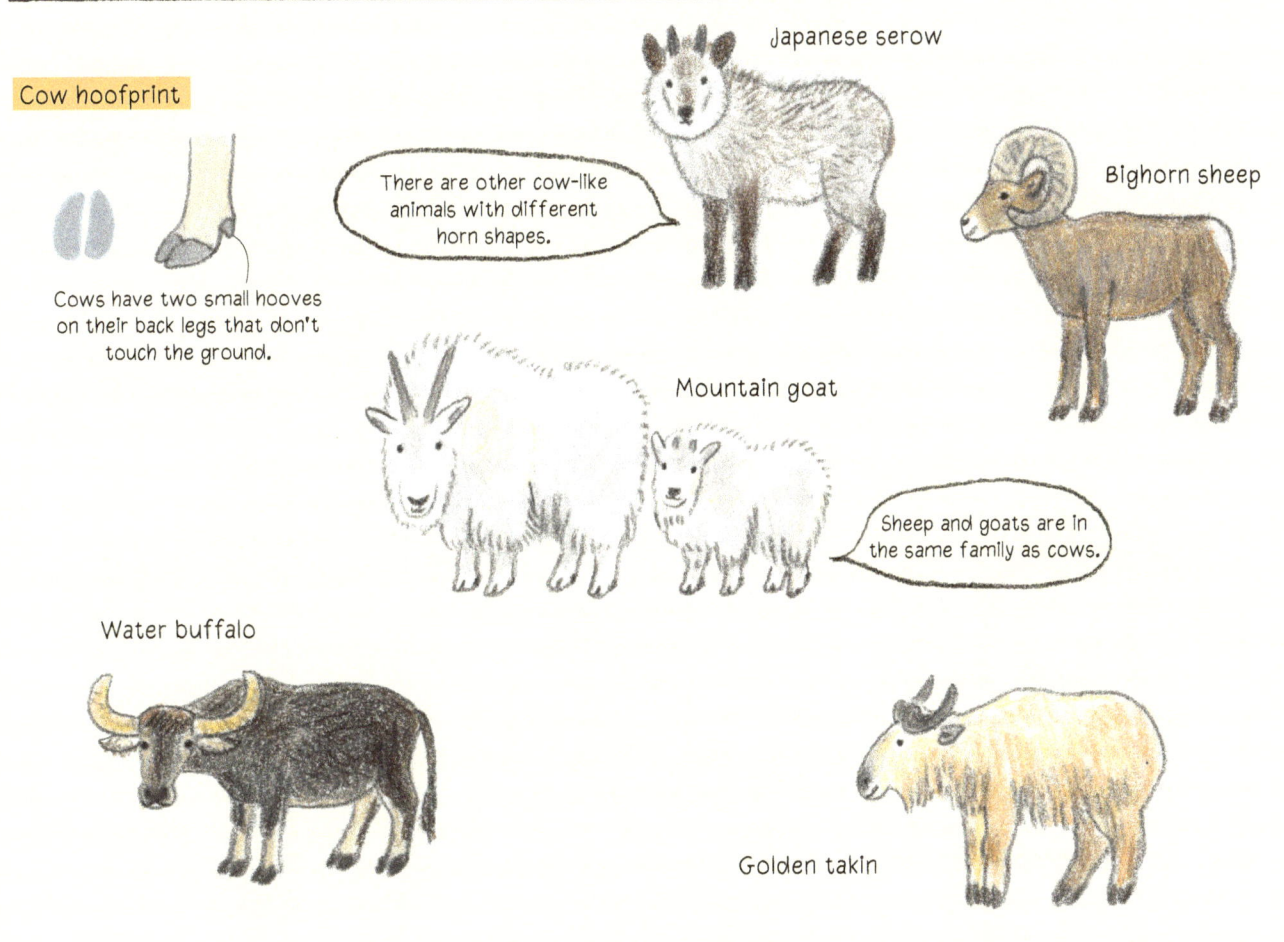

Cow hoofprint

Cows have two small hooves on their back legs that don't touch the ground.

There are other cow-like animals with different horn shapes.

Japanese serow

Bighorn sheep

Mountain goat

Sheep and goats are in the same family as cows.

Water buffalo

Golden takin

GOAT

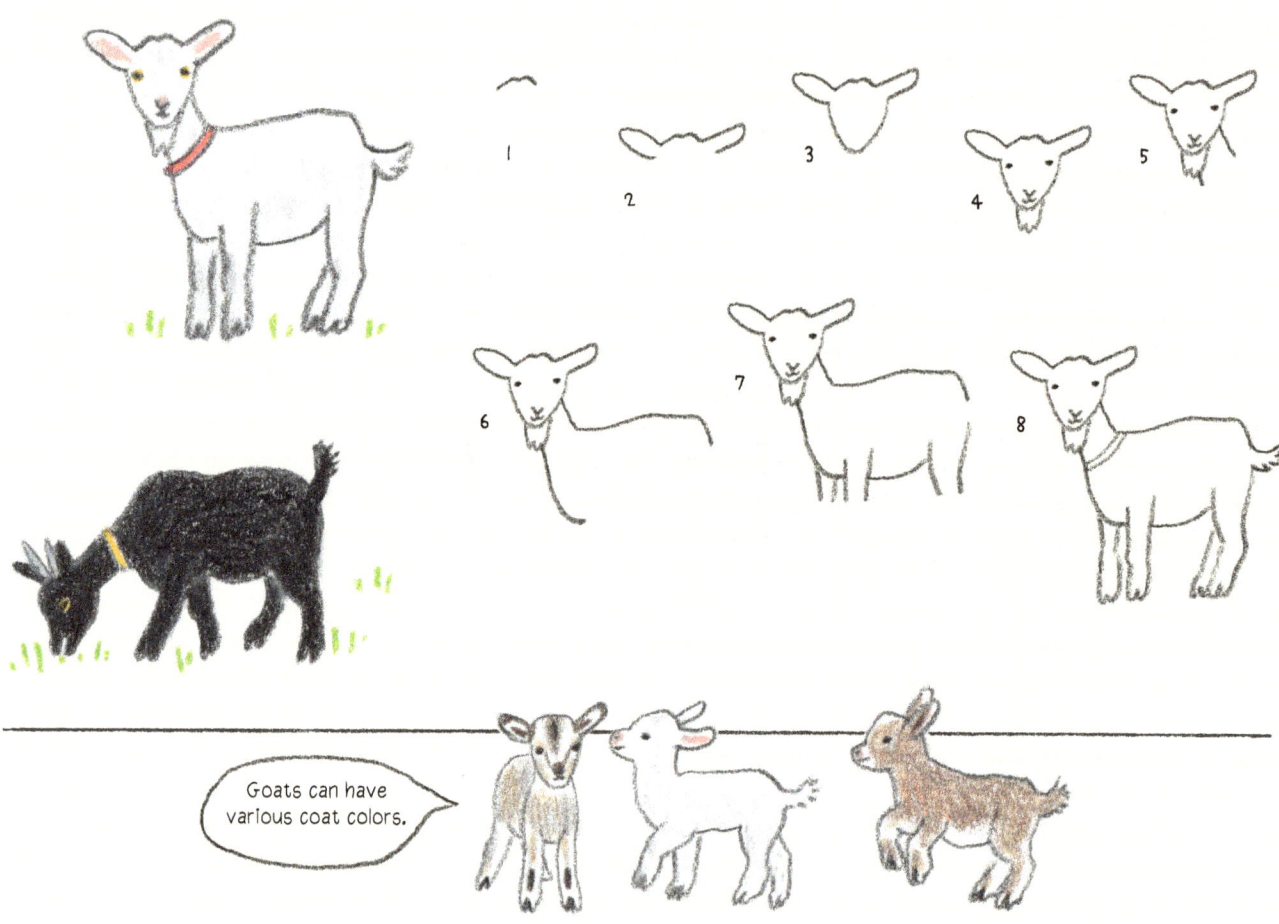

1
2
3
4
5
6
7
8

Goats can have various coat colors.

SHEEP

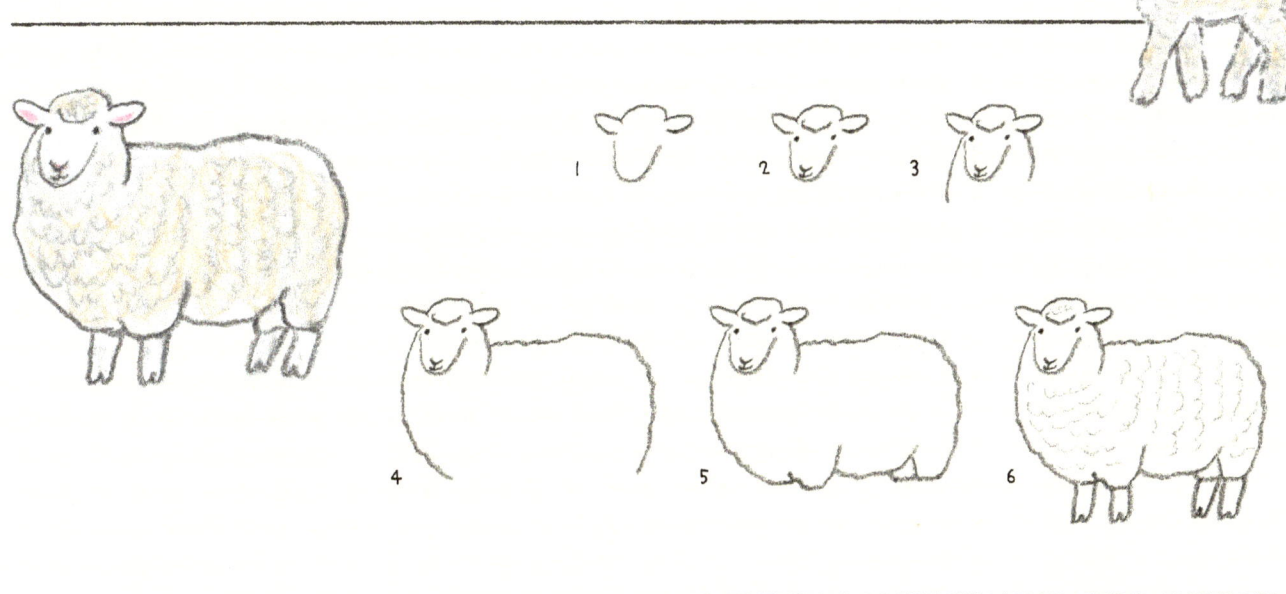

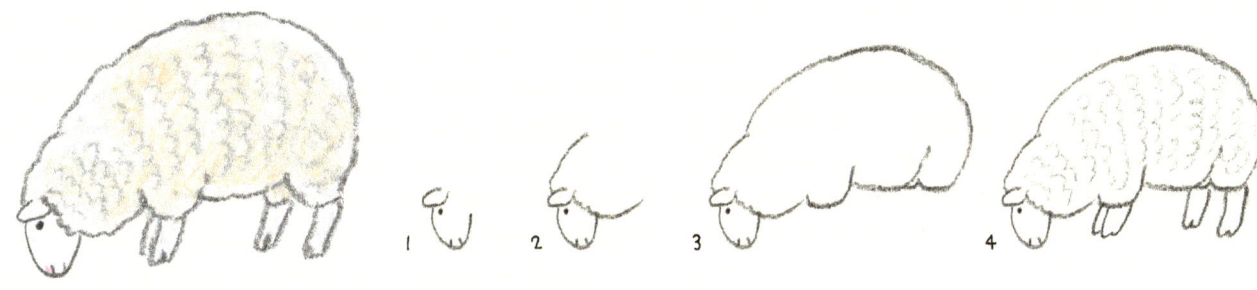

PIG

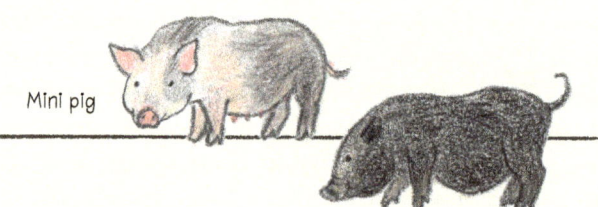

Mini pig

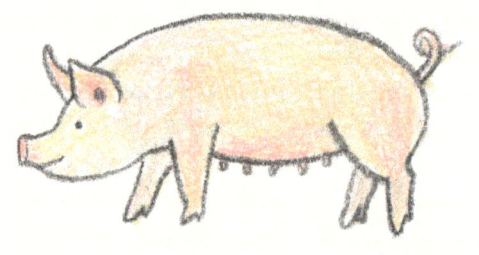

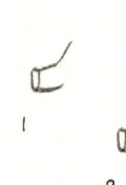

1

2

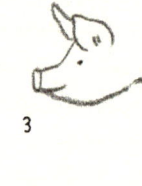

3

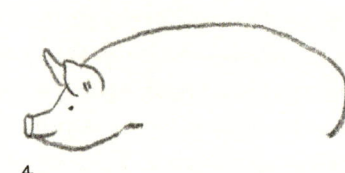

4

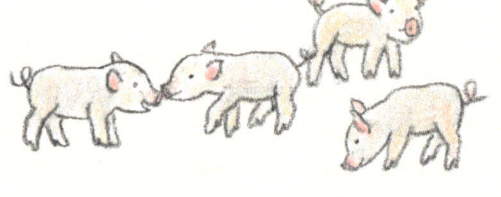

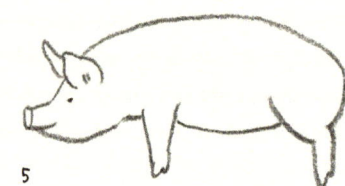

5

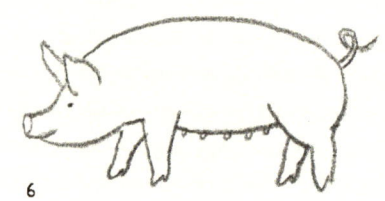

6

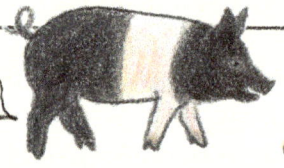

There are pigs with different colors and patterns.

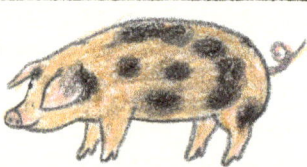

Pig hoofprint

Pig   Wild boar

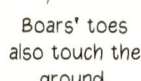

Boars' toes also touch the ground.

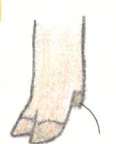

There is a hoof here, also.

060

WILD BOAR

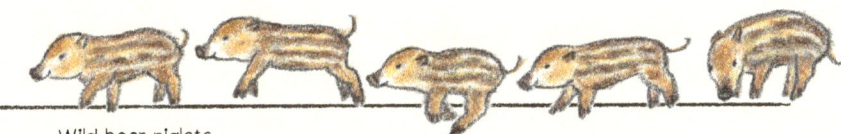

Wild boar piglets

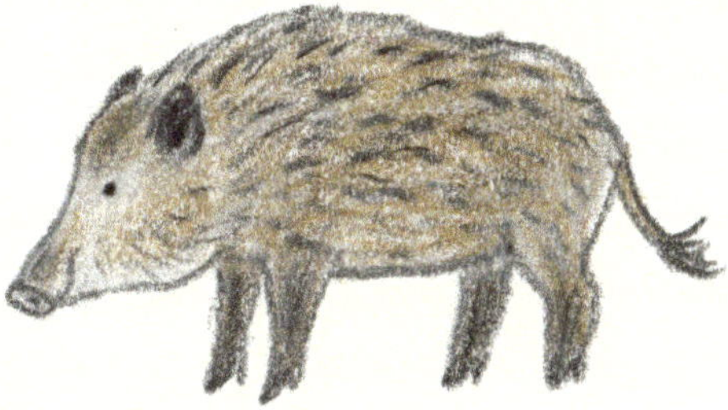

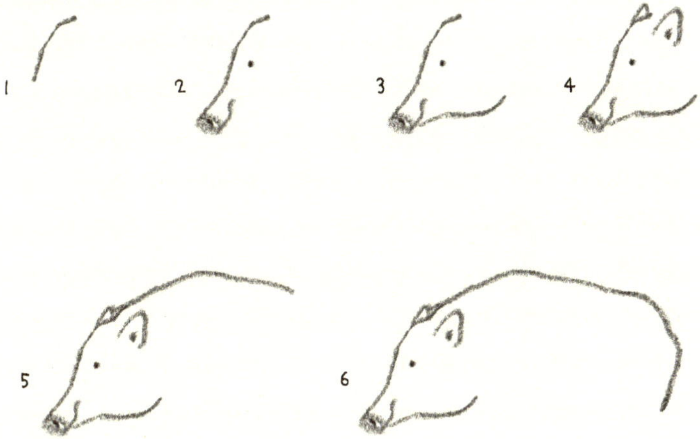

1

2

3

4

5

6

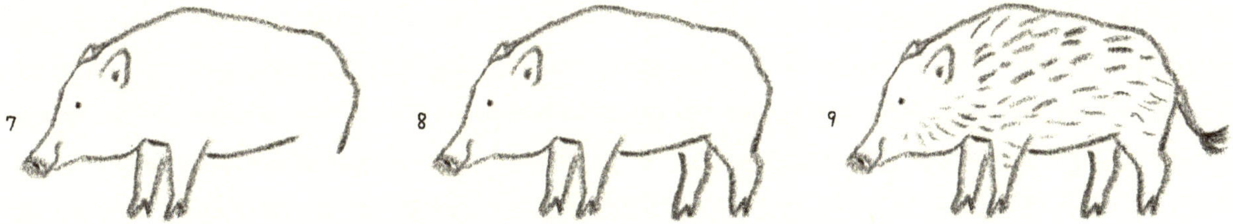

7

8

9

BACTRIAN CAMEL

Camel humps contain fat, which is used as a source of energy. The humps shrink if they haven't eaten much.

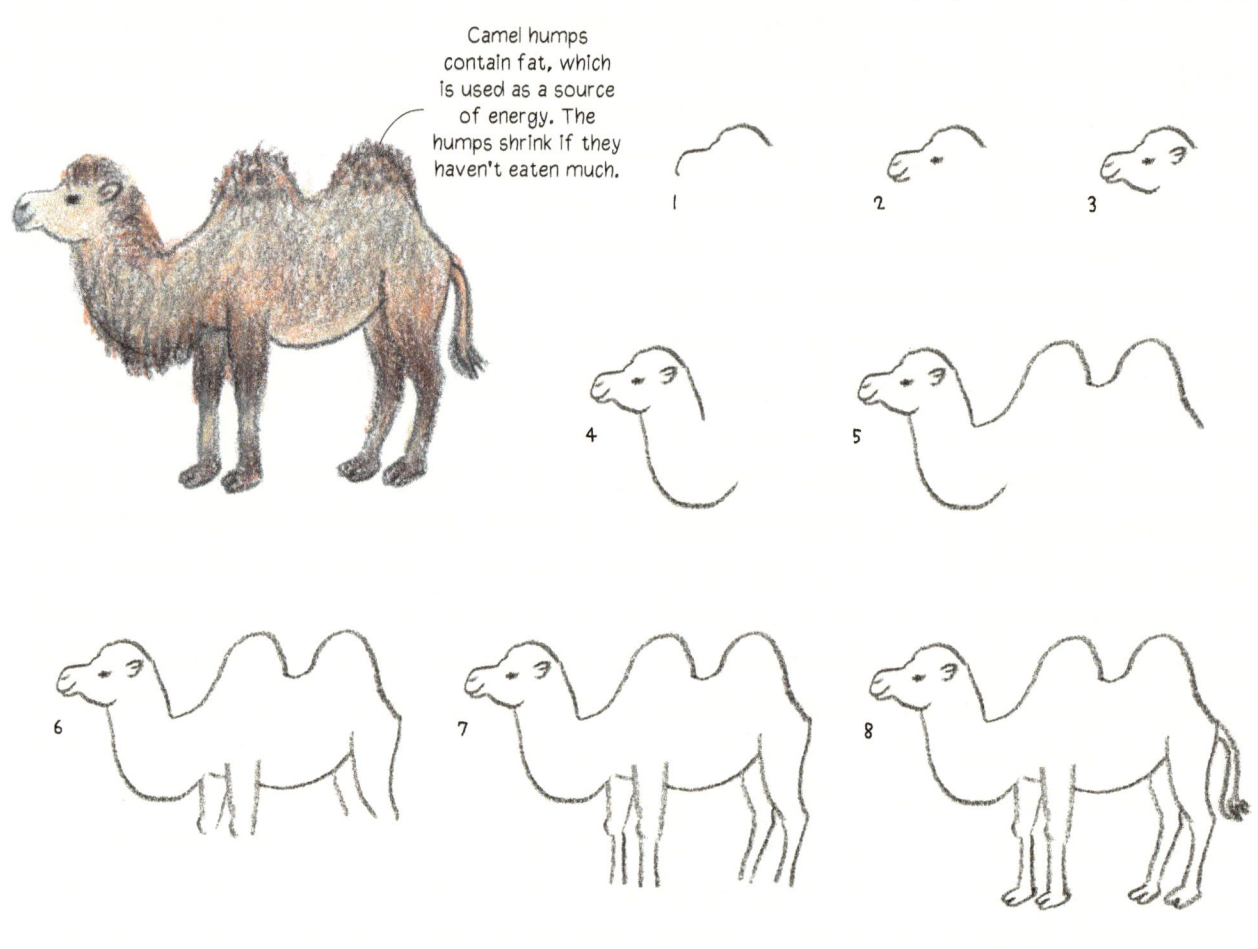

OTHER MEMBERS OF THE CAMEL FAMILY

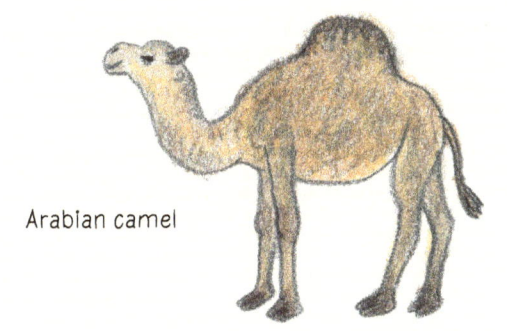

Arabian camel

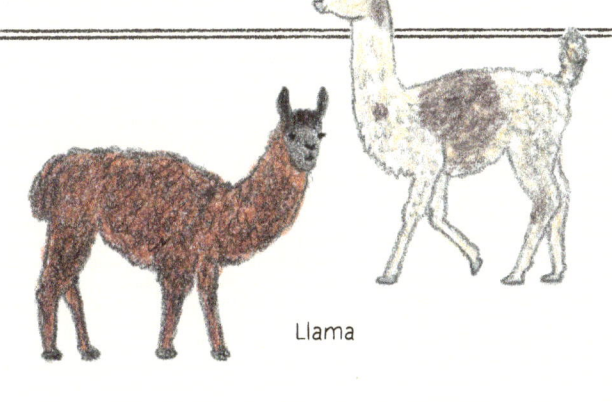

Llama

Camel footprint

Camels have two
toes on each foot.

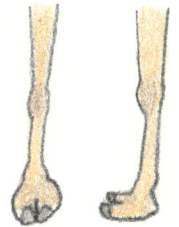

Their feet are big
to help them walk
long distances in the
desert sands.

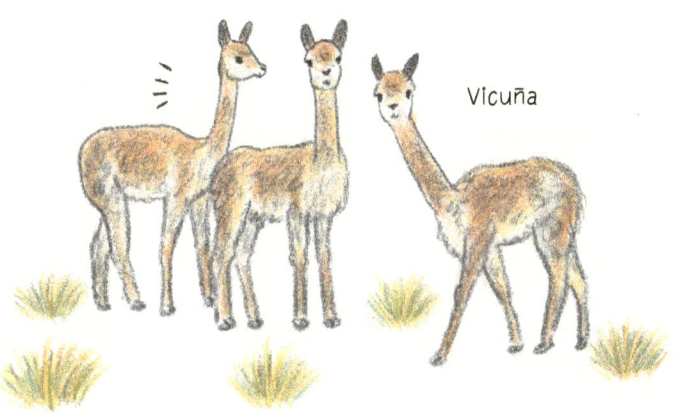

Vicuña

Vicuñas are a wild species and all
have the same colors.

ALPACA

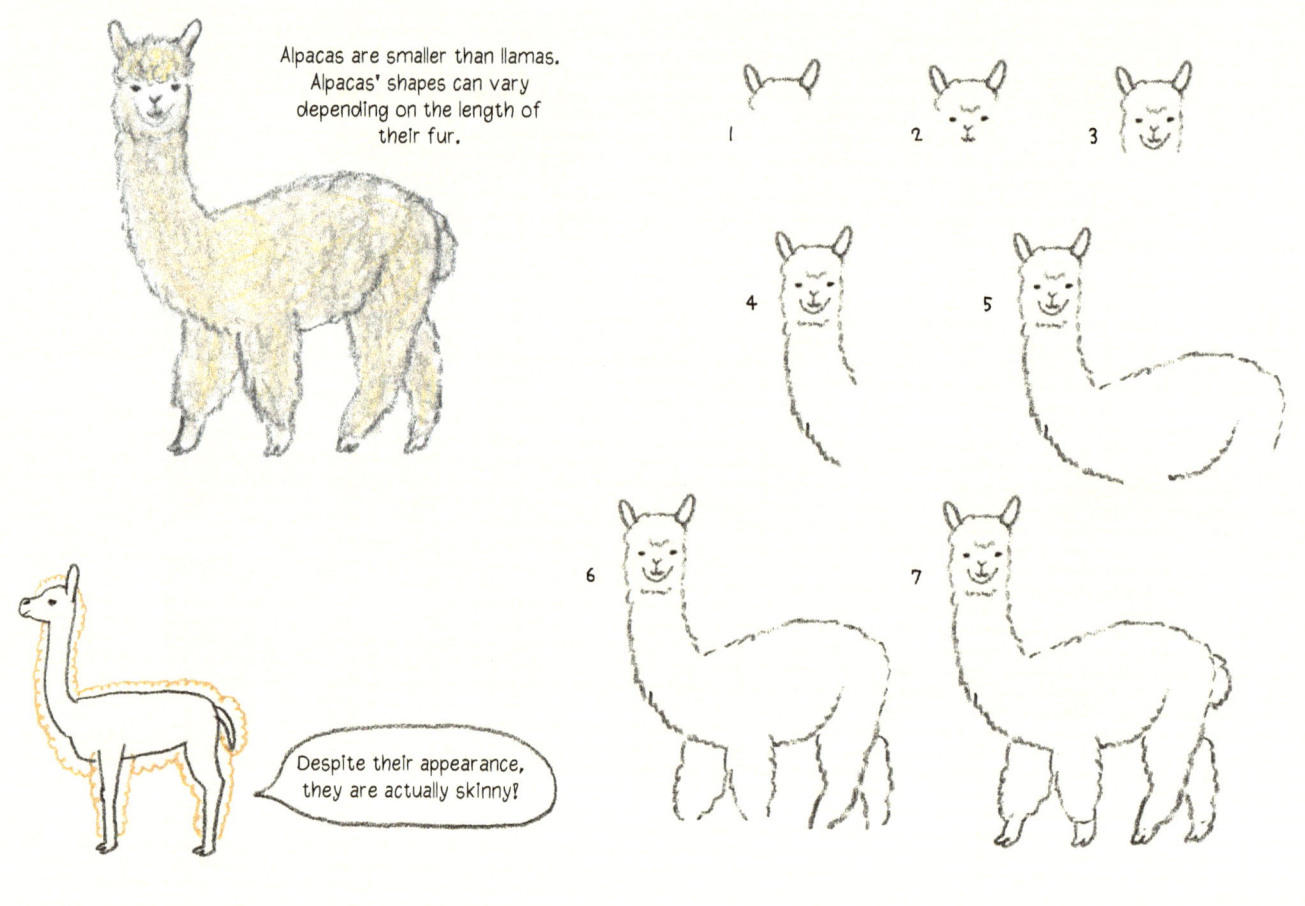

Alpacas are smaller than llamas. Alpacas' shapes can vary depending on the length of their fur.

Despite their appearance, they are actually skinny!

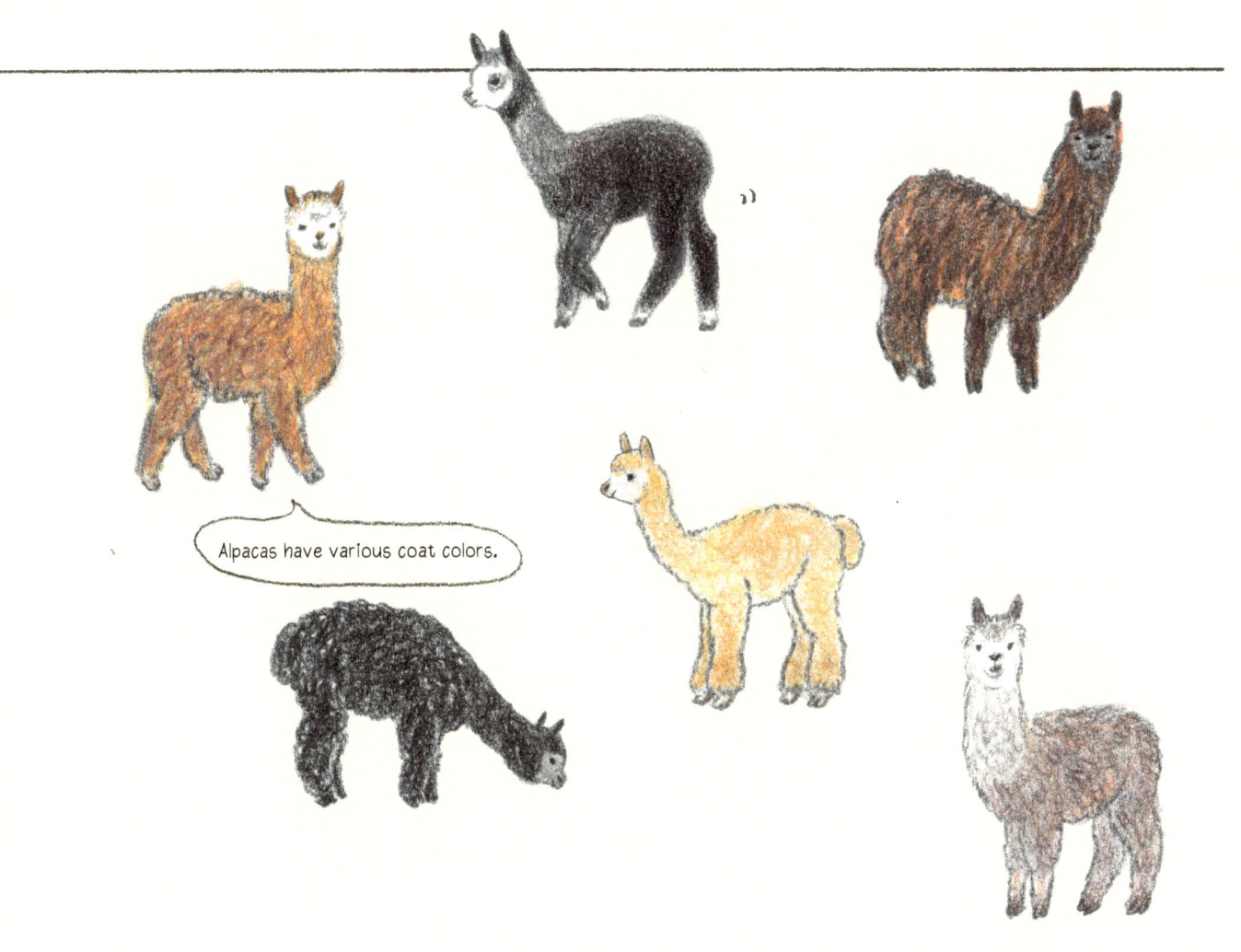

Alpacas have various coat colors.

HORSE

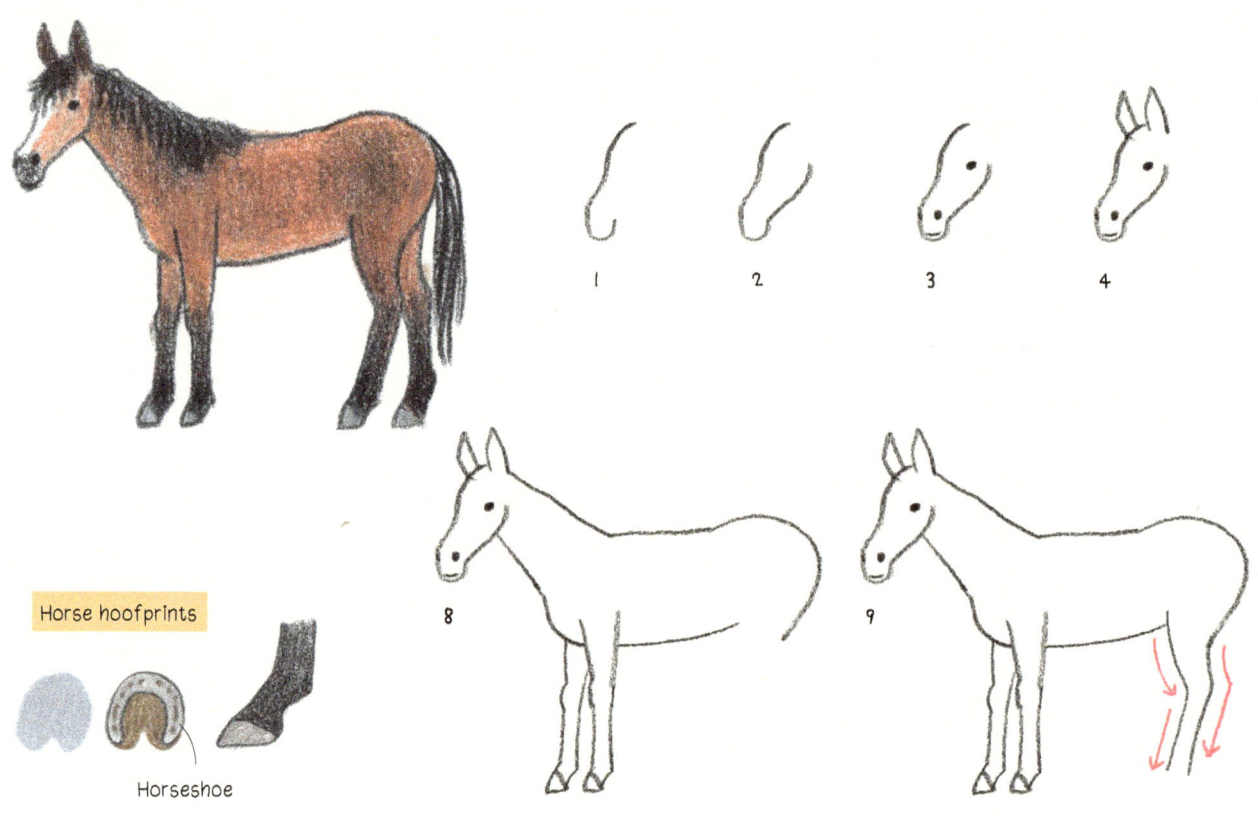

1

2

3

4

8

9

Horse hoofprints

Horseshoe

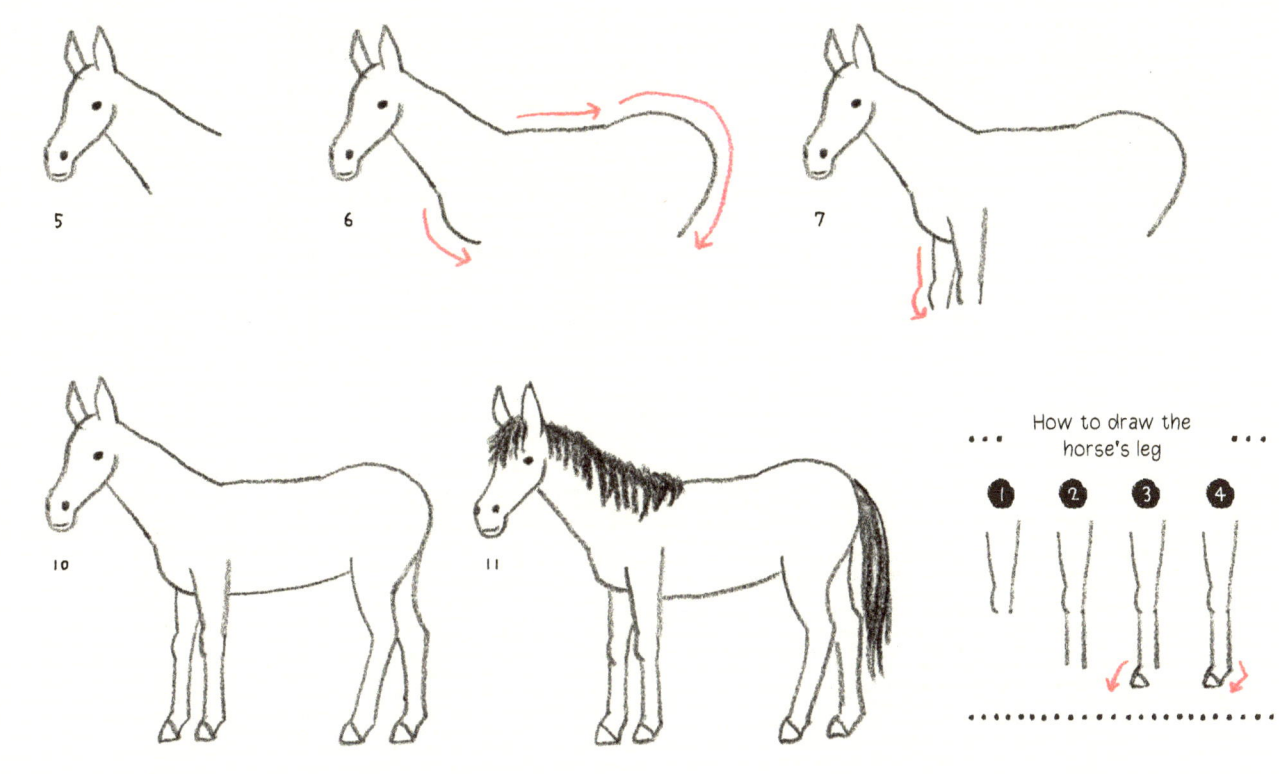

5

6

7

10

11

How to draw the
horse's leg

1 2 3 4

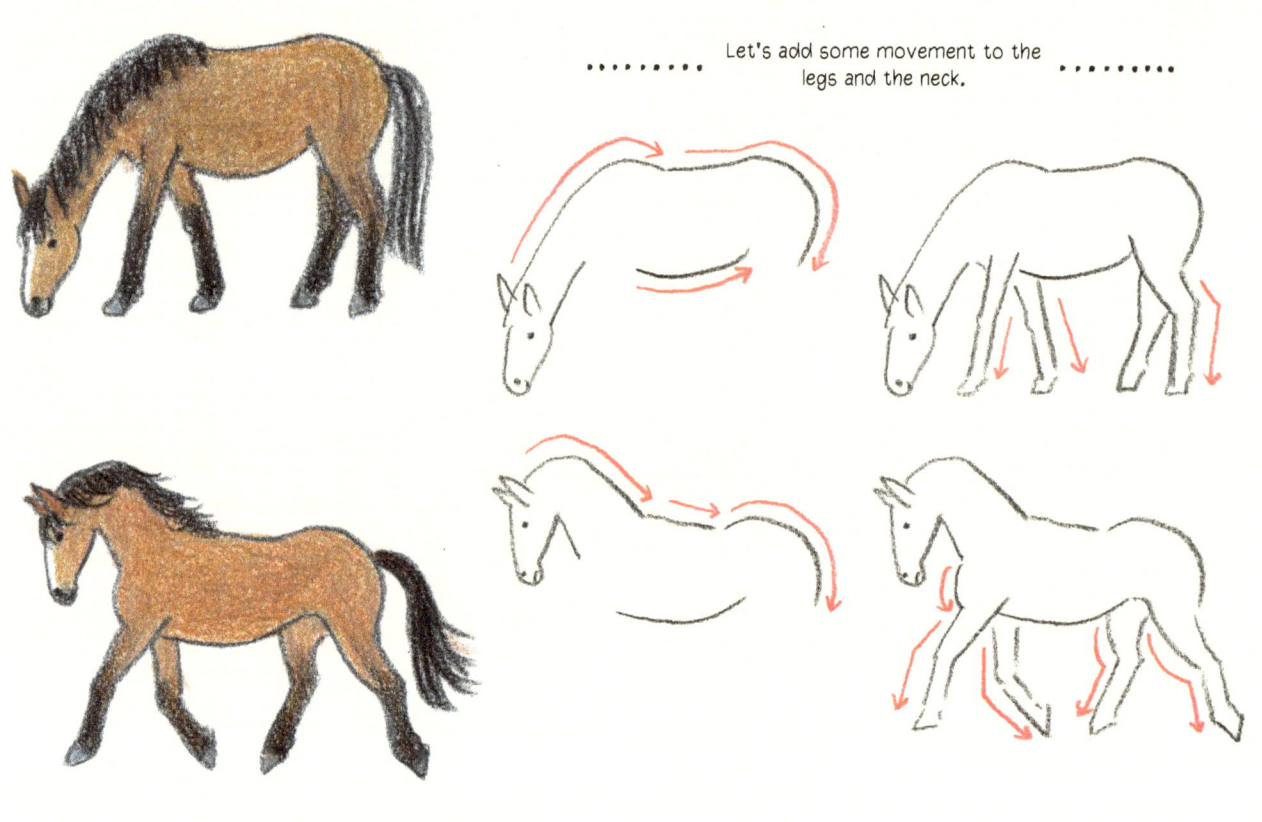

Let's add some movement to the
legs and the neck.

DONKEY

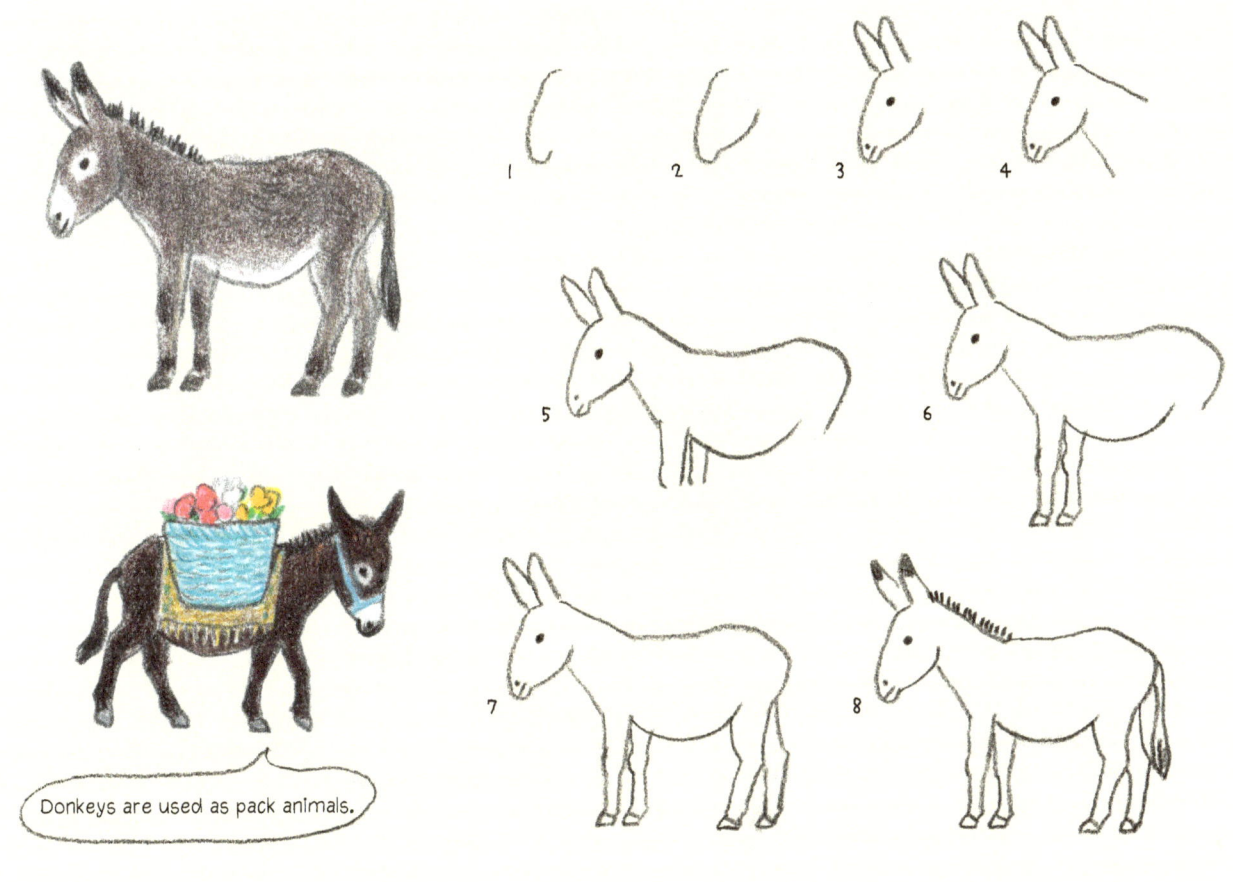

Donkeys are used as pack animals.

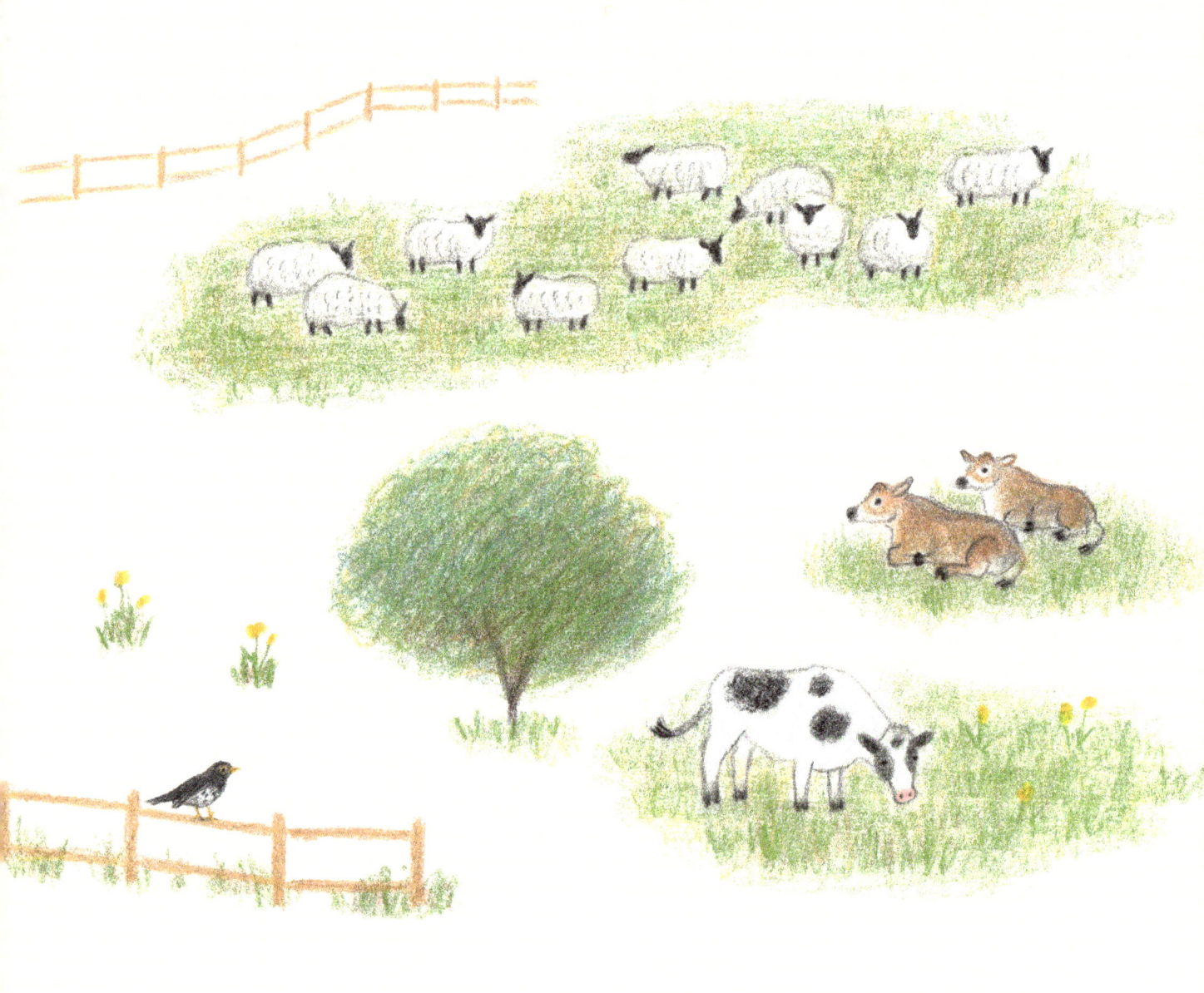

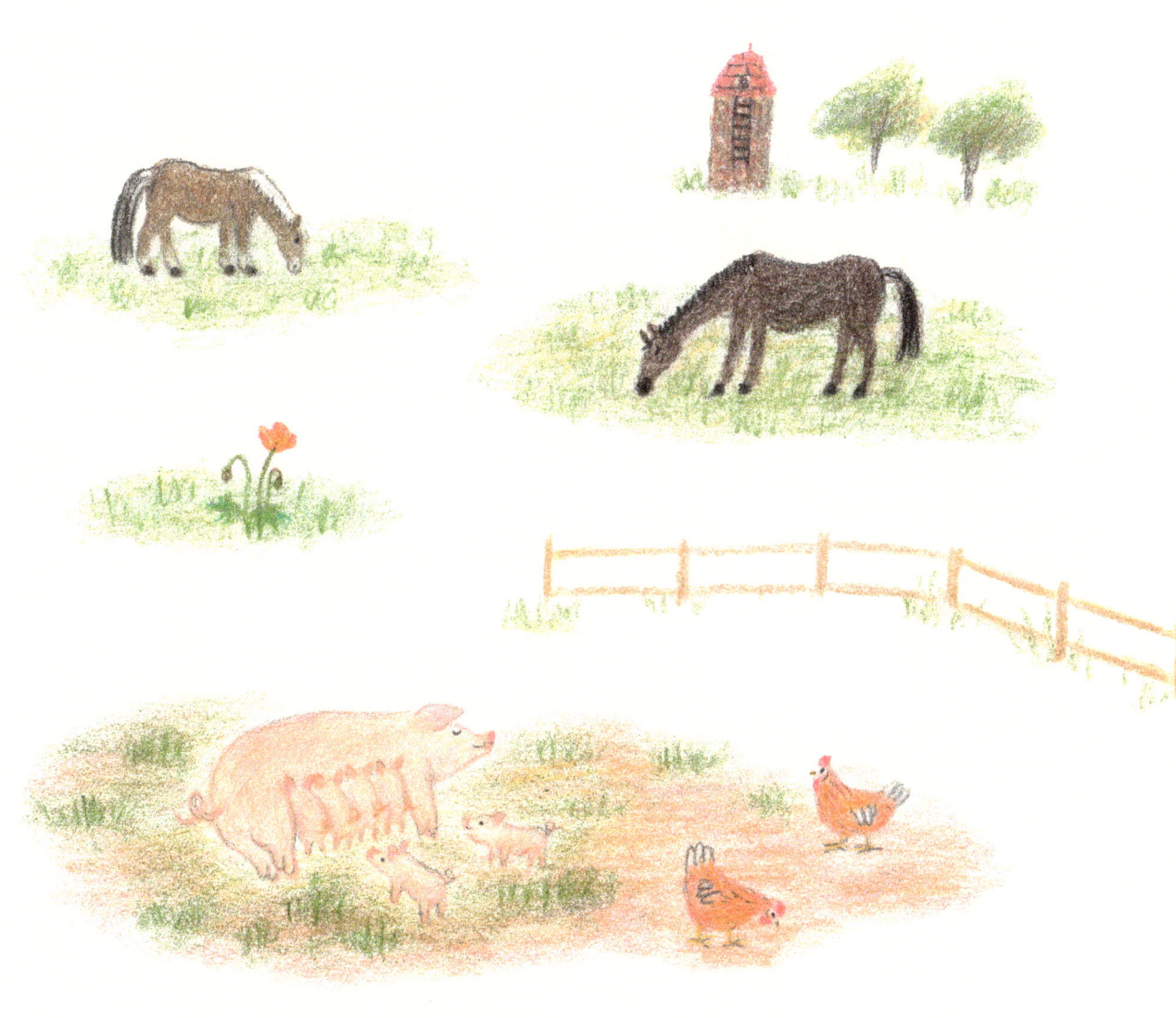

CAT

••• Let's try drawing a cat's face first. •••

| | 1 | 2 | 3 | 4 | 5 | 6 |

Cats have different facial expressions since each has its own character.

•••••• Eye expression ••••••

The pupils get bigger when it's dark and smaller when it's bright.

Squinting eyes

•••••••••••••••••••• Eye color ••••••••••••••••••••

Green   Yellow   Brown   Blue   Odd eye

Odd eye, or heterochromia, occurs when each eye has a different color.

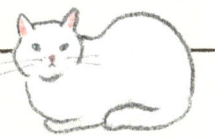

White

Black

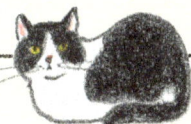

Black and white

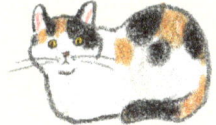

Calico

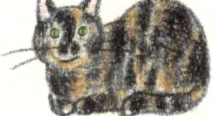

Orange and black

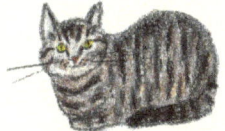

Tabby

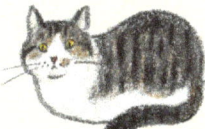

White and tabby

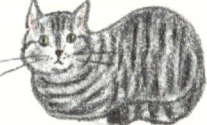

Grey tabby

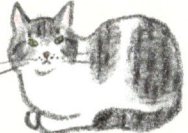

Grey and white tabby

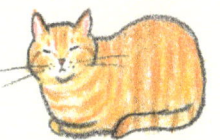

Orange tiger

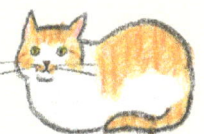

Orange and white tiger

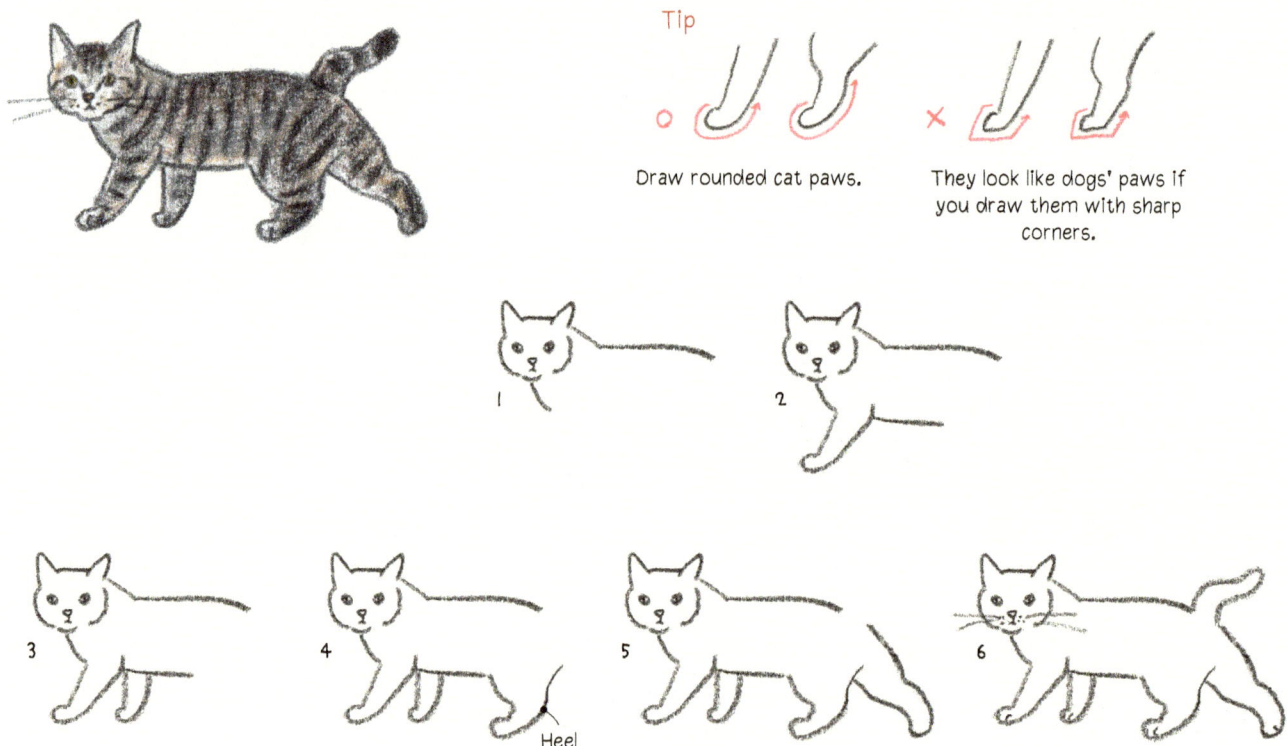

Tip

Draw rounded cat paws.

They look like dogs' paws if you draw them with sharp corners.

1

2

3

4

Heel

5

6

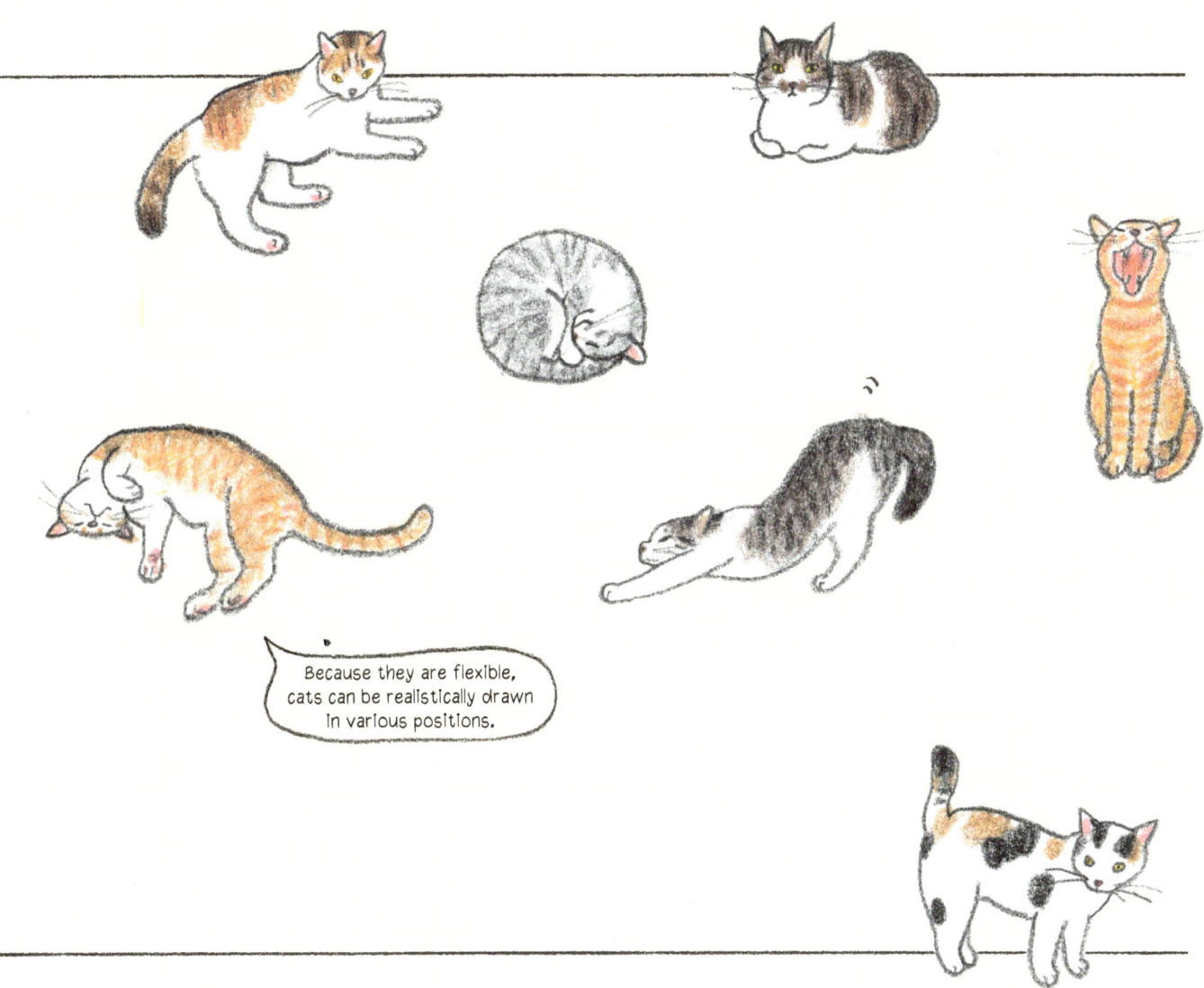

Because they are flexible,
cats can be realistically drawn
in various positions.

DIFFERENT TYPES OF CATS

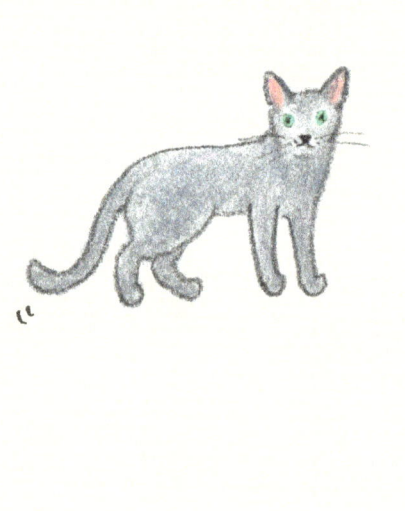
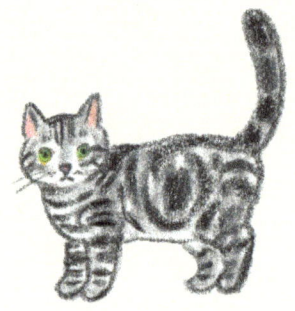
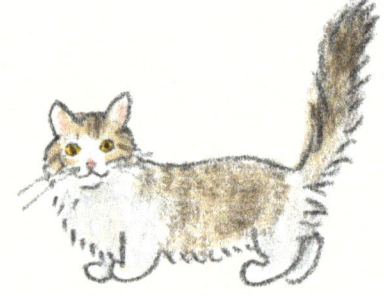
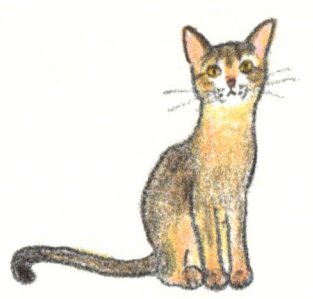
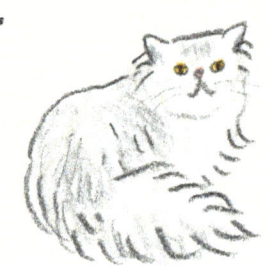

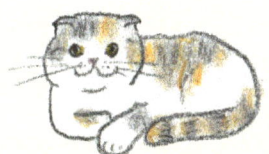
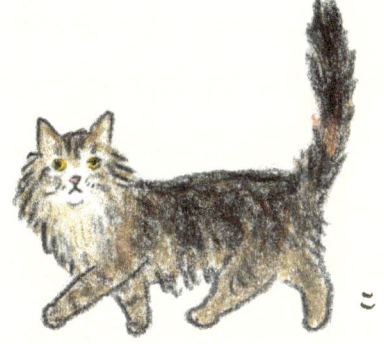
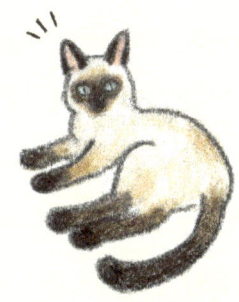
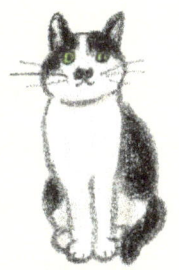
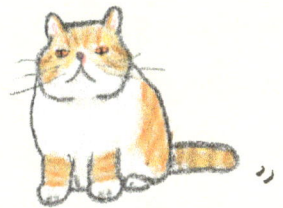

LION

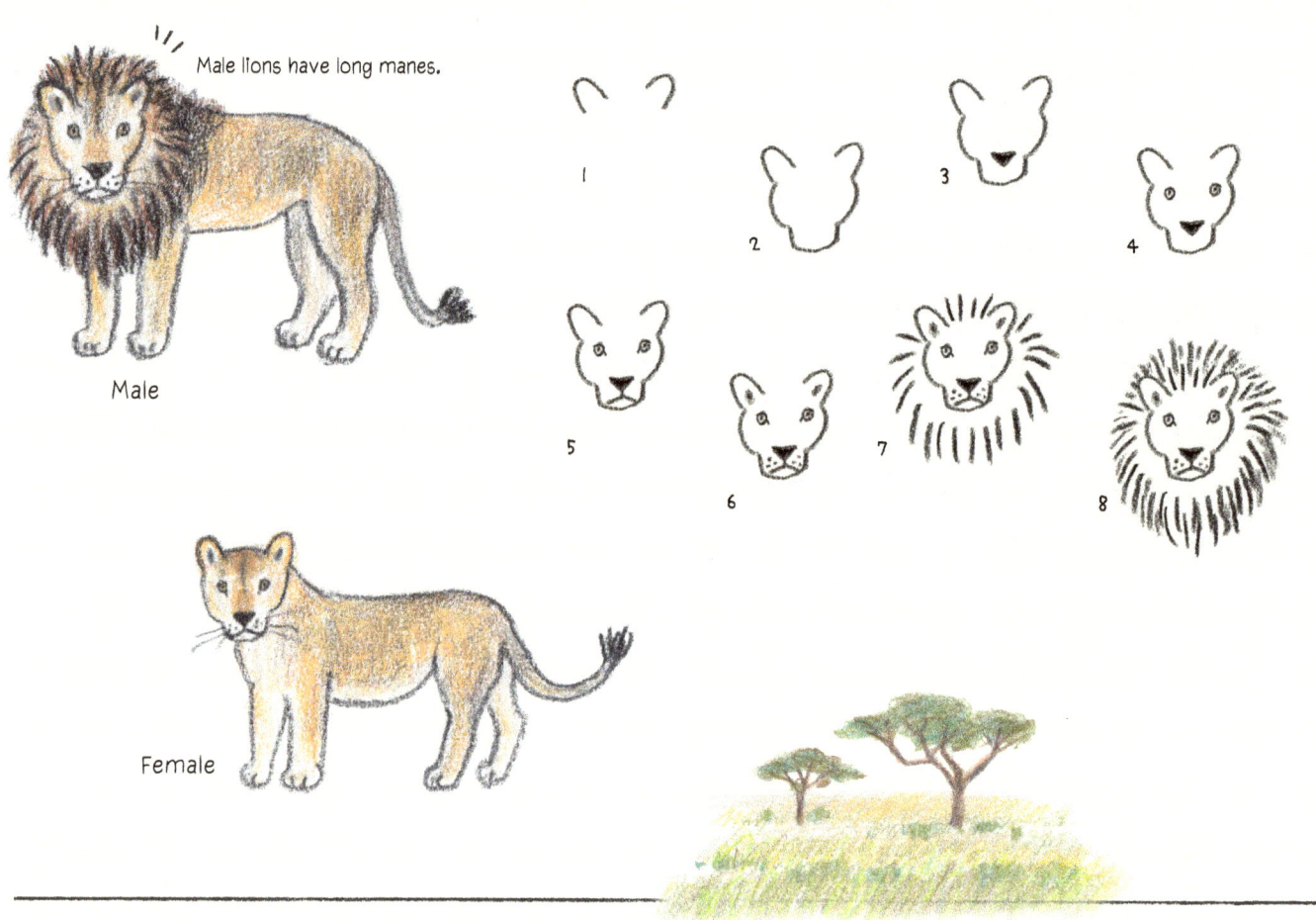

Male lions have long manes.

Male

Female

1

2

3

4

5

6

7

8

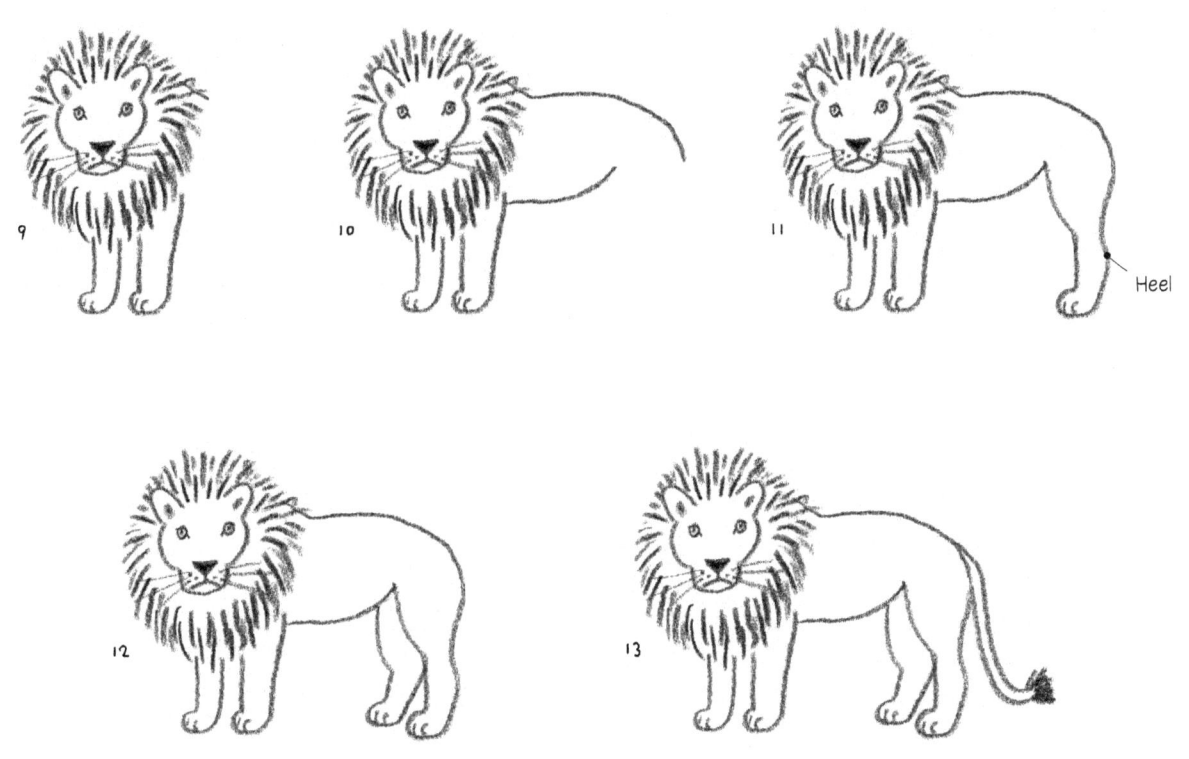

9

10

11

Heel

12

13

TIGER

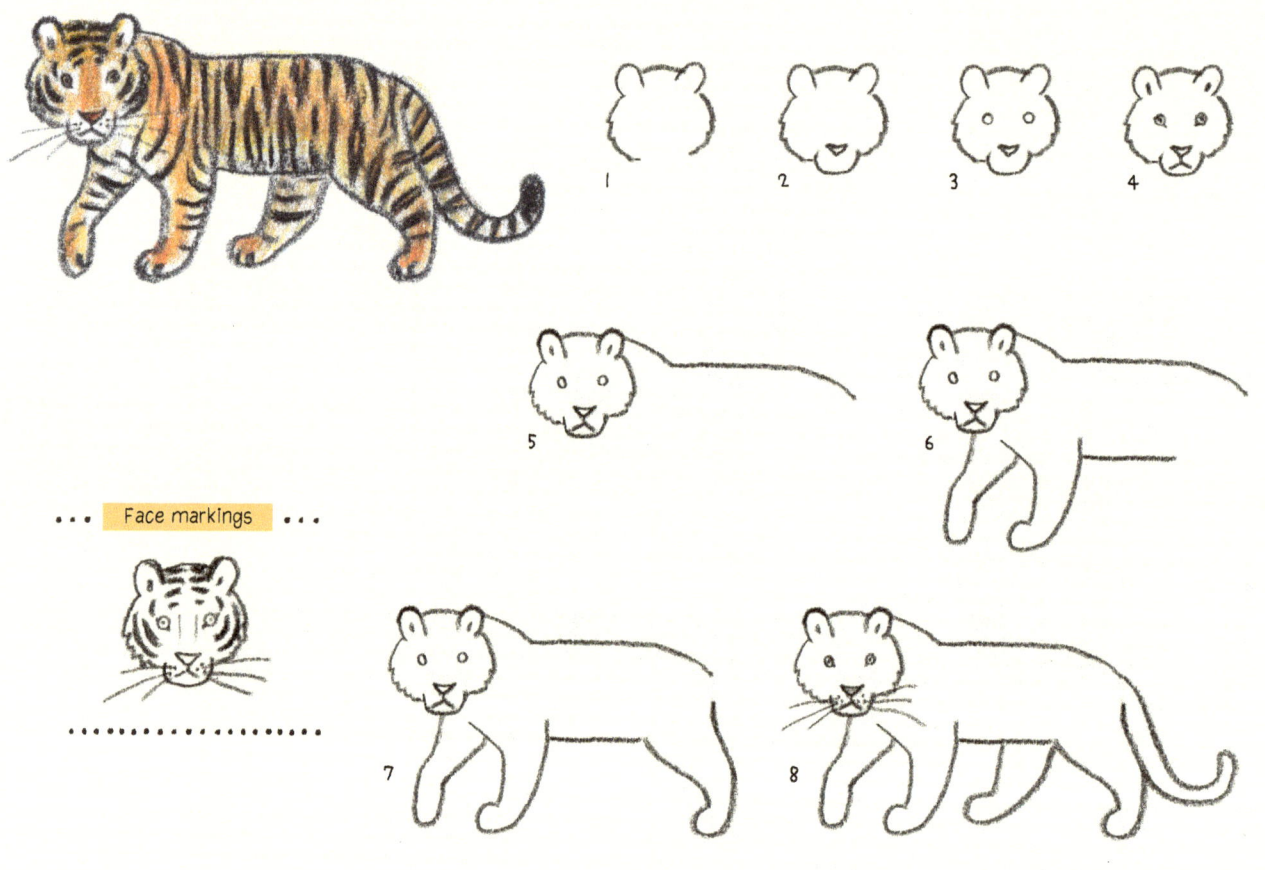

Face markings

CHEETAH

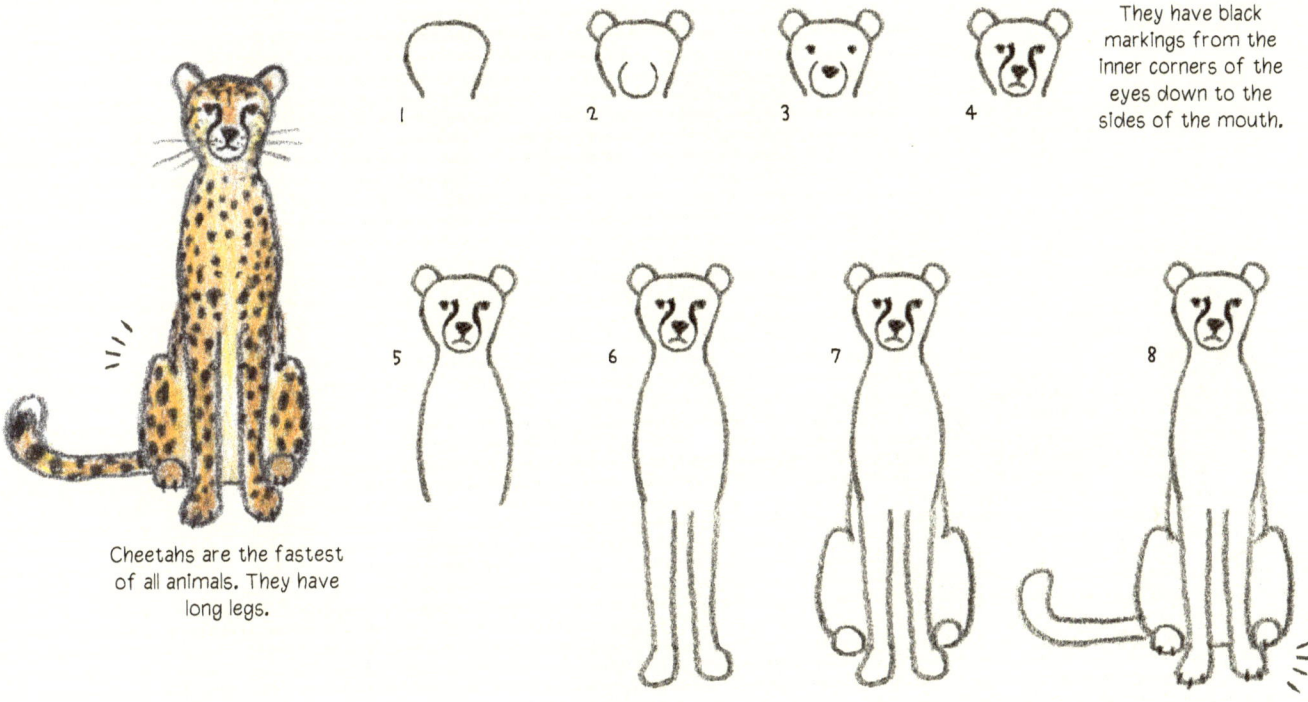

1

2

3

4

They have black
markings from the
inner corners of the
eyes down to the
sides of the mouth.

5

6

7

8

Cheetahs are the fastest
of all animals. They have
long legs.

Among the big cats, only
cheetahs are unable to
retract their claws fully.

BIG CATS AND THEIR COATS

Let's compare big cats' patterns.

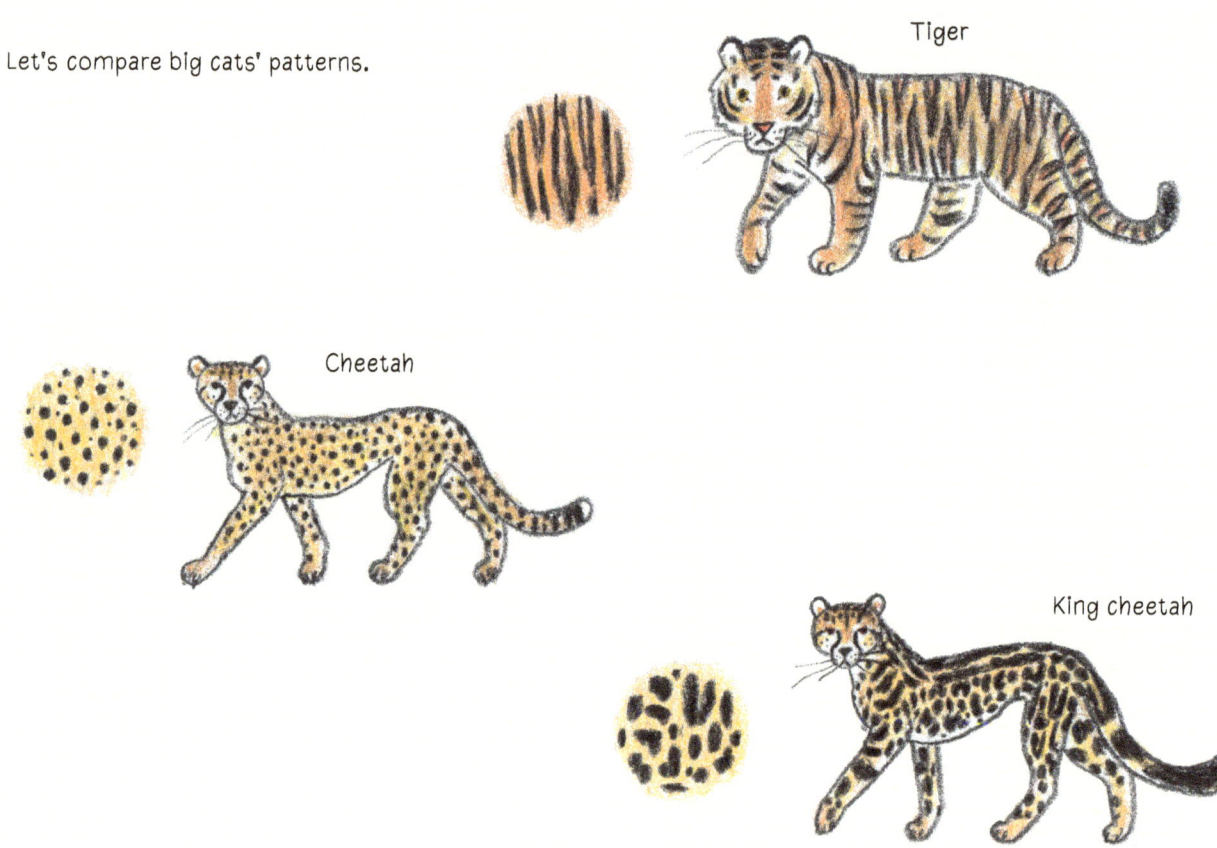

Tiger

Cheetah

King cheetah

King cheetahs are genetically mutated cheetahs,
causing them to have larger dark splotches.

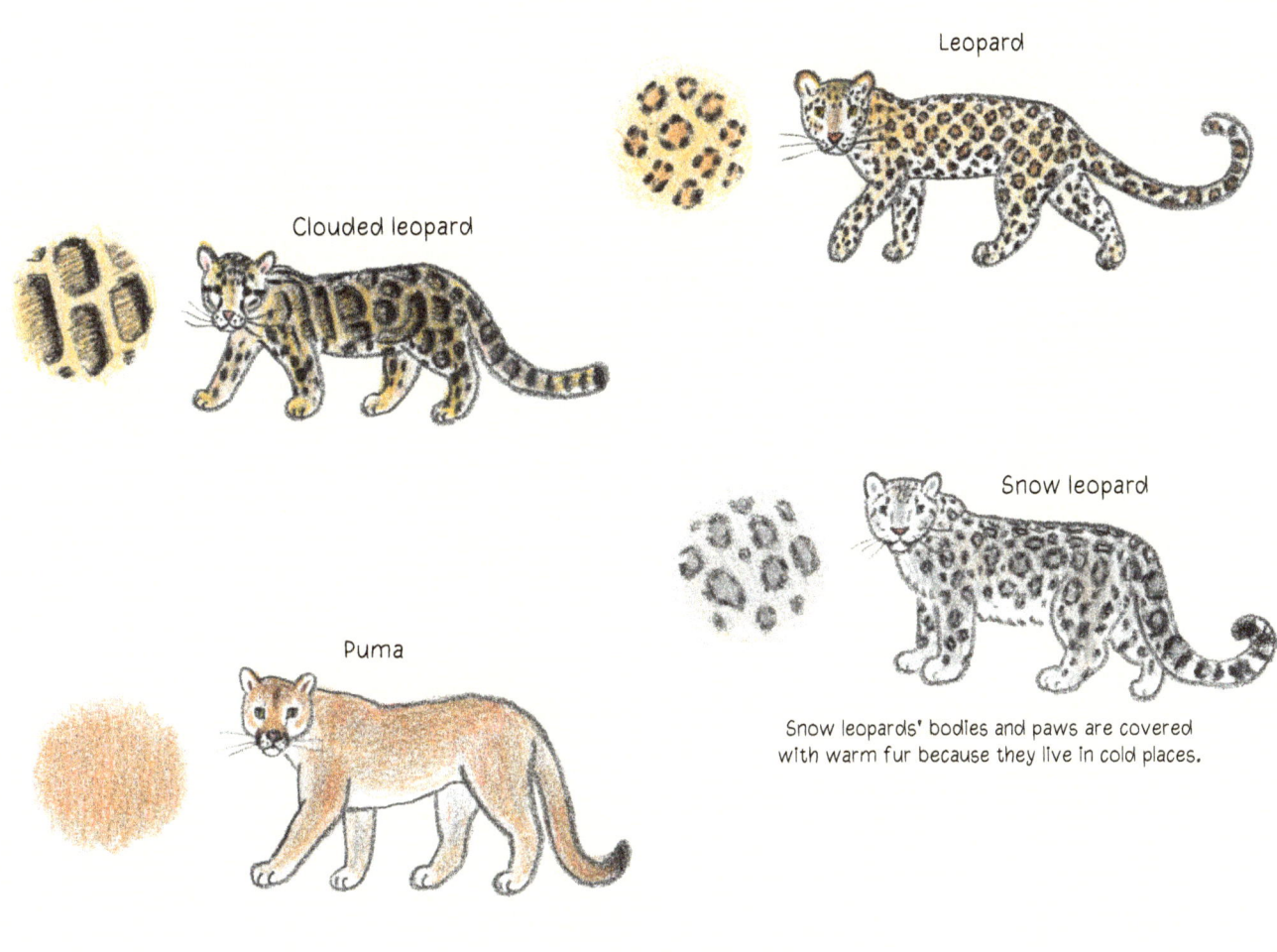

Leopard

Clouded leopard

Snow leopard

Snow leopards' bodies and paws are covered with warm fur because they live in cold places.

Puma

GIRAFFE

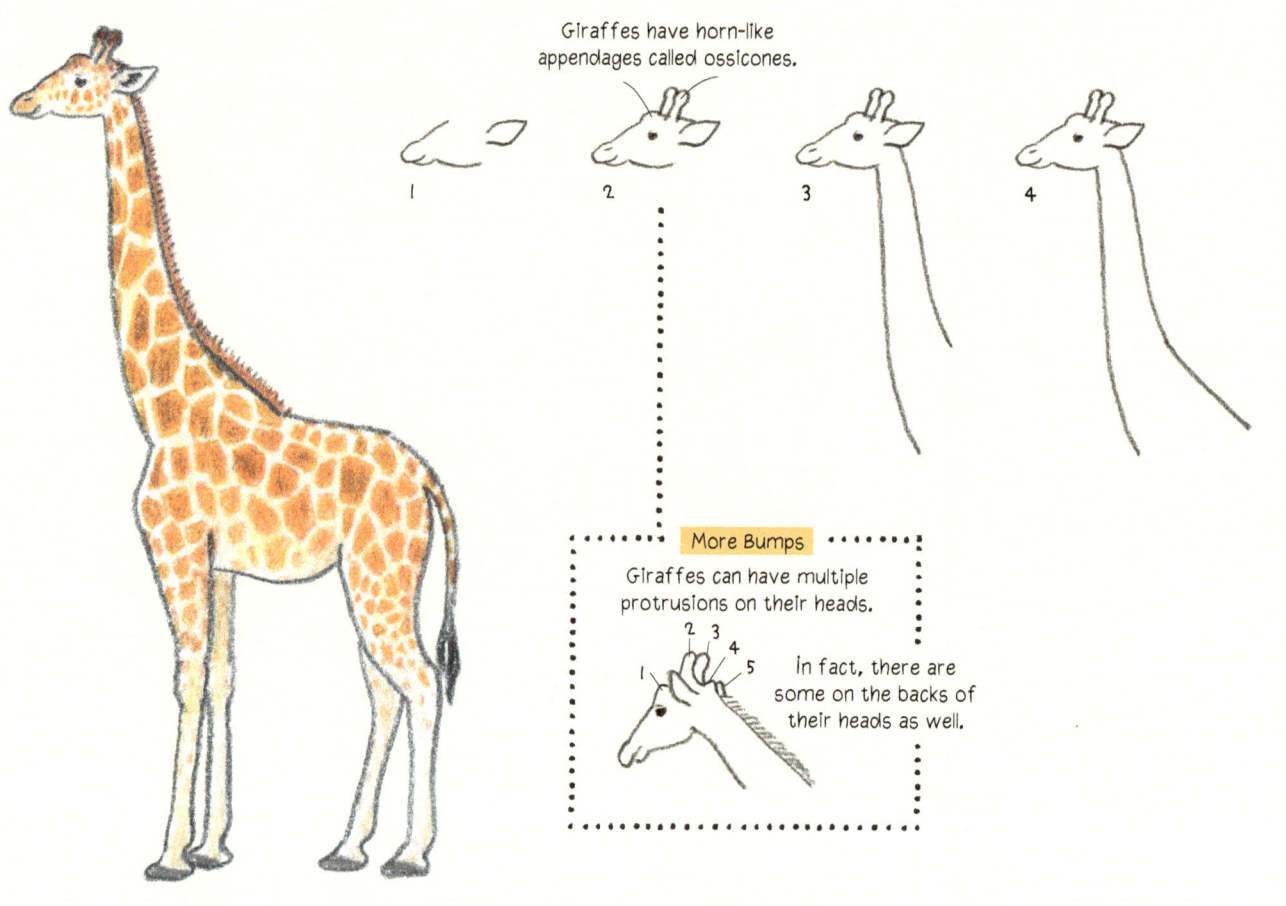

Giraffes have horn-like appendages called ossicones.

1 2 3 4

More Bumps

Giraffes can have multiple protrusions on their heads.

1 2 3 4 5

In fact, there are some on the backs of their heads as well.

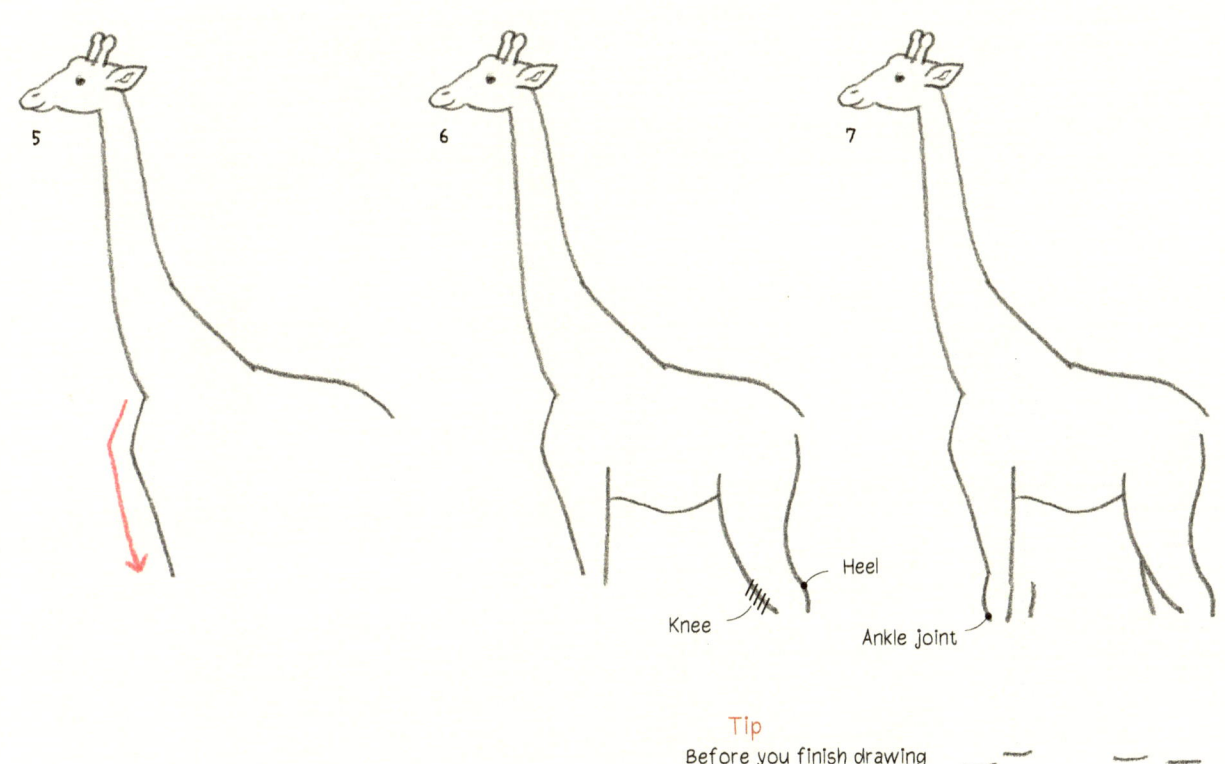

5

6

7

Knee

Heel

Ankle joint

Tip
Before you finish drawing
the giraffe's legs, lightly
sketch in the hooves.

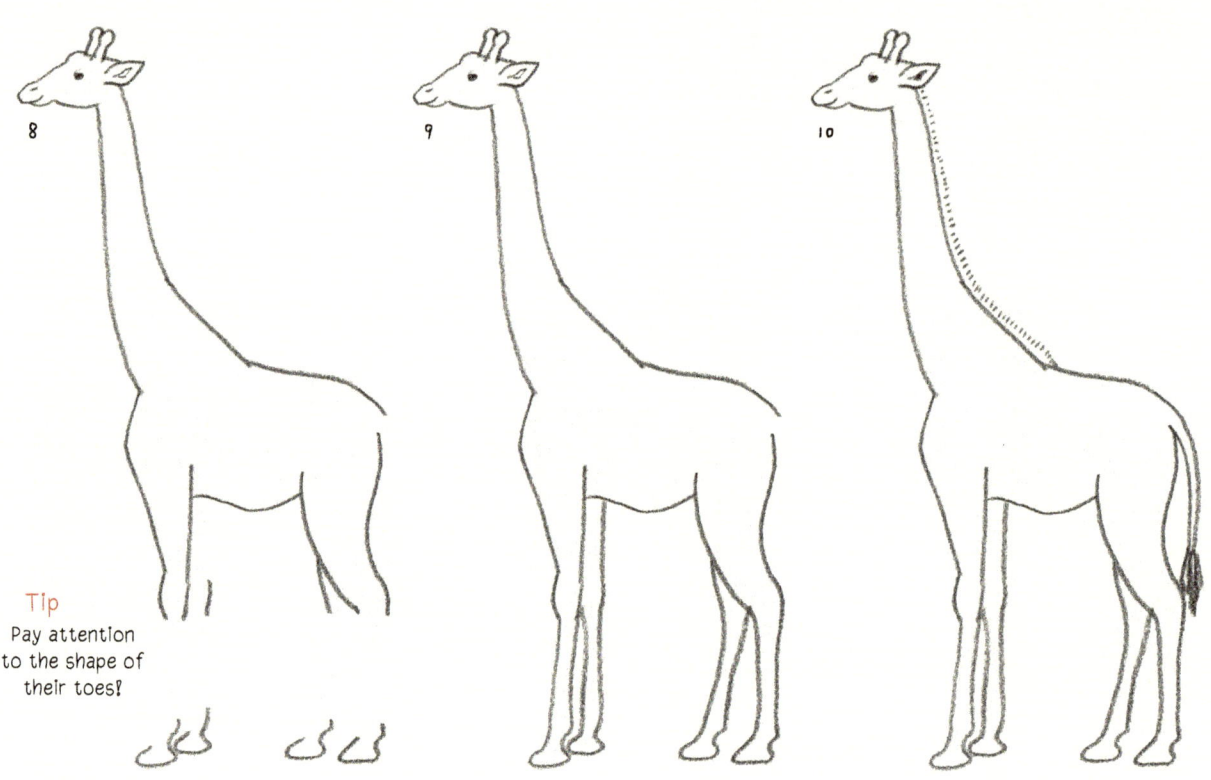

8

9

10

Tip
Pay attention
to the shape of
their toes!

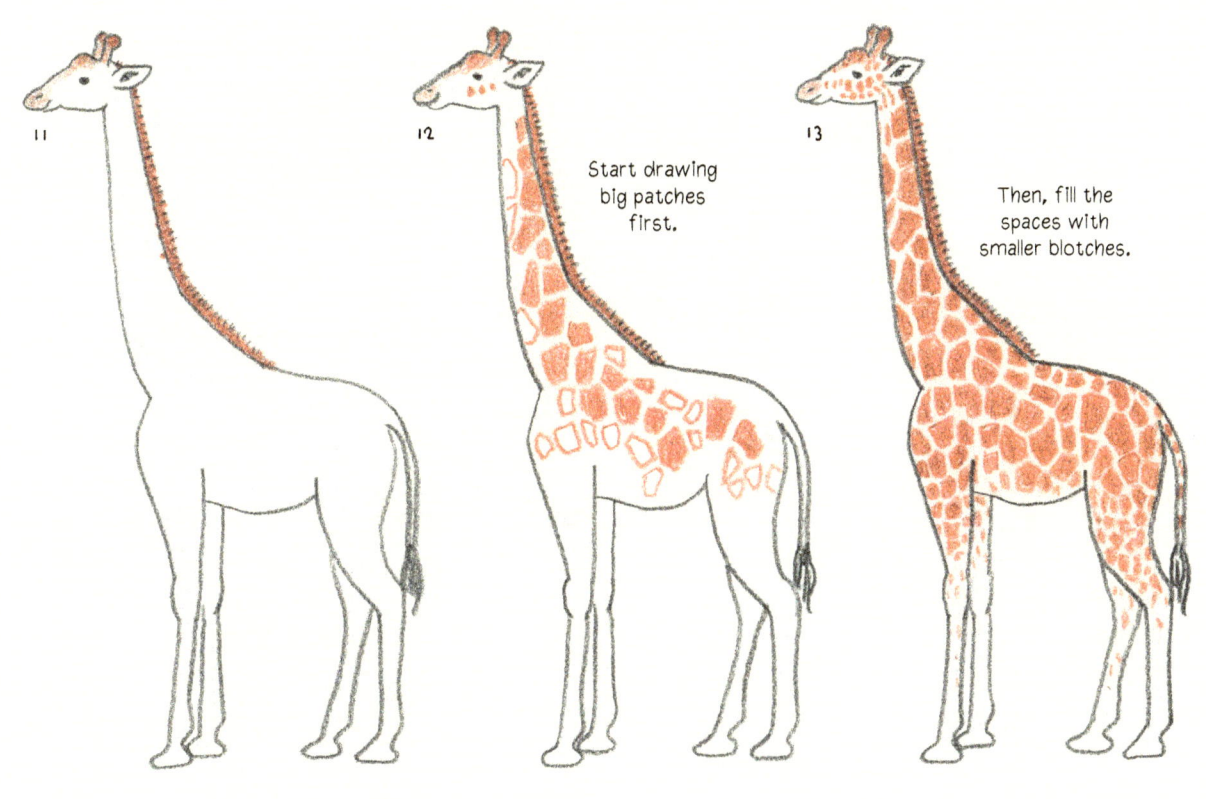

11

12 Start drawing
big patches
first.

13 Then, fill the
spaces with
smaller blotches.

OKAPI

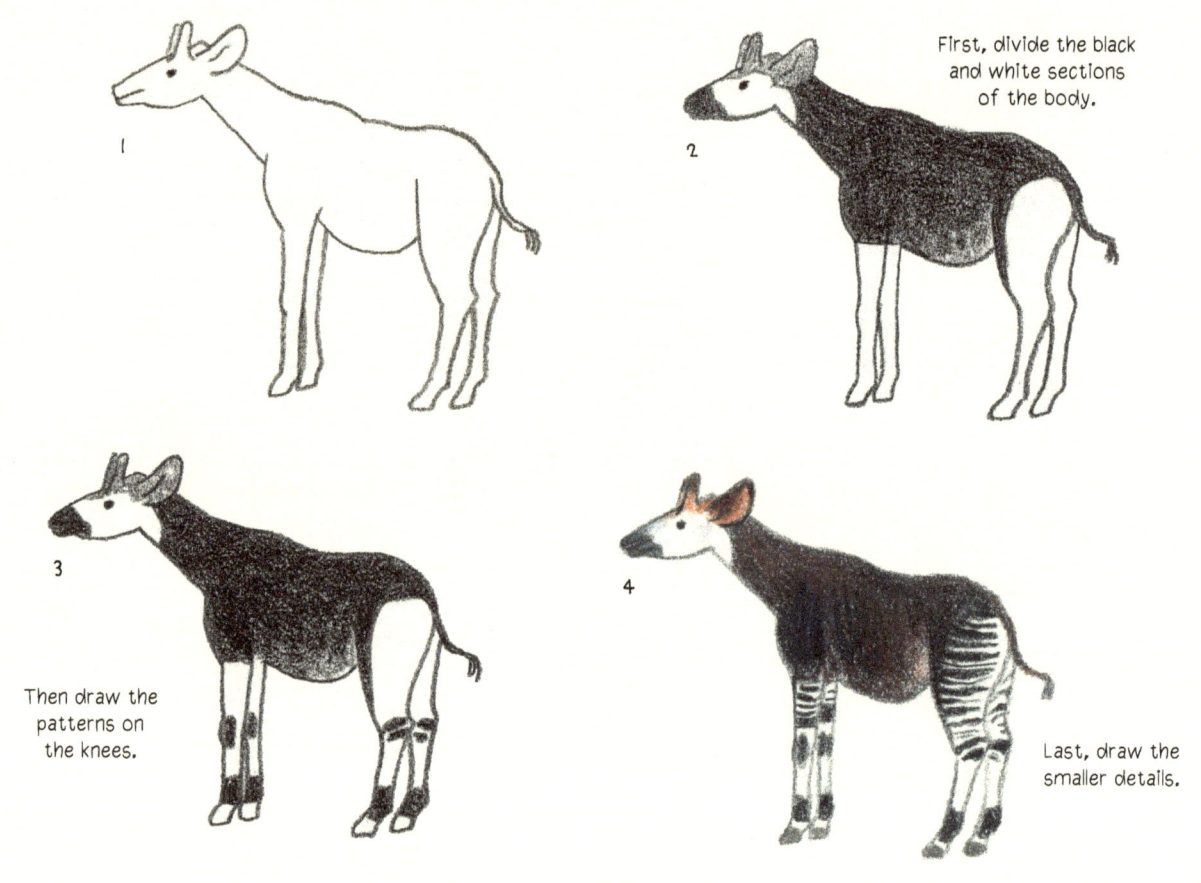

1

2 First, divide the black and white sections of the body.

3 Then draw the patterns on the knees.

4 Last, draw the smaller details.

ZEBRA

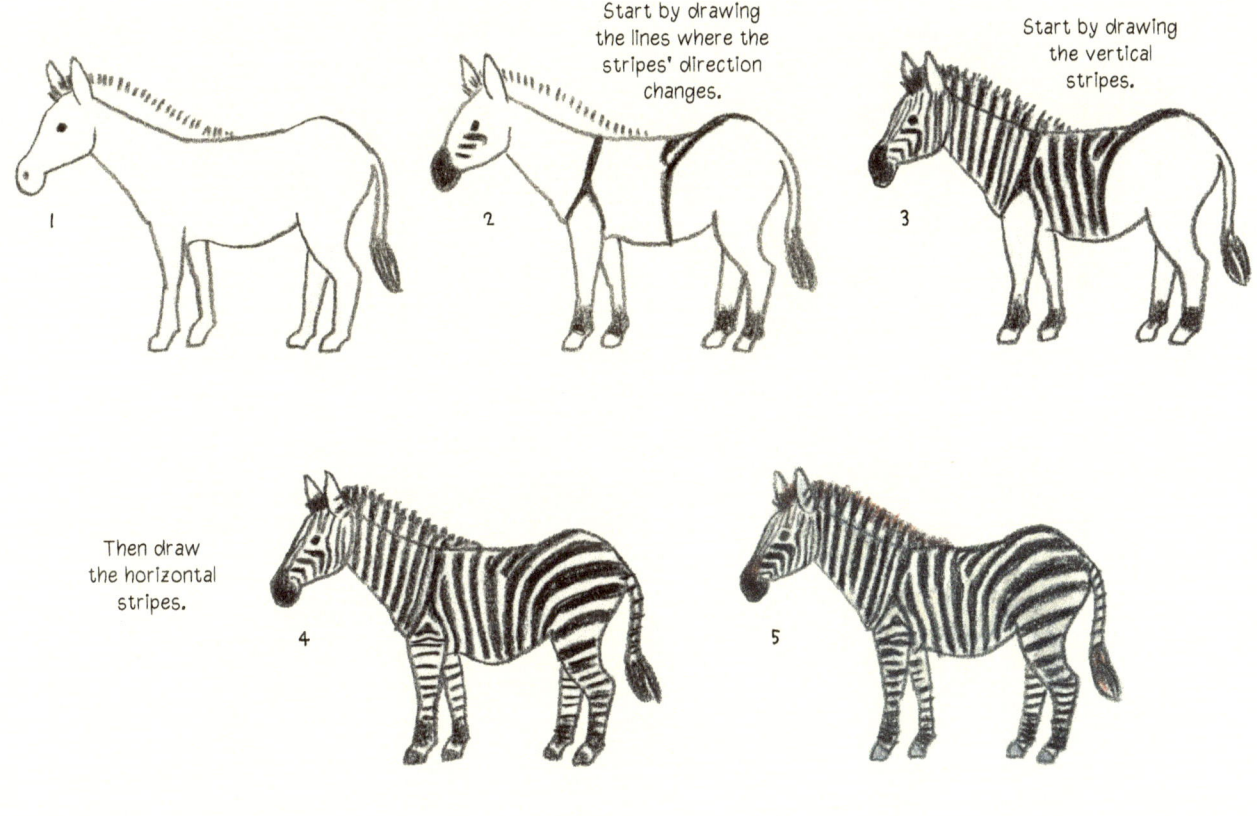

1

Start by drawing
the lines where the
stripes' direction
changes.

2

Start by drawing
the vertical
stripes.

3

Then draw
the horizontal
stripes.

4

5

HIPPOPOTAMUS

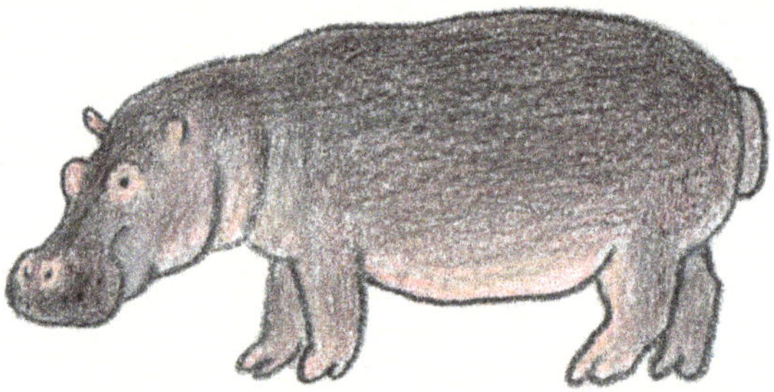

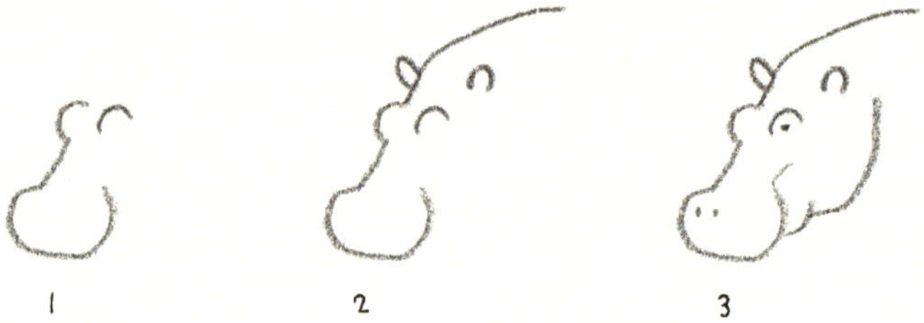

1

2

3

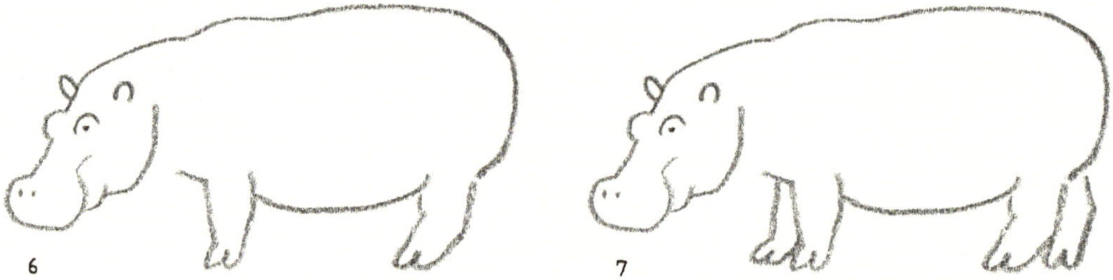

6

7

The ears, eyes, and nose emerge from
the water at the same time.

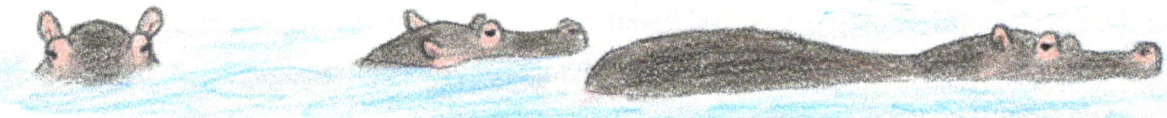

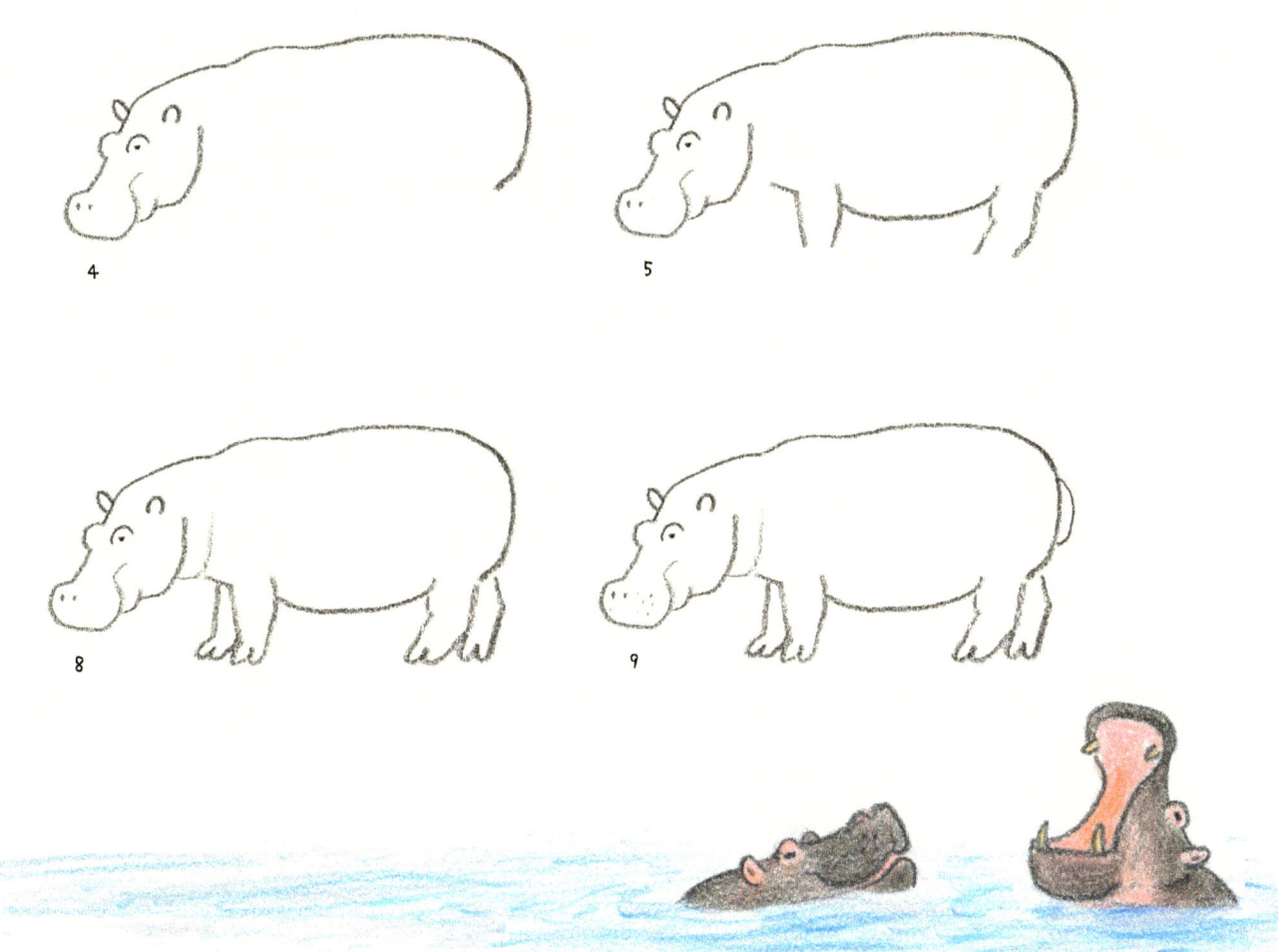

4

5

8

9

RHINOCEROS

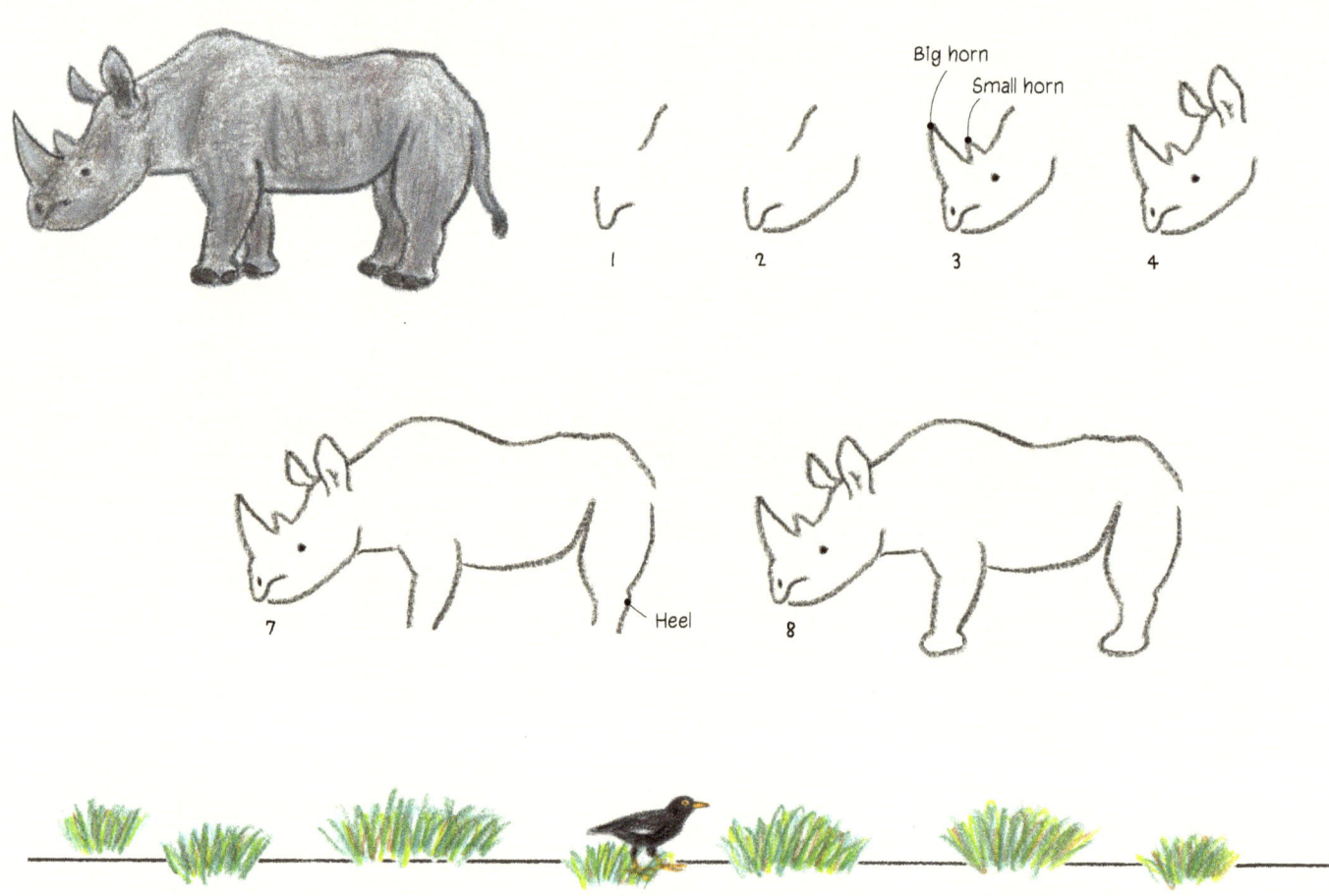

Big horn
Small horn

1

2

3

4

7

Heel

8

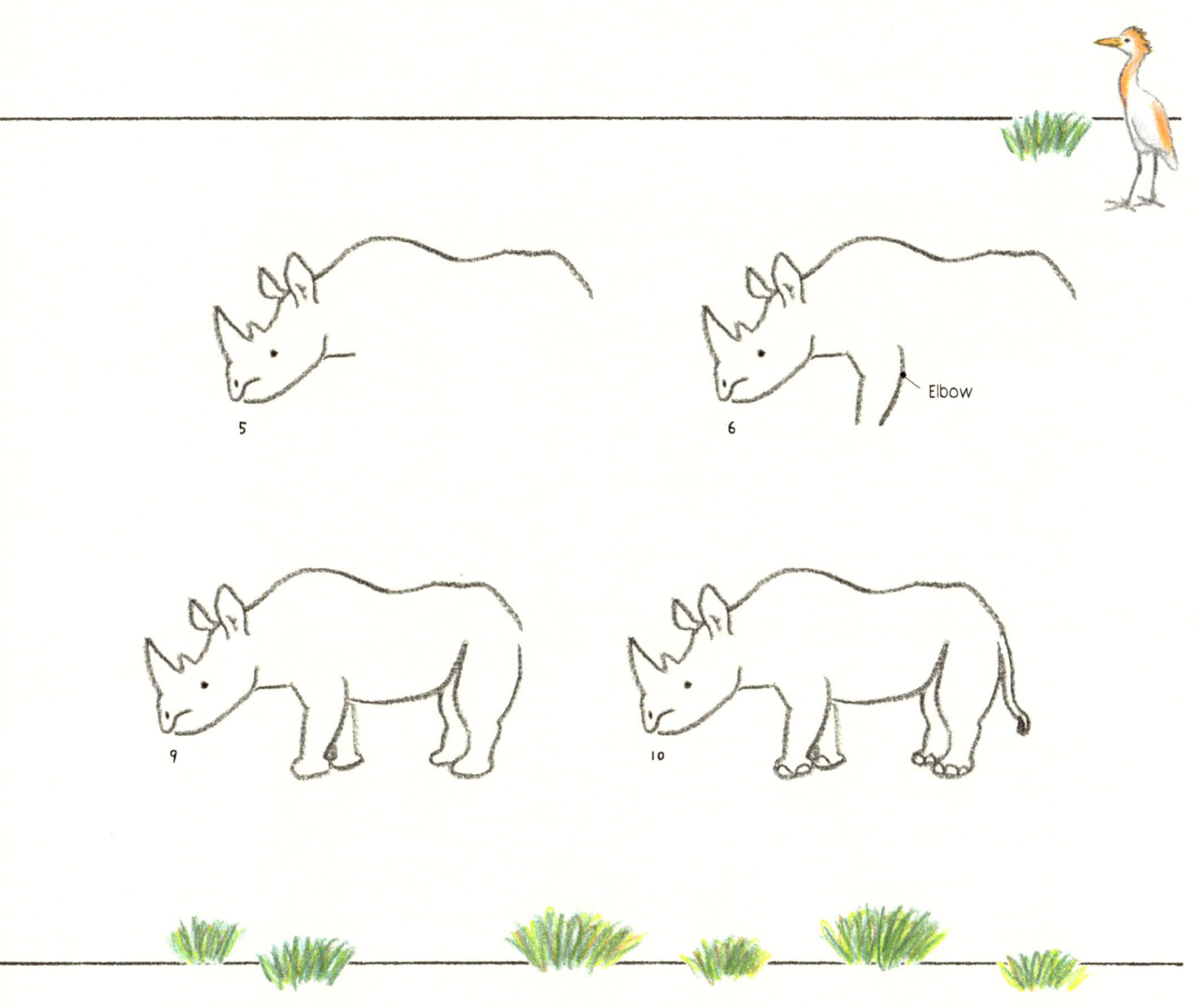

5

6 Elbow

9

10

AFRICAN ELEPHANT

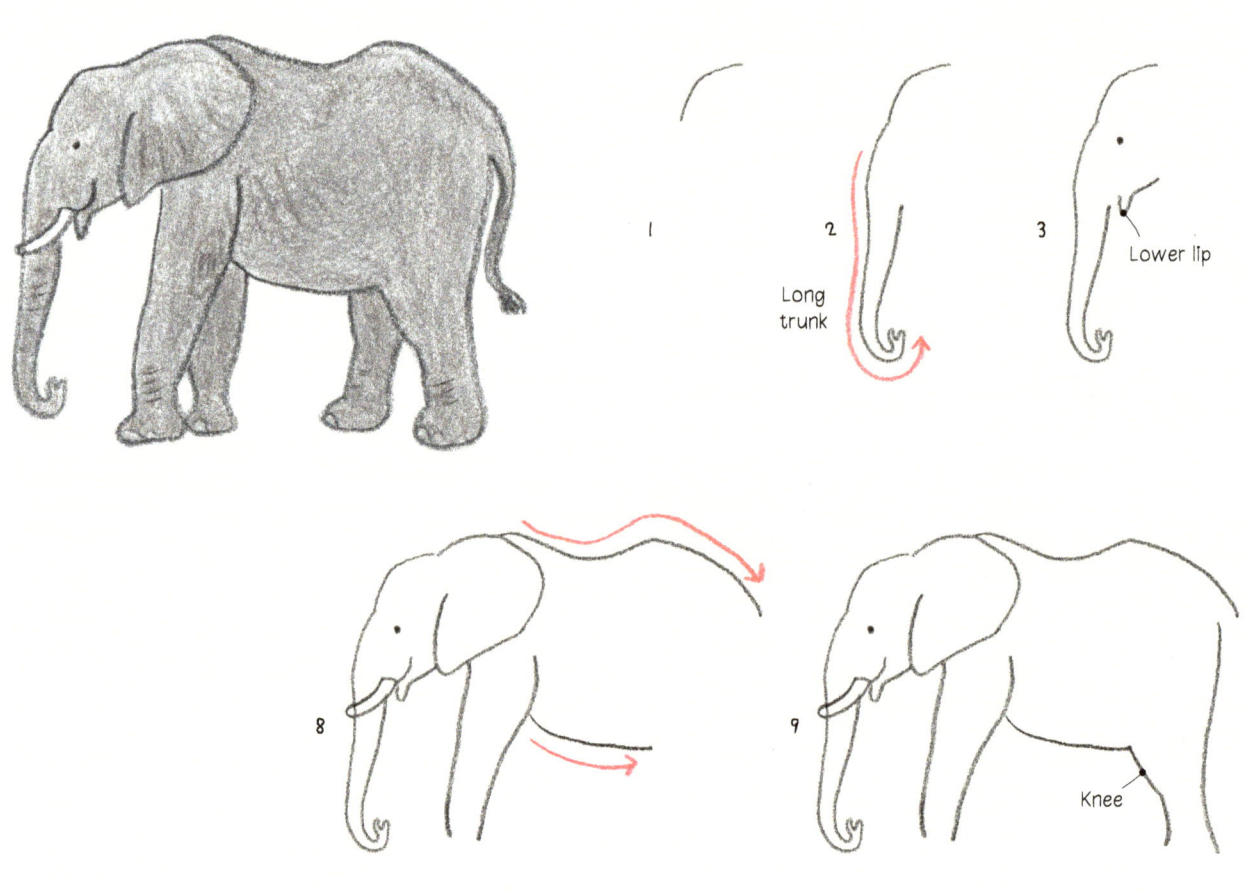

1

2

Long
trunk

3

Lower lip

8

9

Knee

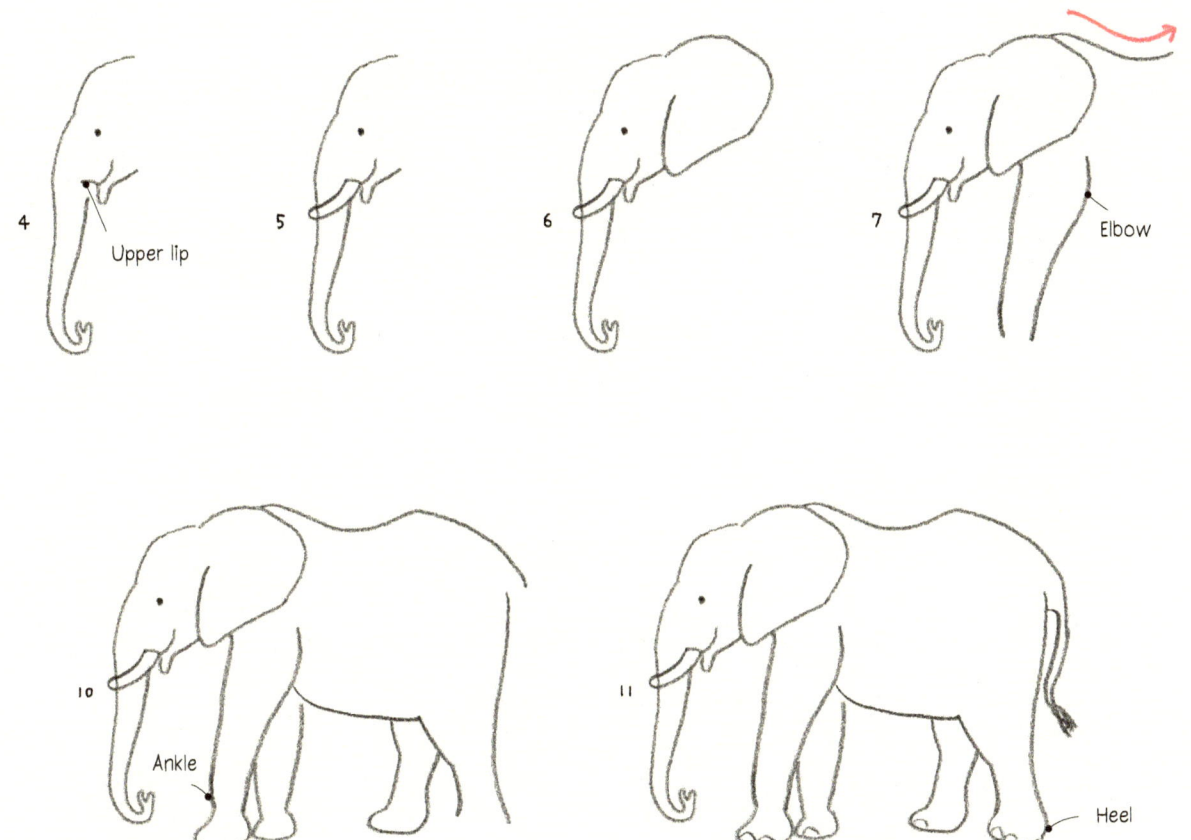

4 Upper lip

5

6

7 Elbow

10 Ankle

11 Heel

Big ears

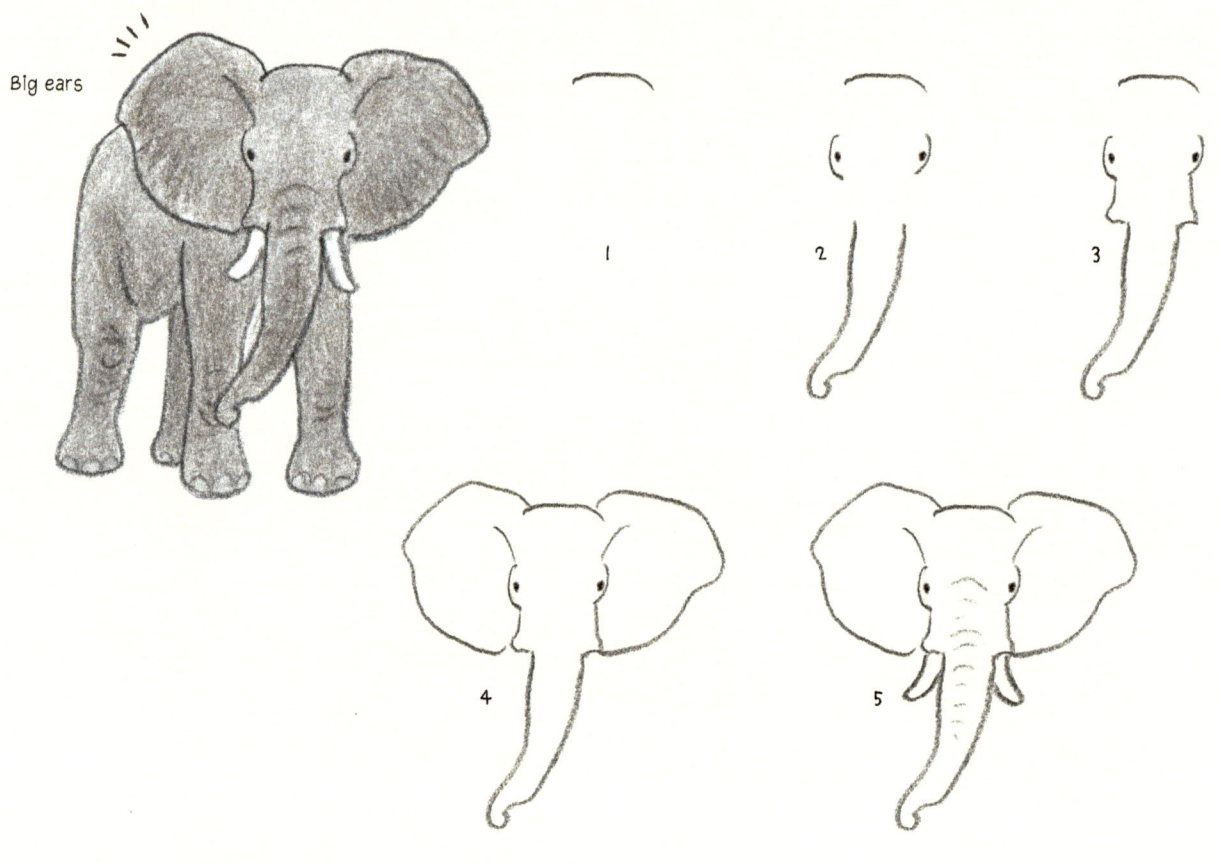

1

2

3

4

5

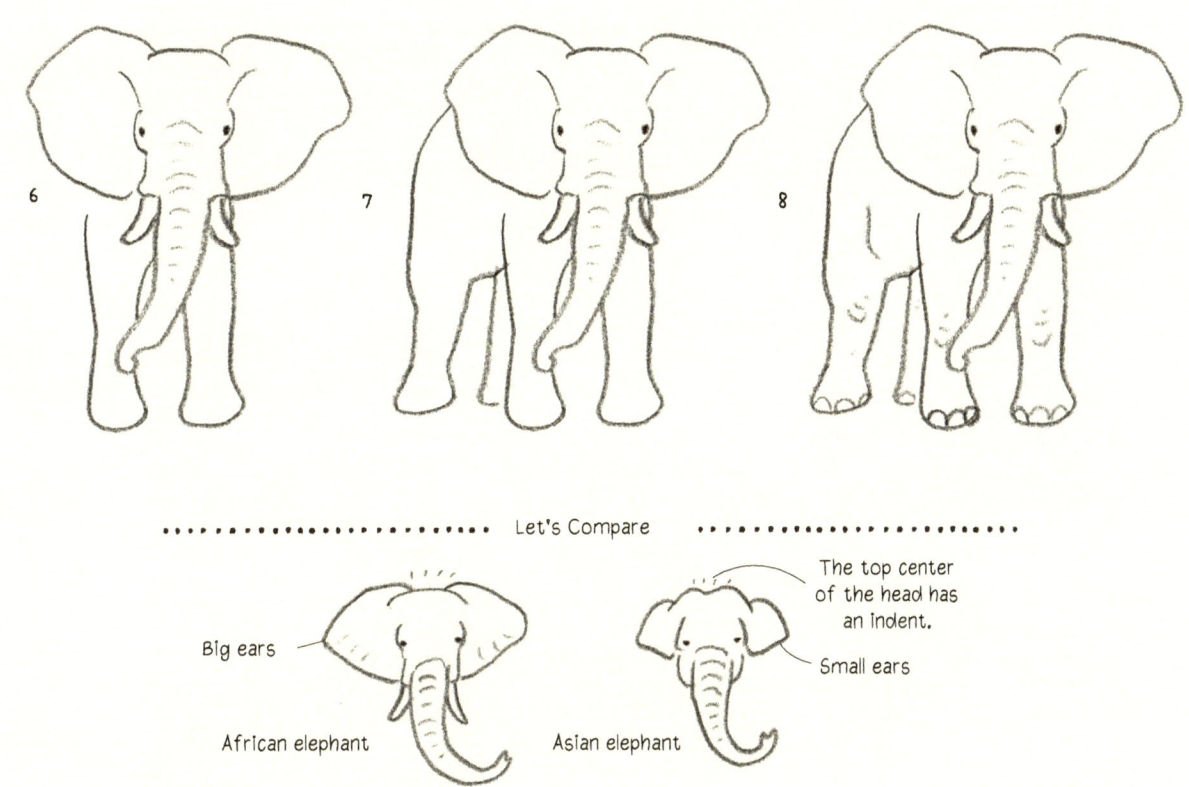

6

7

8

· Let's Compare ·

Big ears

African elephant

The top center
of the head has
an indent.

Small ears

Asian elephant

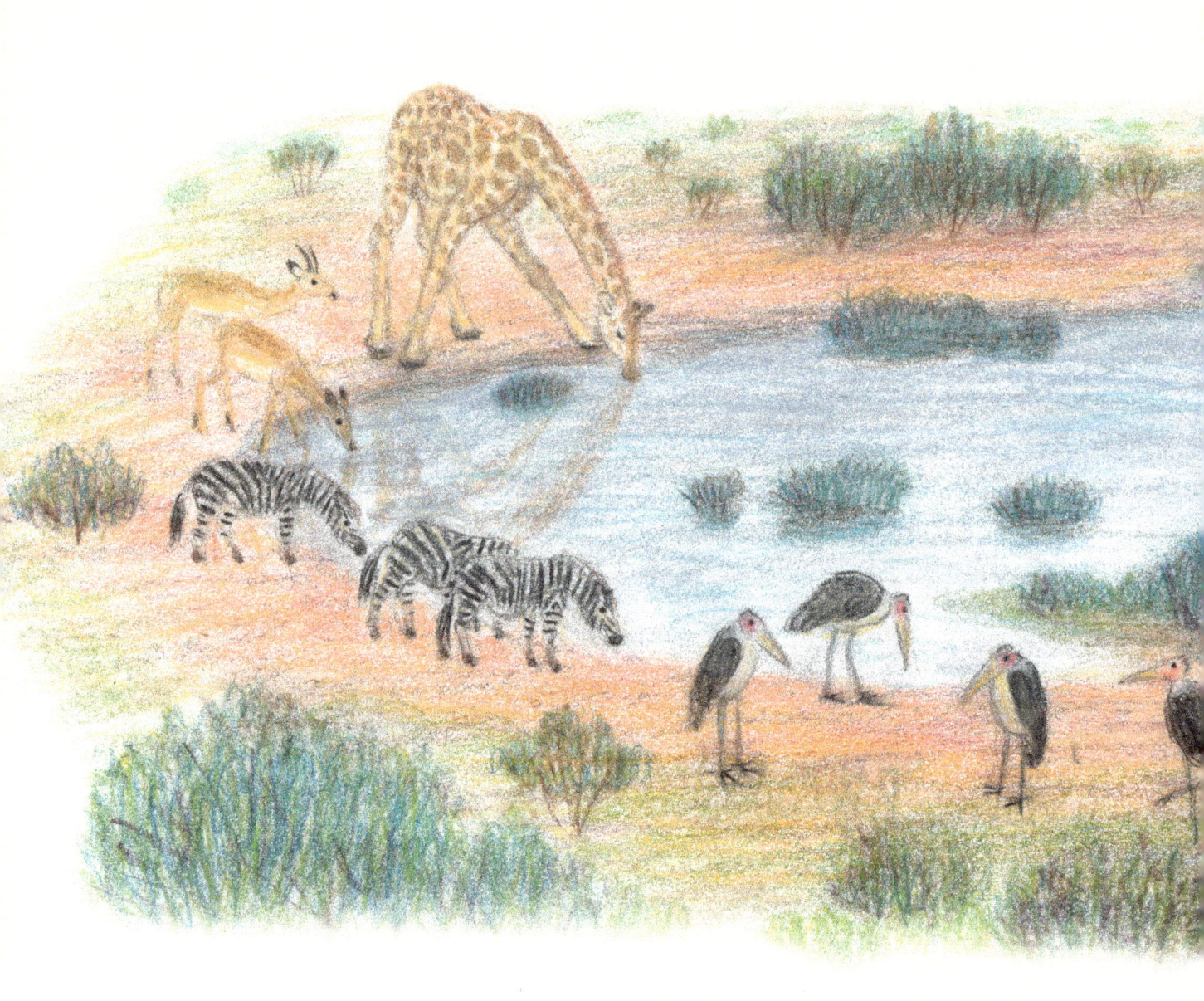

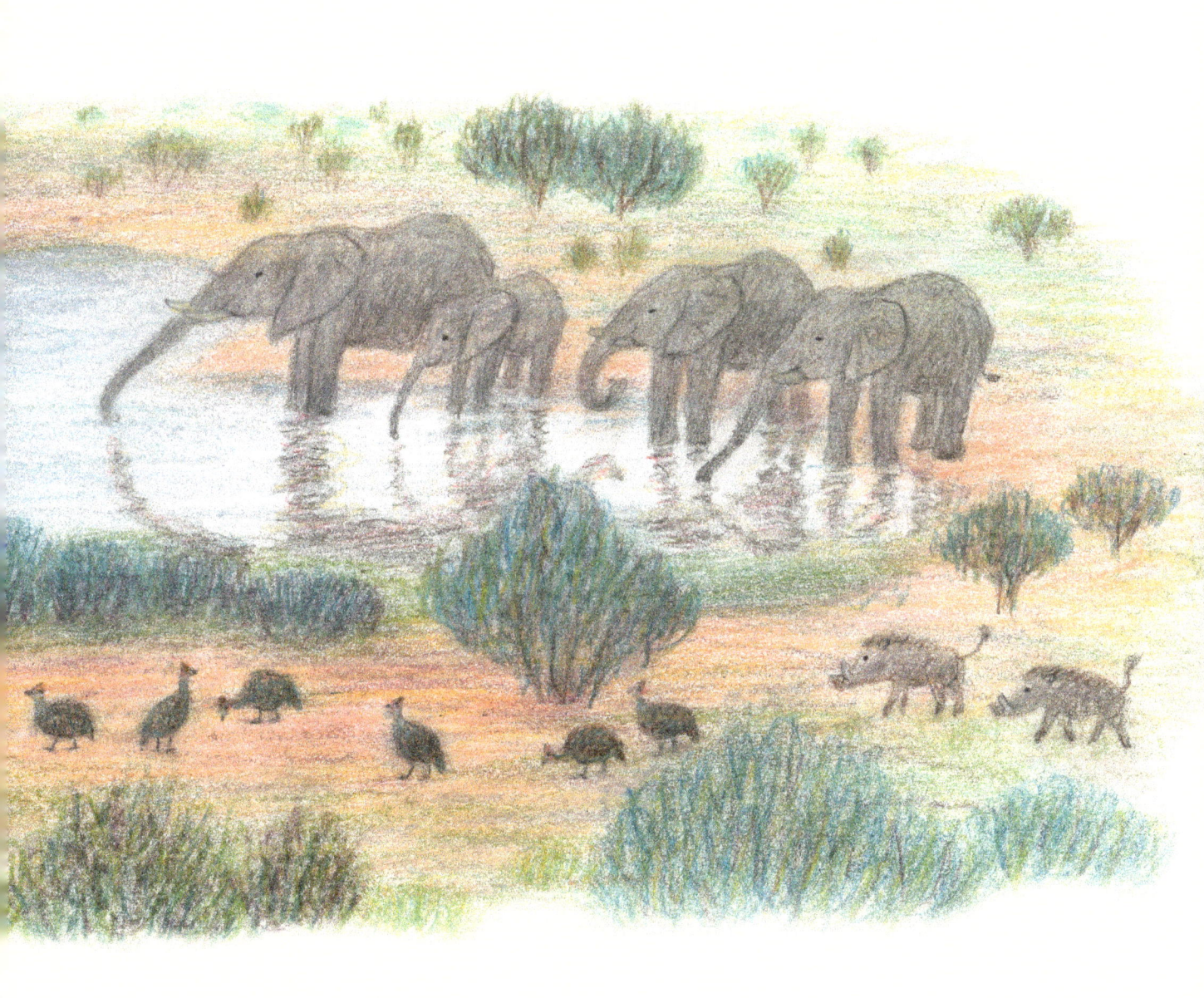

JAPANESE MACAQUE

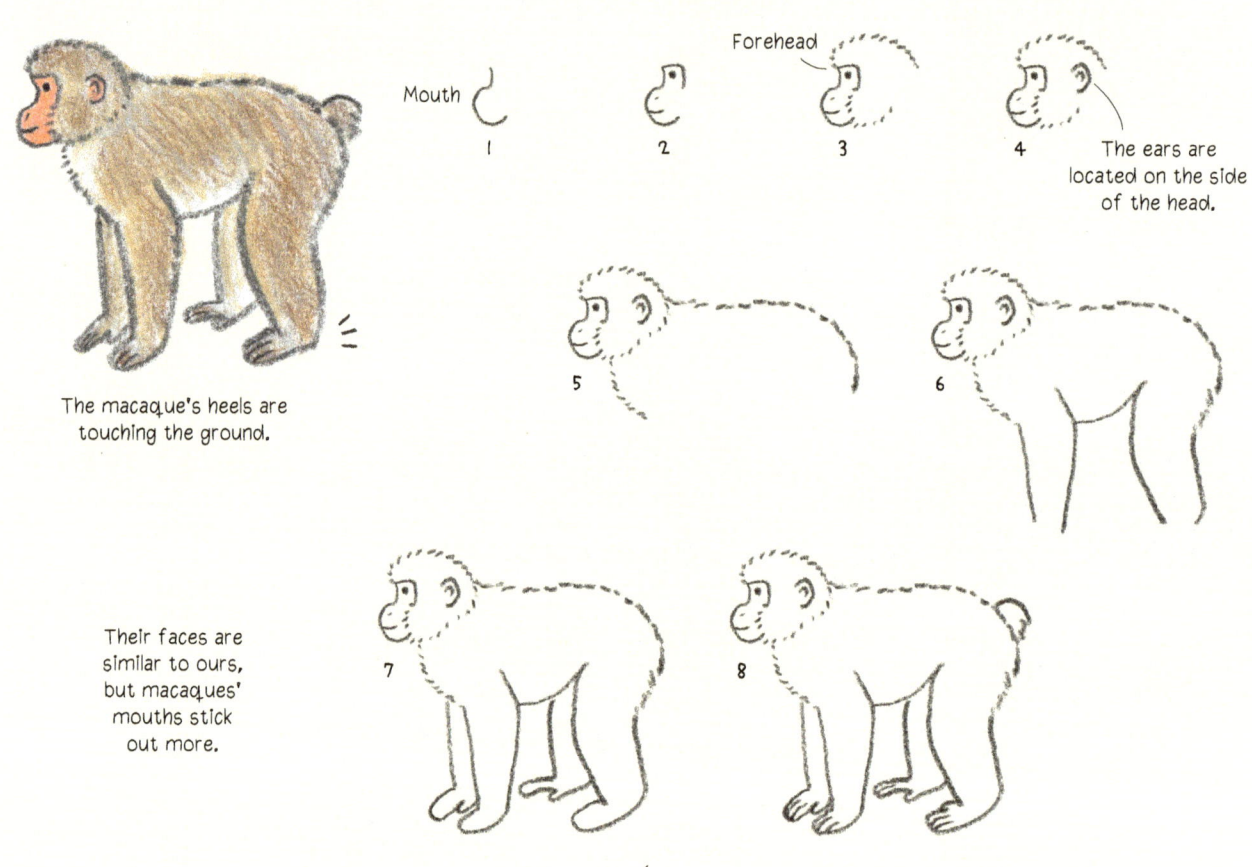

The macaque's heels are touching the ground.

Mouth

1

2

Forehead

3

4

The ears are located on the side of the head.

5

6

Their faces are similar to ours, but macaques' mouths stick out more.

7

8

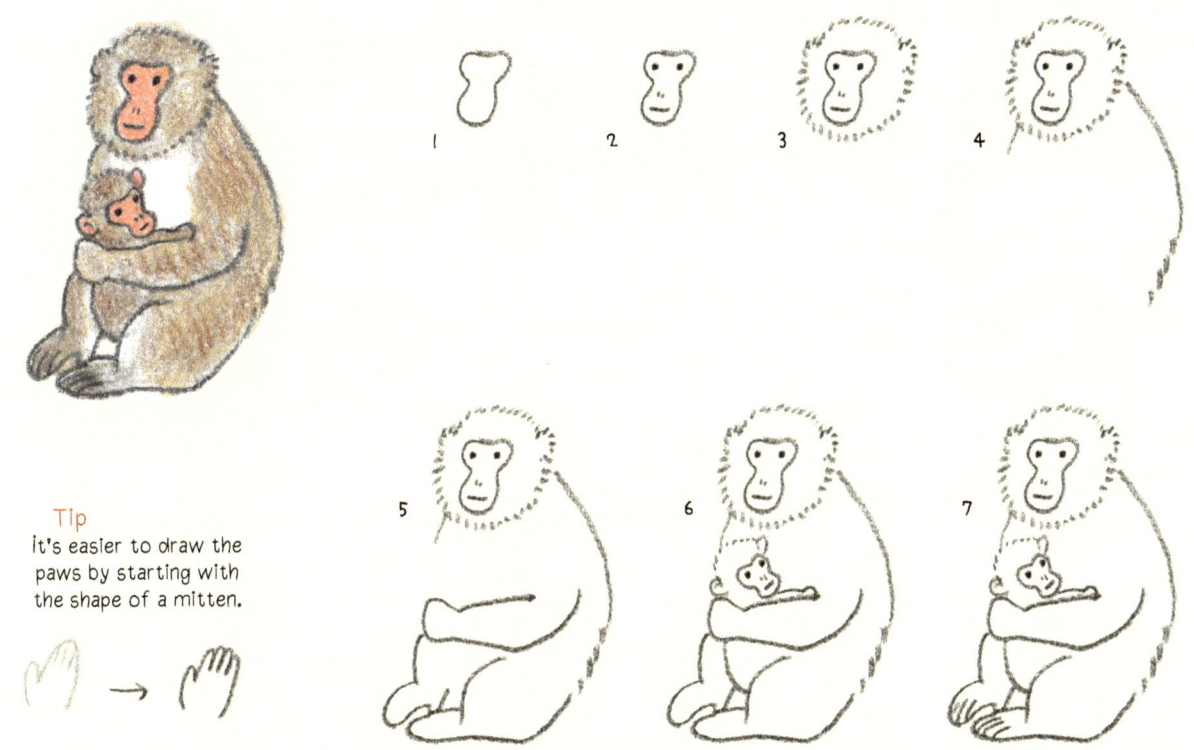

Tip
It's easier to draw the paws by starting with the shape of a mitten.

1   2   3   4

5   6   7

RING-TAILED LEMUR

1

2

3

4

5

6

7

8

9

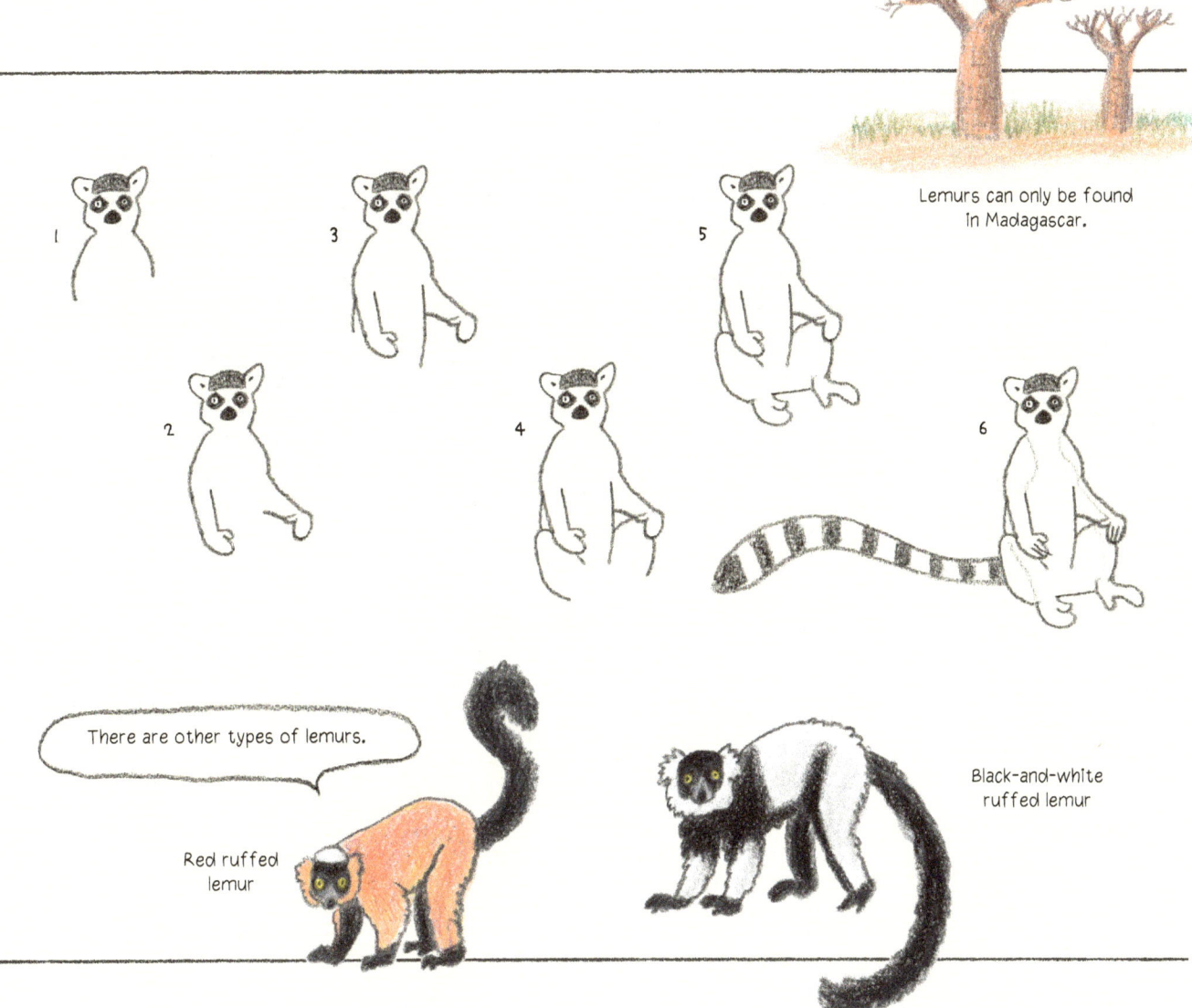

1

2

3

4

5

Lemurs can only be found in Madagascar.

6

There are other types of lemurs.

Red ruffed lemur

Black-and-white ruffed lemur

OTHER PRIMATES

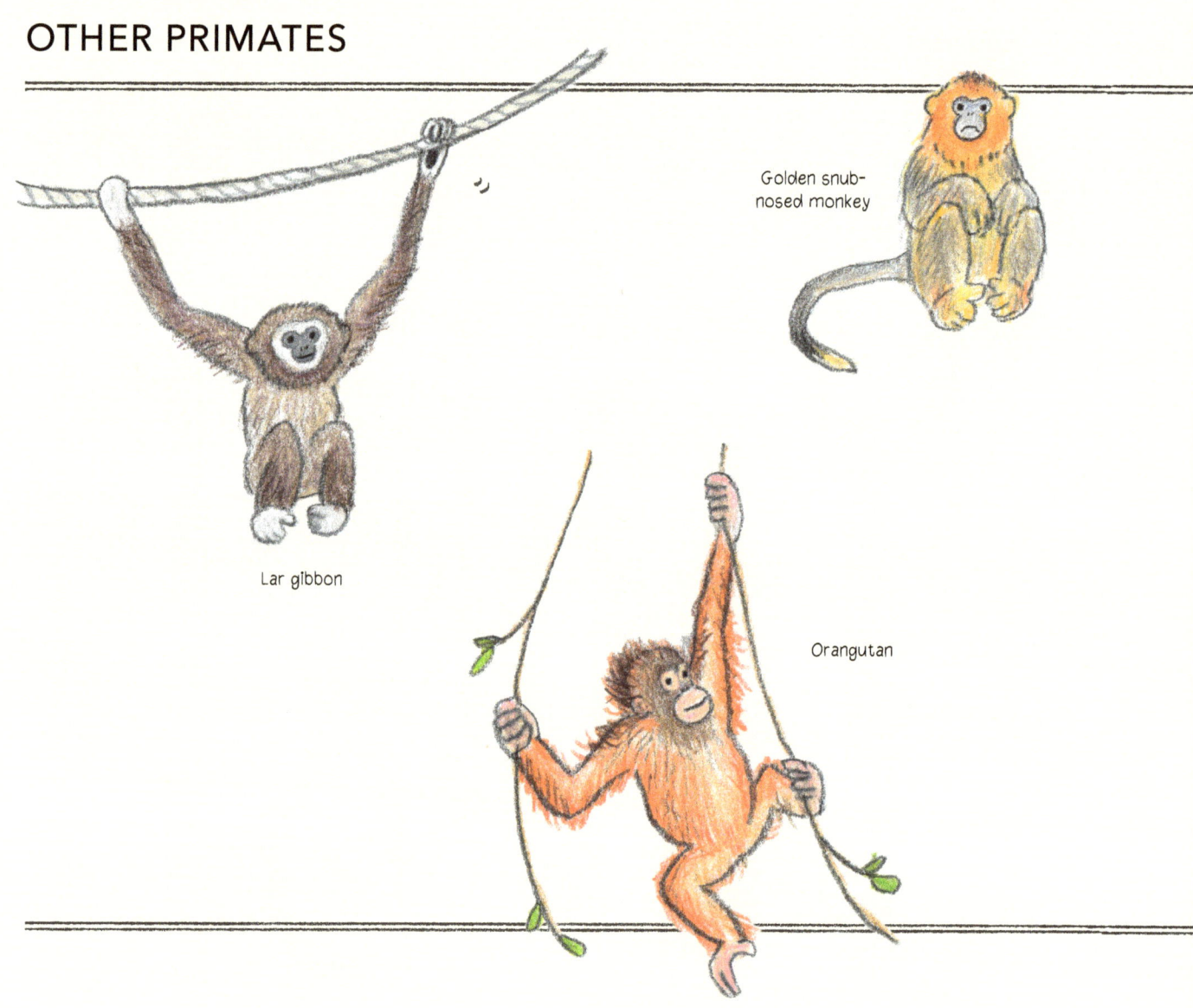

Lar gibbon

Golden snub-nosed monkey

Orangutan

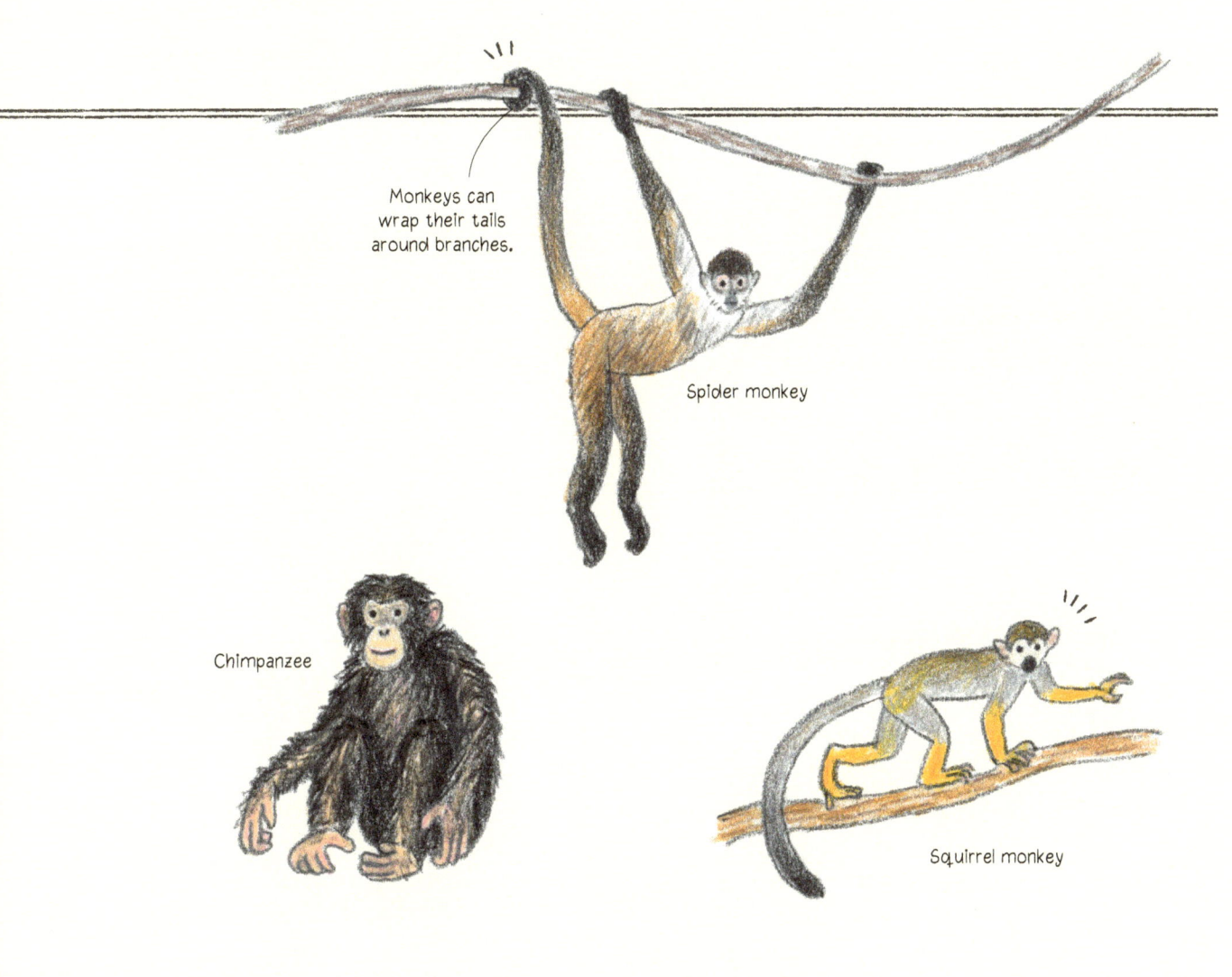

Monkeys can wrap their tails around branches.

Spider monkey

Chimpanzee

Squirrel monkey

KANGAROO

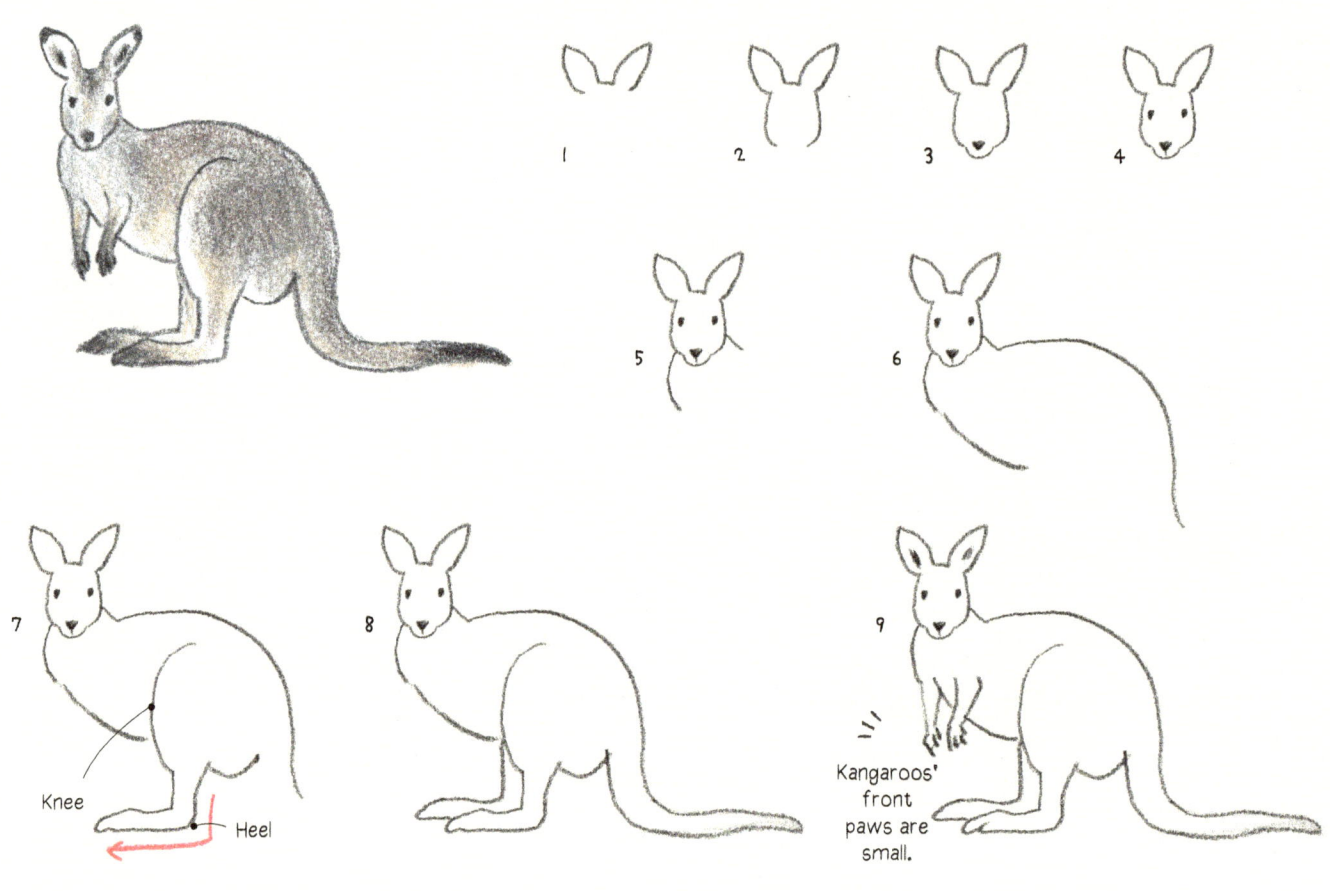

Knee

Heel

Kangaroos' front paws are small.

106

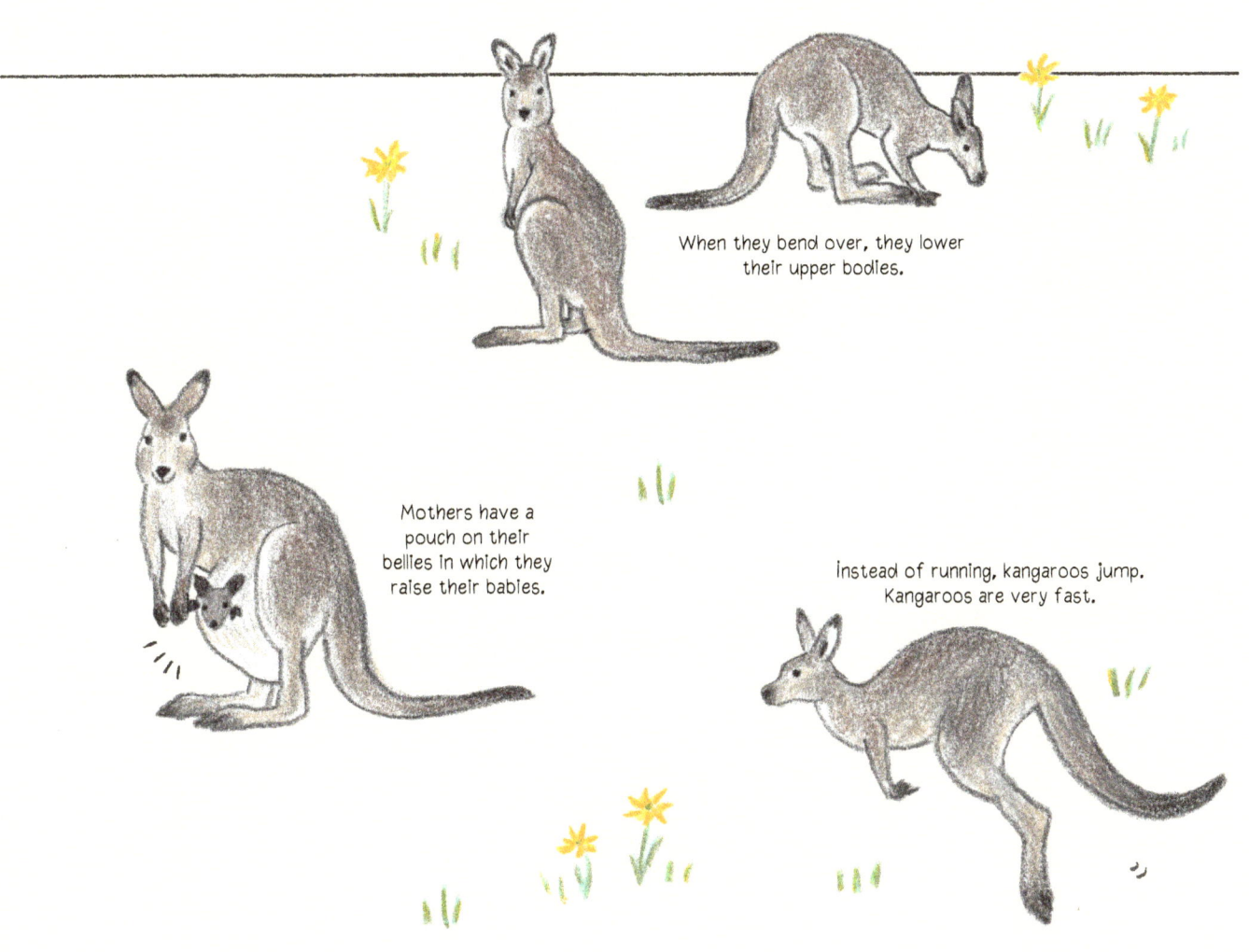

When they bend over, they lower their upper bodies.

Mothers have a pouch on their bellies in which they raise their babies.

Instead of running, kangaroos jump. Kangaroos are very fast.

KOALA BEAR

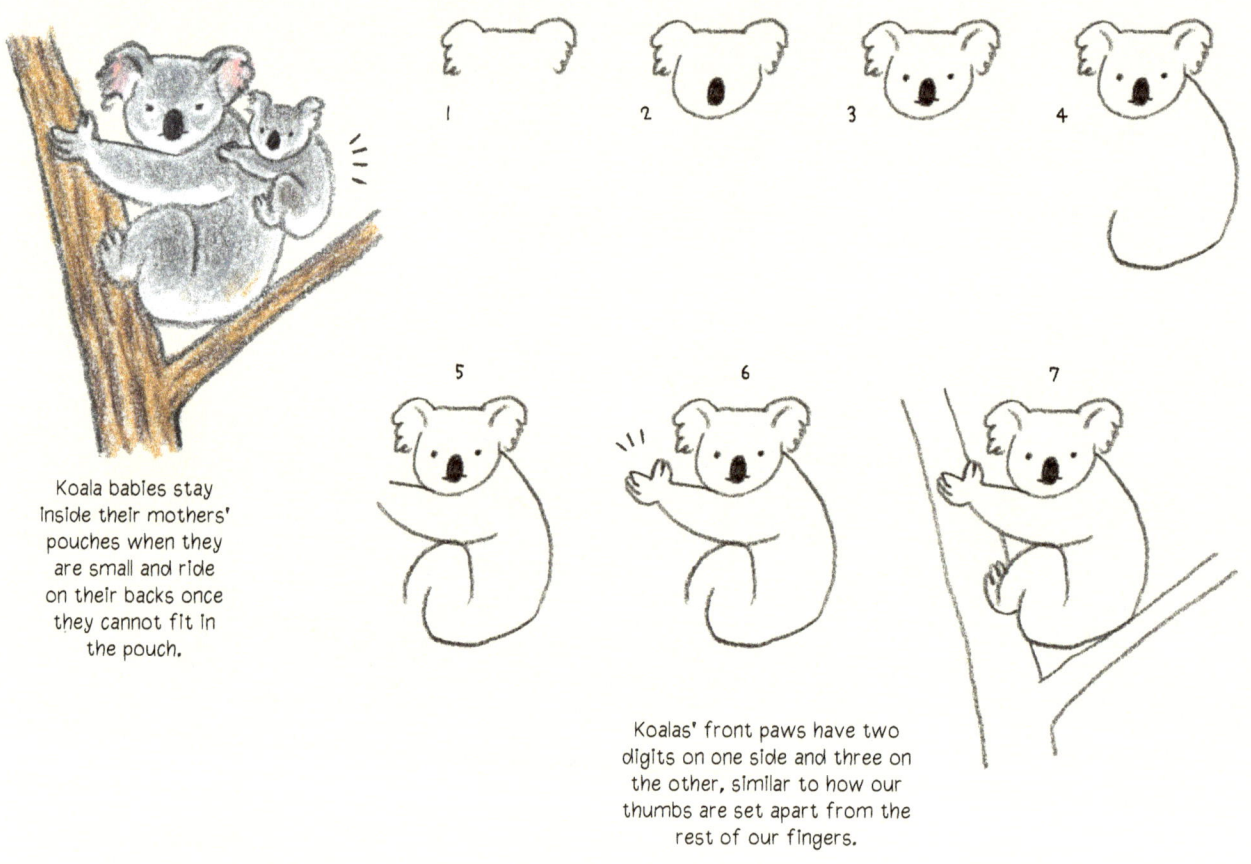

Koala babies stay inside their mothers' pouches when they are small and ride on their backs once they cannot fit in the pouch.

Koalas' front paws have two digits on one side and three on the other, similar to how our thumbs are set apart from the rest of our fingers.

1 2 3 4 5 6 7

PLATYPUS

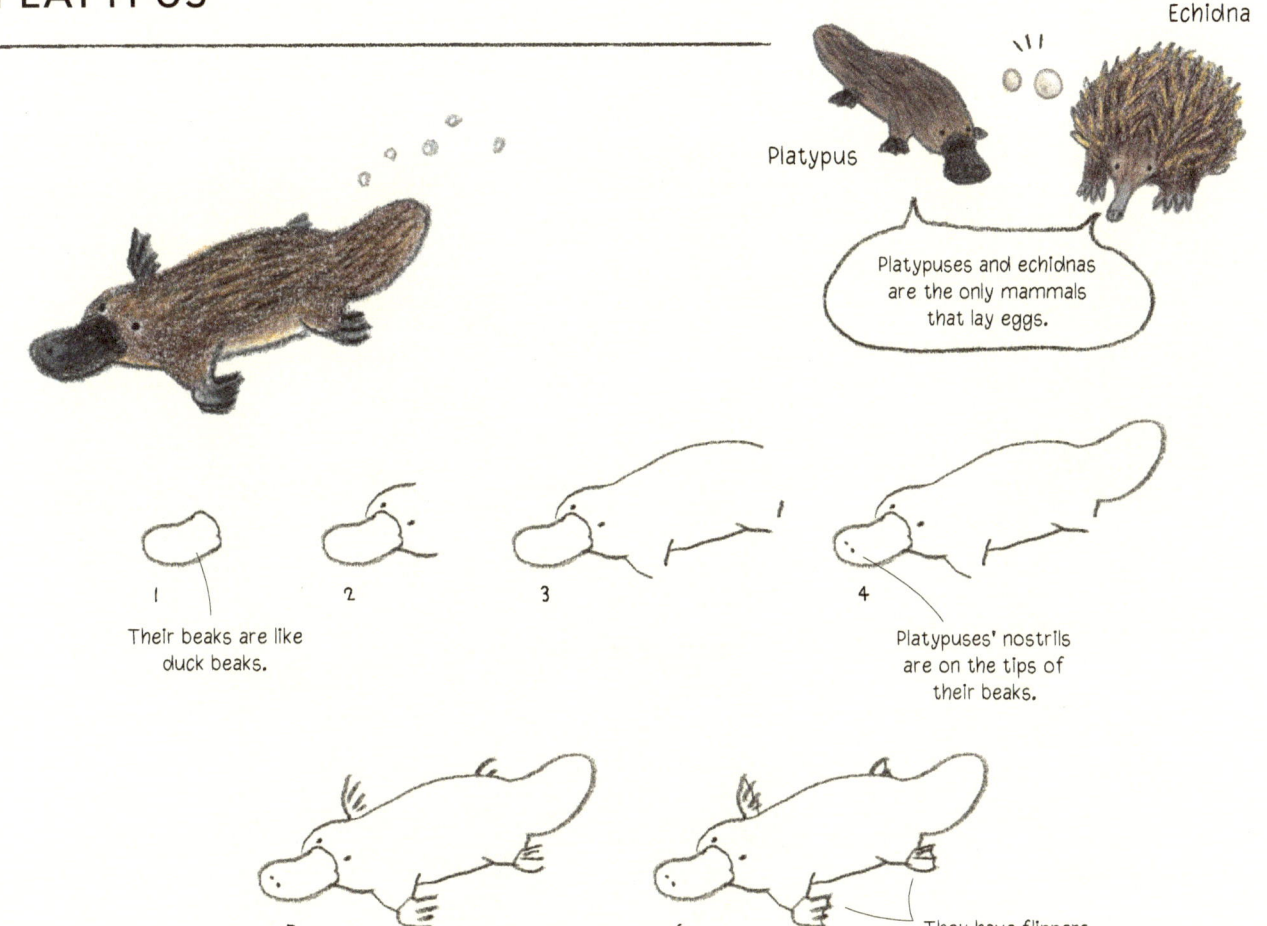

Echidna

Platypus

Platypuses and echidnas are the only mammals that lay eggs.

1

Their beaks are like duck beaks.

2

3

4

Platypuses' nostrils are on the tips of their beaks.

5

6

They have flippers.

SLOTH

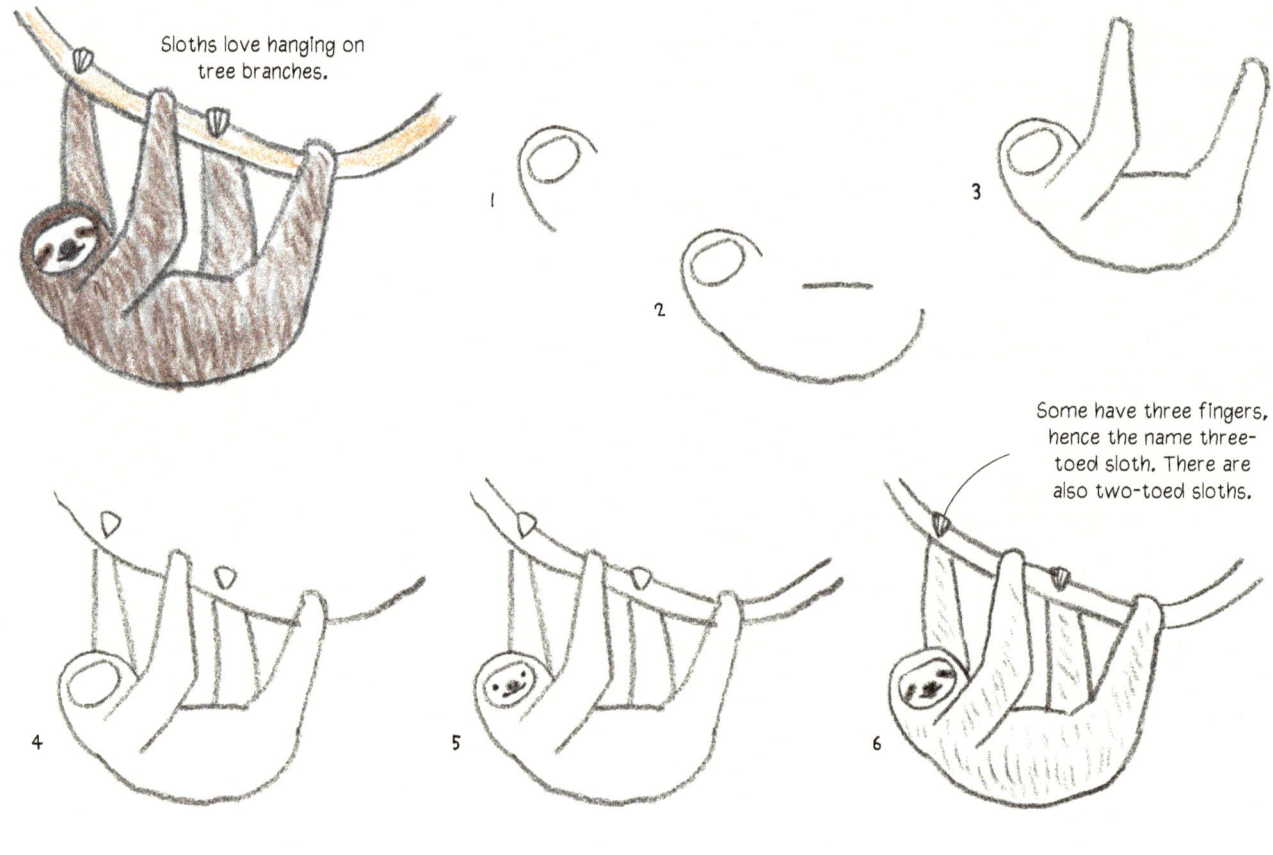

Sloths love hanging on tree branches.

1

2

3

4

5

6

Some have three fingers, hence the name three-toed sloth. There are also two-toed sloths.

BAT

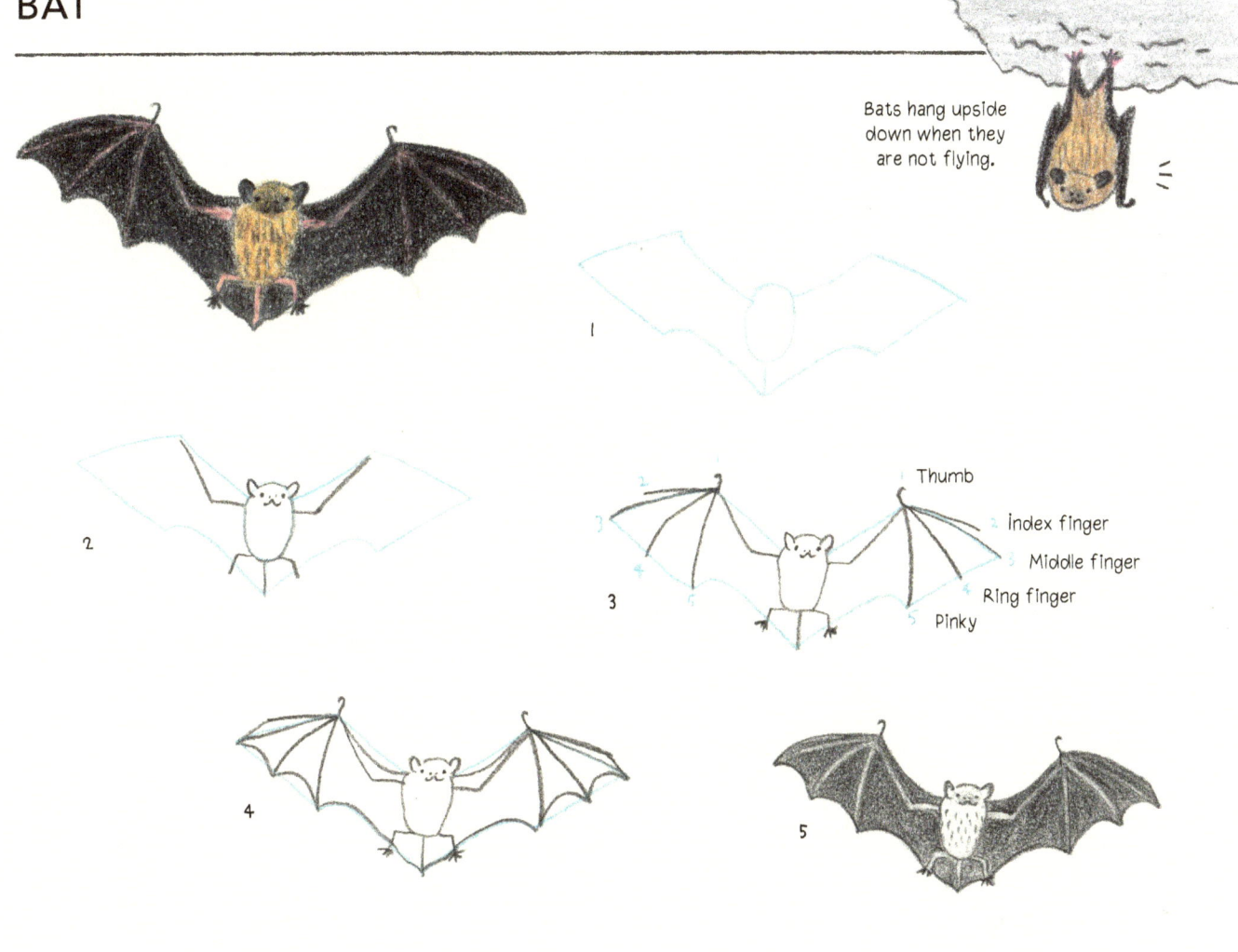

Bats hang upside down when they are not flying.

1

2

3

Thumb
Index finger
Middle finger
Ring finger
Pinky

4

5

ARMADILLO

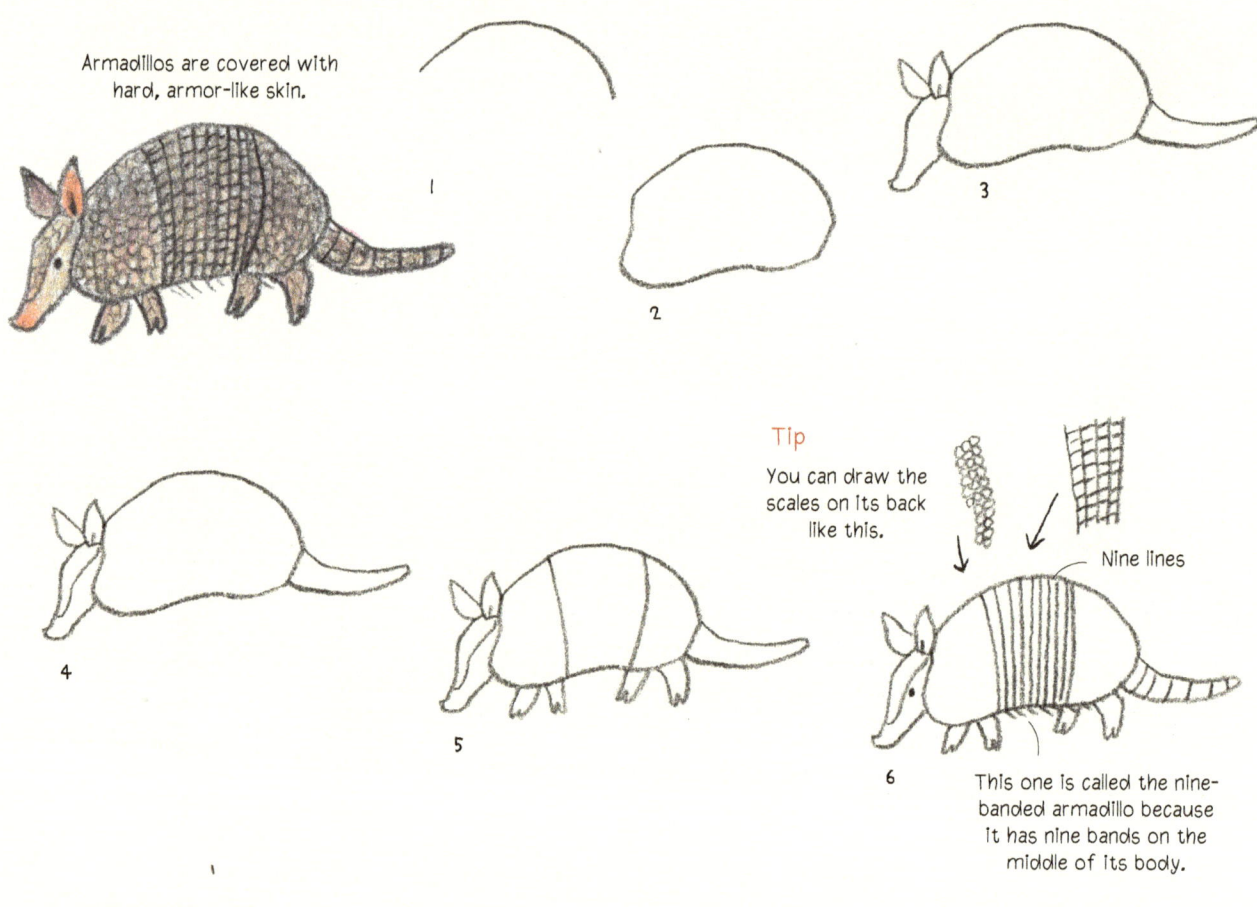

Armadillos are covered with hard, armor-like skin.

1

2

3

4

5

Tip

You can draw the scales on its back like this.

Nine lines

6

This one is called the nine-banded armadillo because it has nine bands on the middle of its body.

AARDVARK

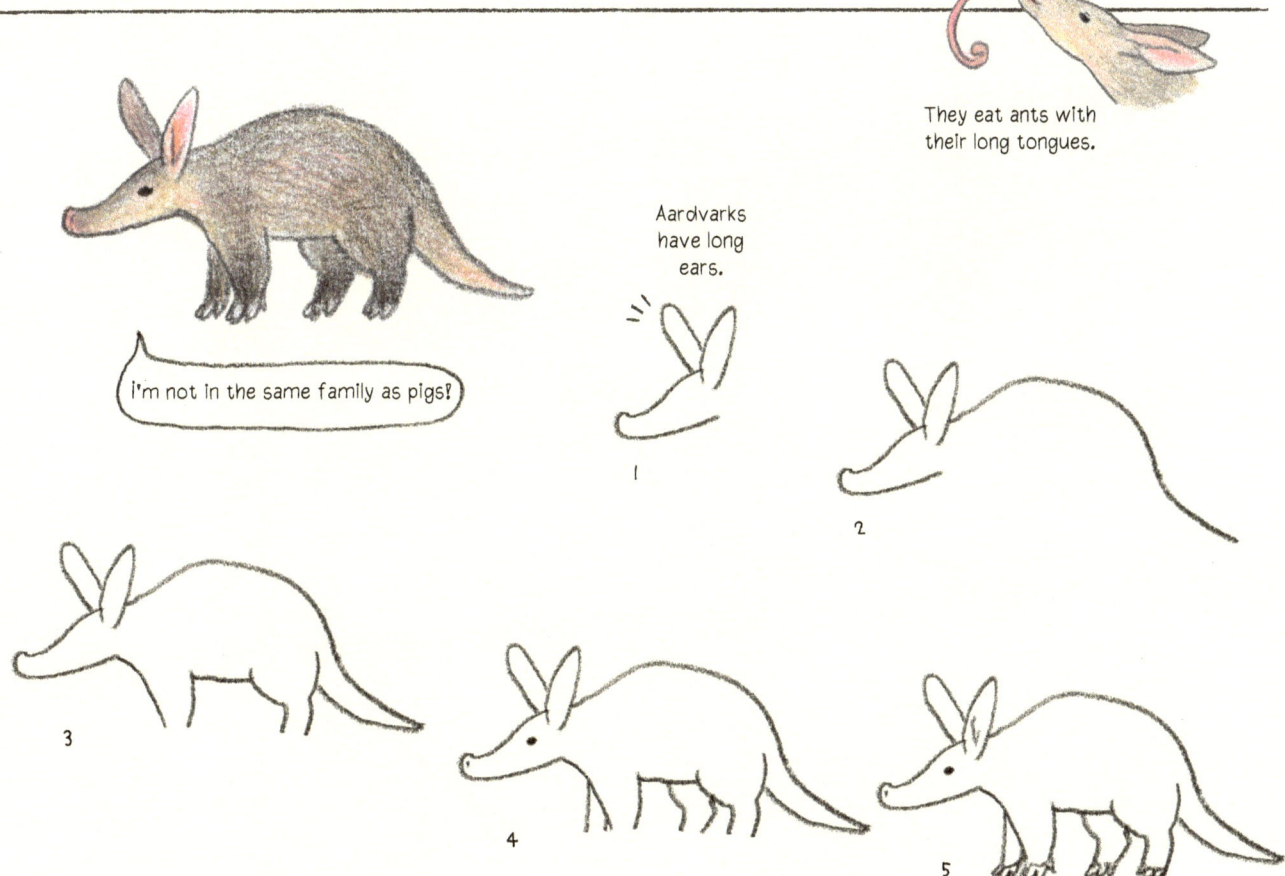

They eat ants with their long tongues.

I'm not in the same family as pigs!

Aardvarks have long ears.

1

2

3

4

5

GIANT ANTEATER

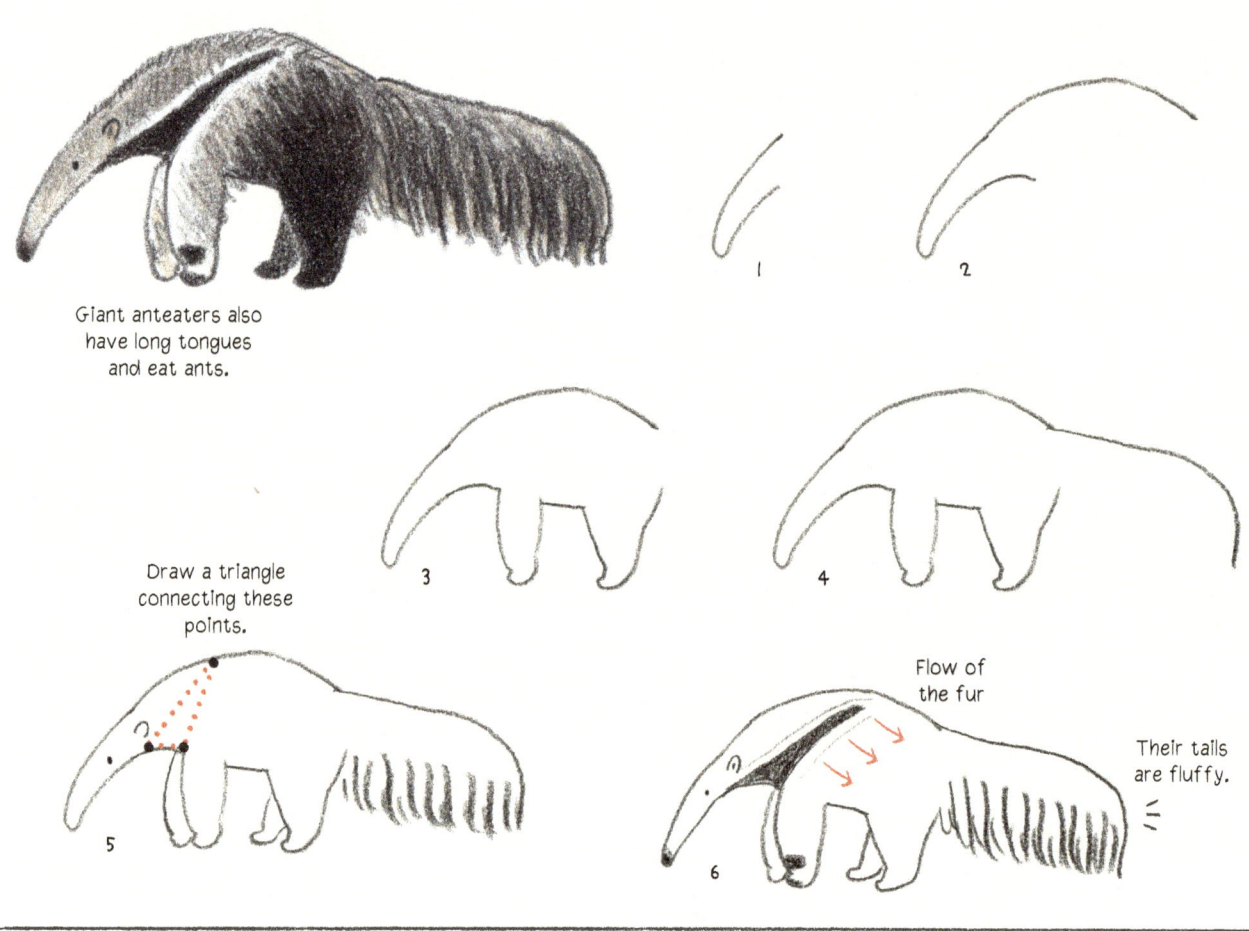

Giant anteaters also
have long tongues
and eat ants.

1

2

3

4

Draw a triangle
connecting these
points.

5

Flow of
the fur

Their tails
are fluffy.

6

TAMANDUA

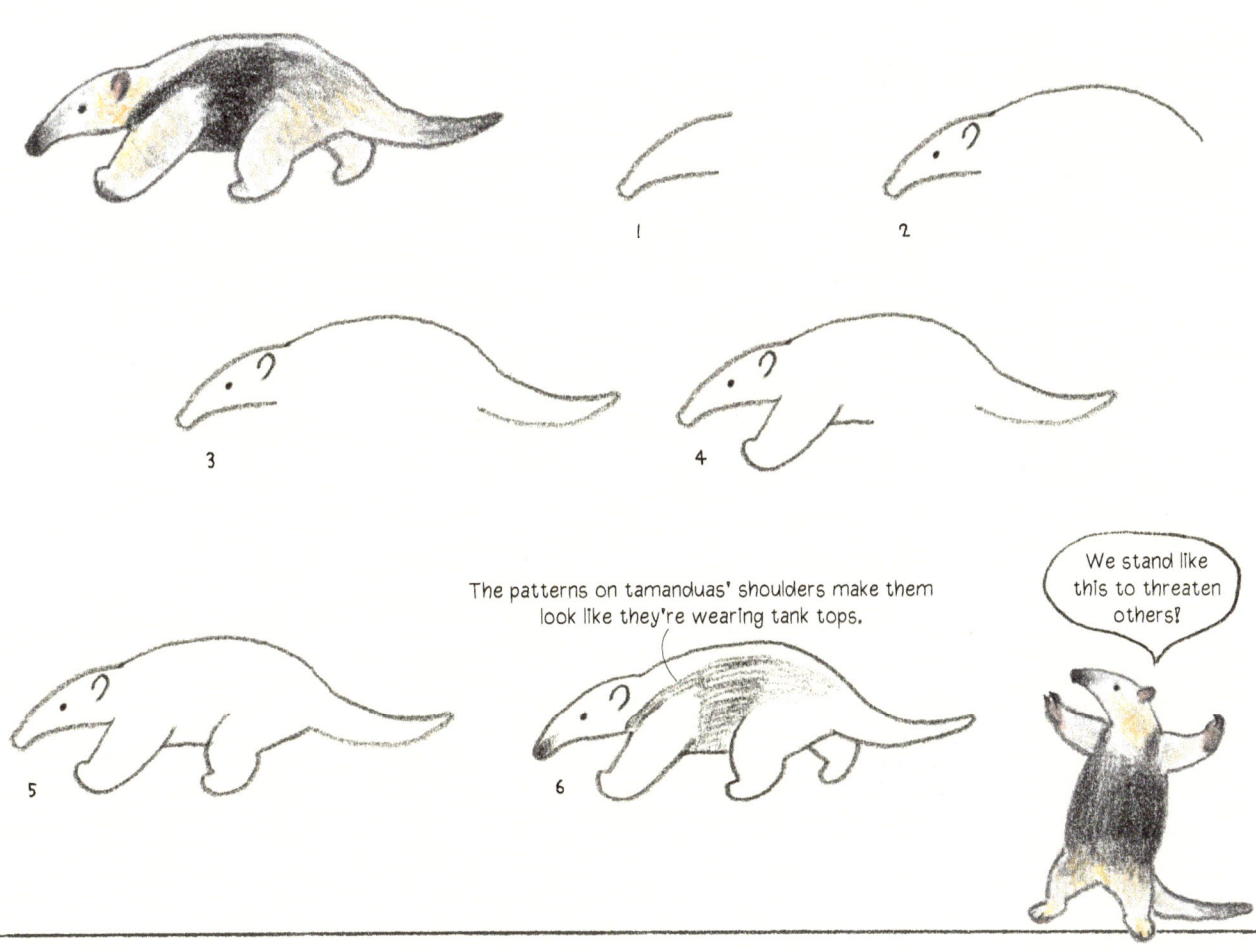

1

2

3

4

The patterns on tamanduas' shoulders make them look like they're wearing tank tops.

5

6

We stand like this to threaten others!

TAPIR

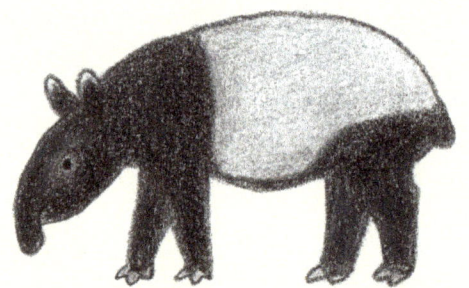

This is the Malayan tapir. It has a black-and-white pattern.

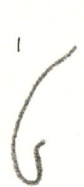

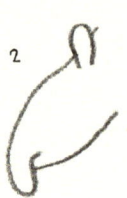

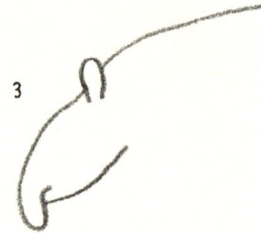

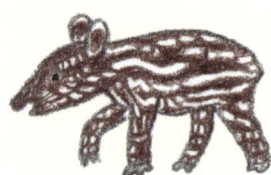

Their babies have almost the same pattern as wild boar piglets!

Tapirs' patterns begin to change as they become adults.

The front paws have four toes.

The back paws have three toes.

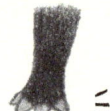

They spread their toes when they touch the ground so they don't sink into muddy places.

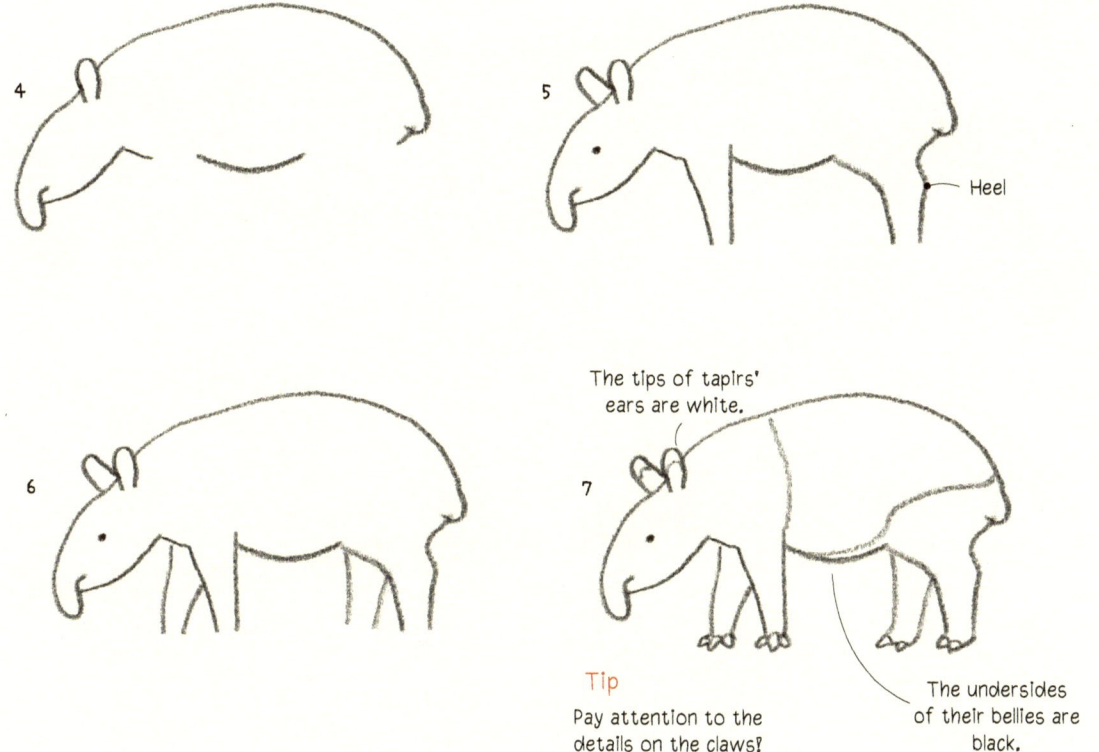

4

5 Heel

6

7

The tips of tapirs' ears are white.

The undersides of their bellies are black.

Tip

Pay attention to the details on the claws!

117

PANDA BEAR

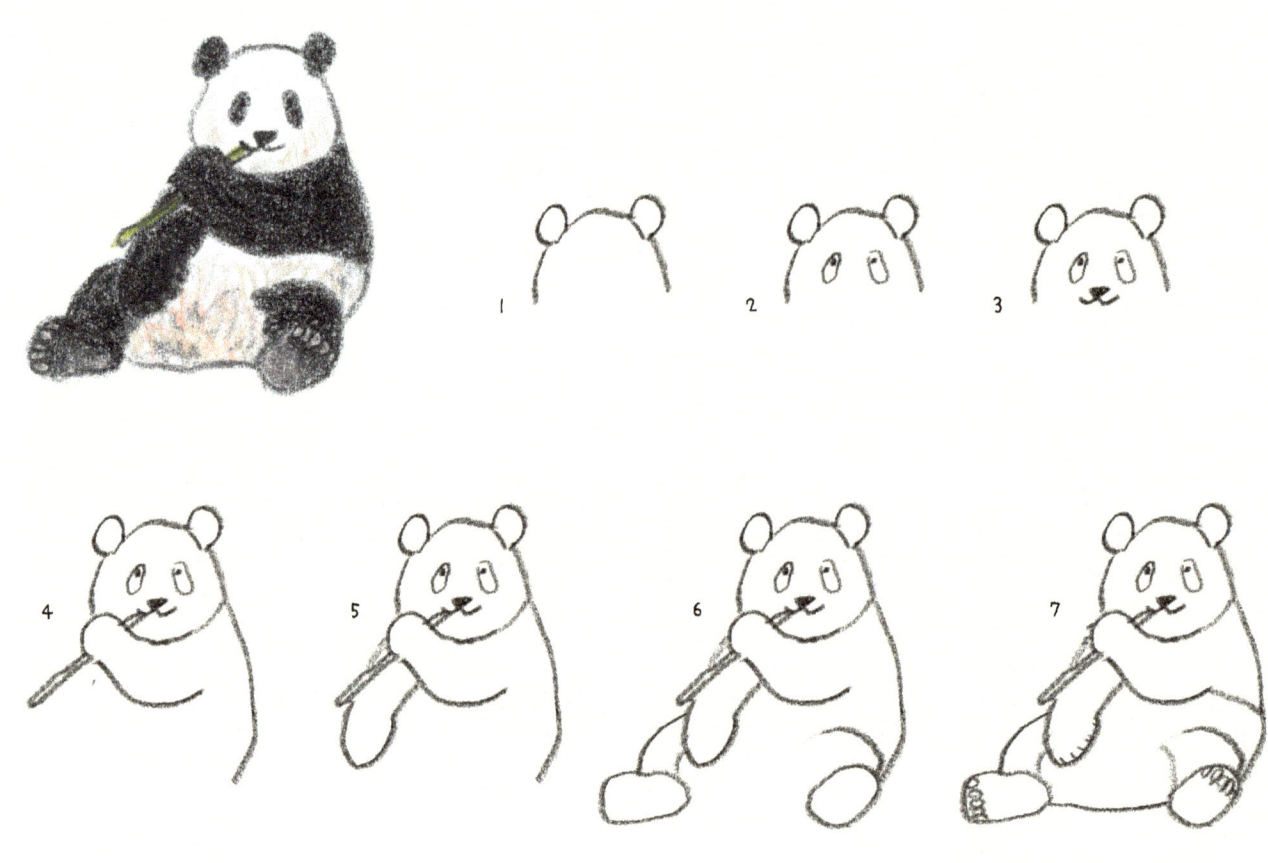

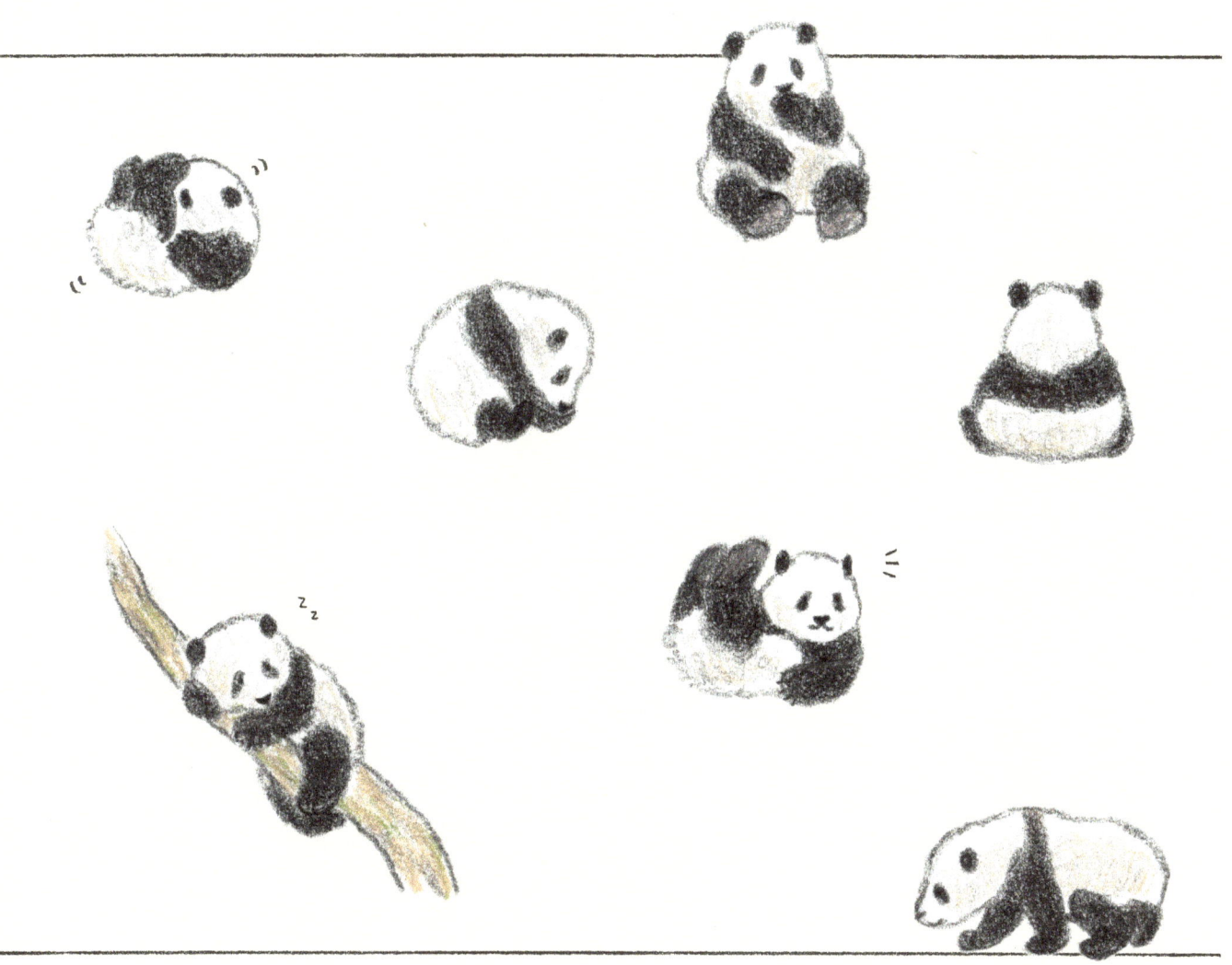

SEAL

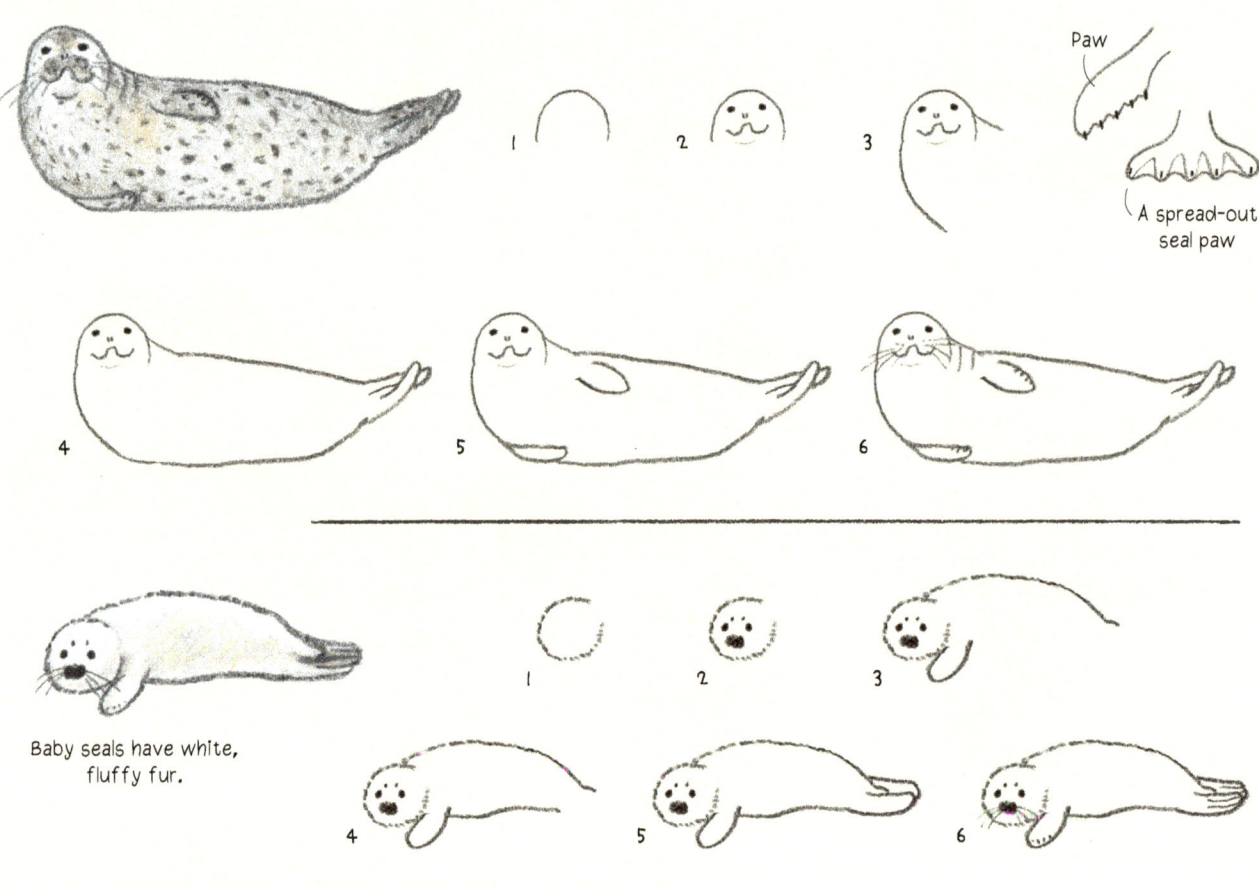

Paw

A spread-out
seal paw

1   2   3

4   5   6

Baby seals have white,
fluffy fur.

1   2   3

4   5   6

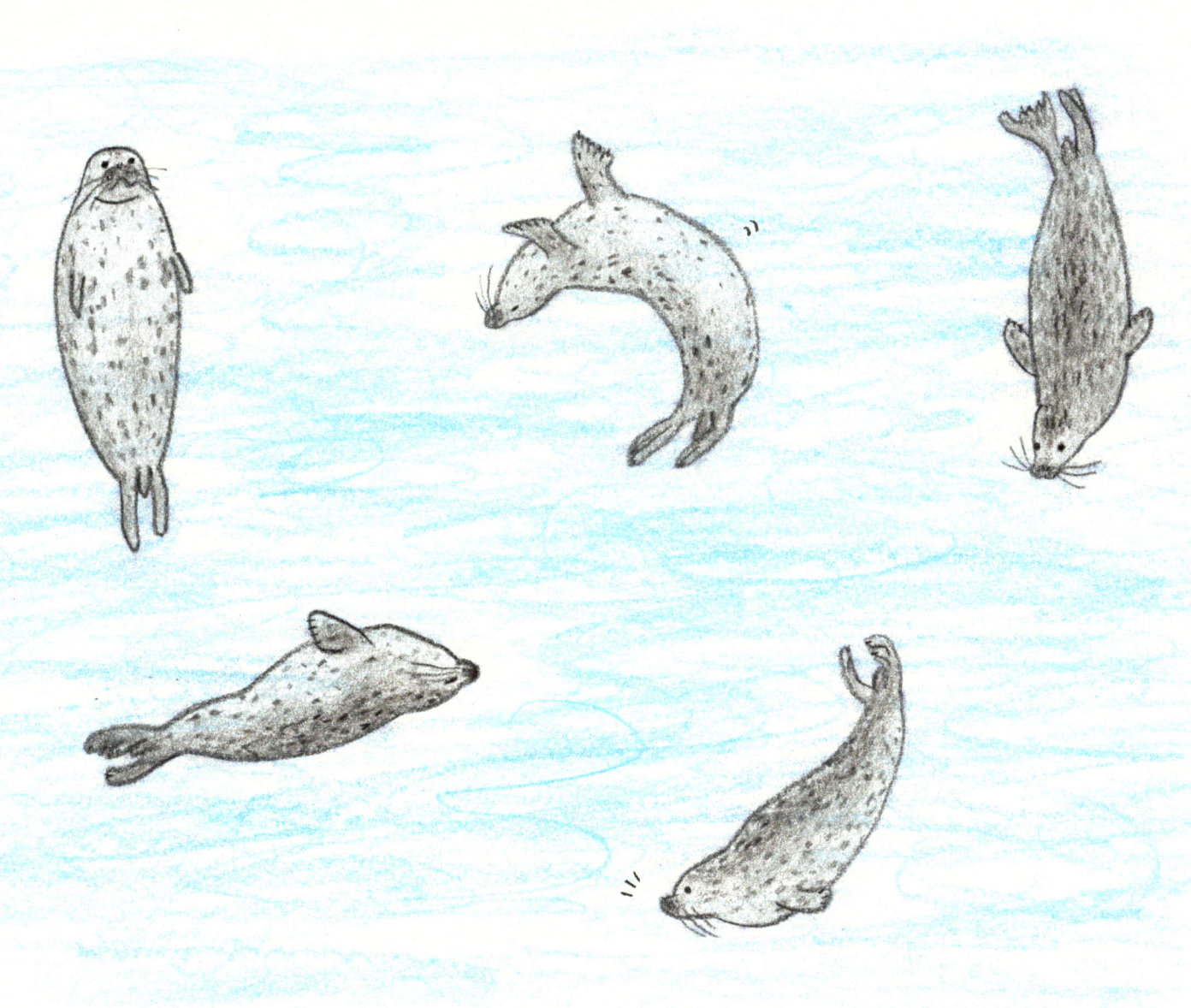

SEA LION

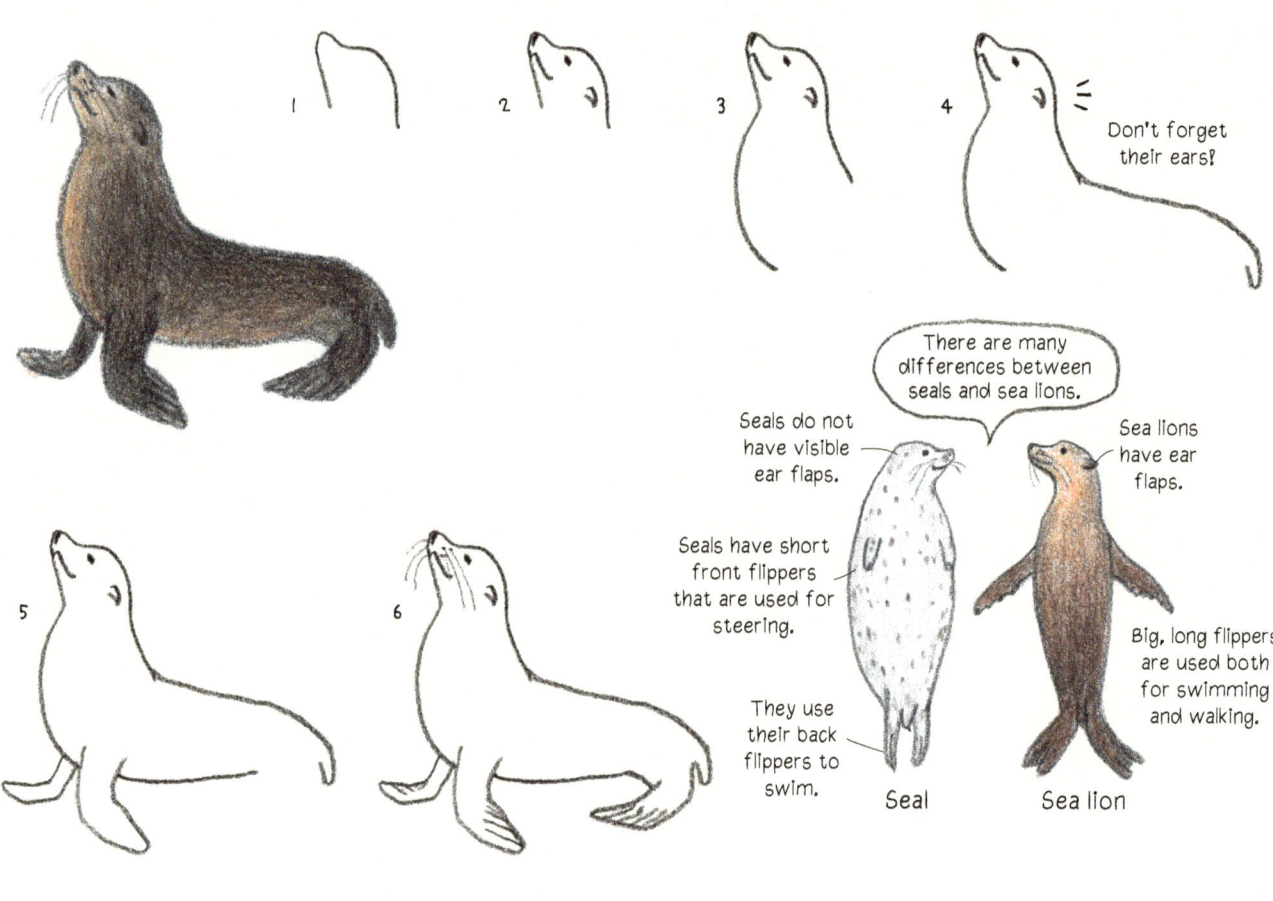

1

2

3

4 Don't forget their ears!

5

6

There are many differences between seals and sea lions.

Seals do not have visible ear flaps.

Seals have short front flippers that are used for steering.

They use their back flippers to swim.

Seal

Sea lions have ear flaps.

Big, long flippers are used both for swimming and walking.

Sea lion

WALRUS

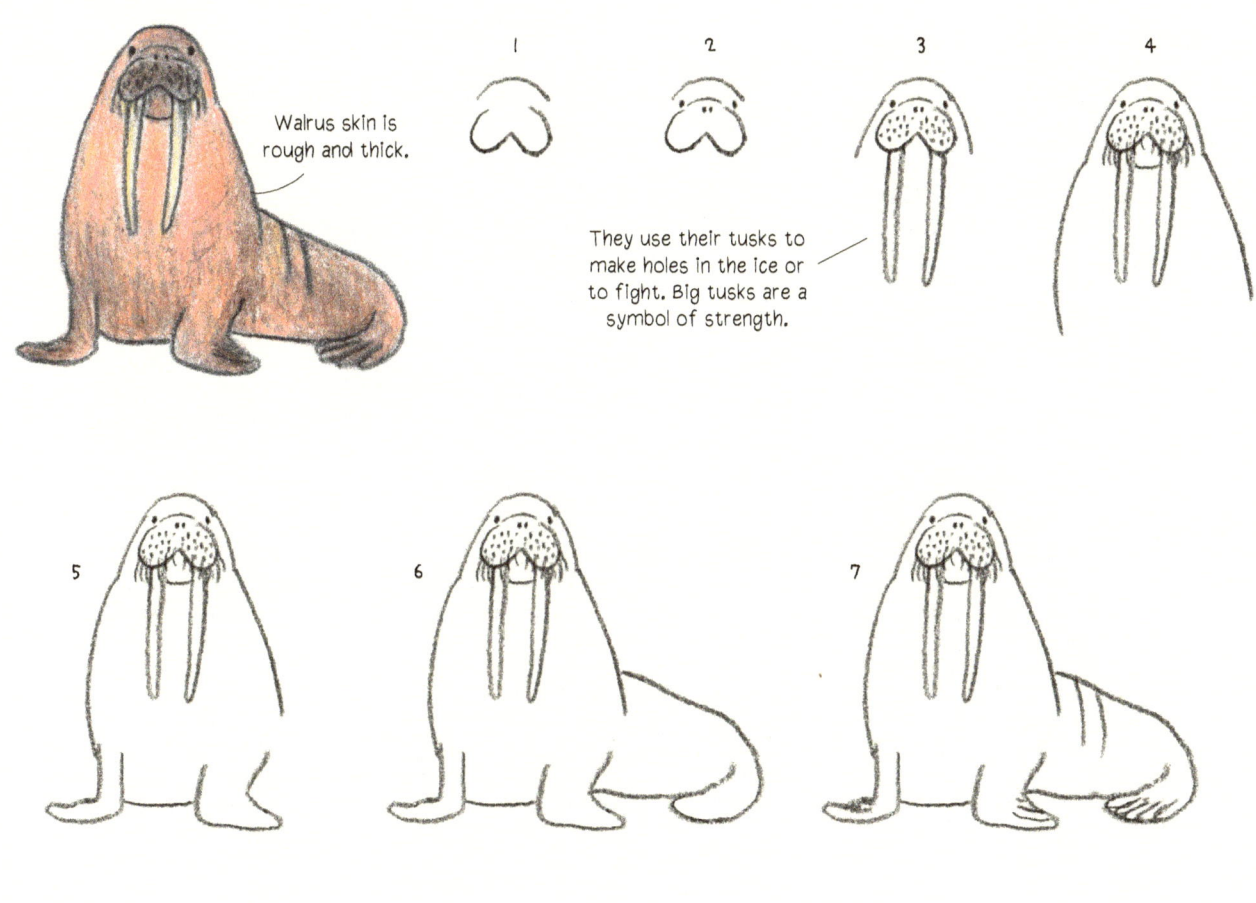

Walrus skin is rough and thick.

1

2

They use their tusks to make holes in the ice or to fight. Big tusks are a symbol of strength.

3

4

5

6

7

ABOUT THE AUTHOR

Ai Akikusa is a Japanese artist, illustrator, and picture book author based in Tokyo. She graduated from the Department of Graphic Design at Tama Art University. After working at Nakamori Design Office, she became an independent artist. Her publications include *Drawing Cute Animals in Colored Pencil*, and *Drawing Cute Birds in Colored Pencil*.

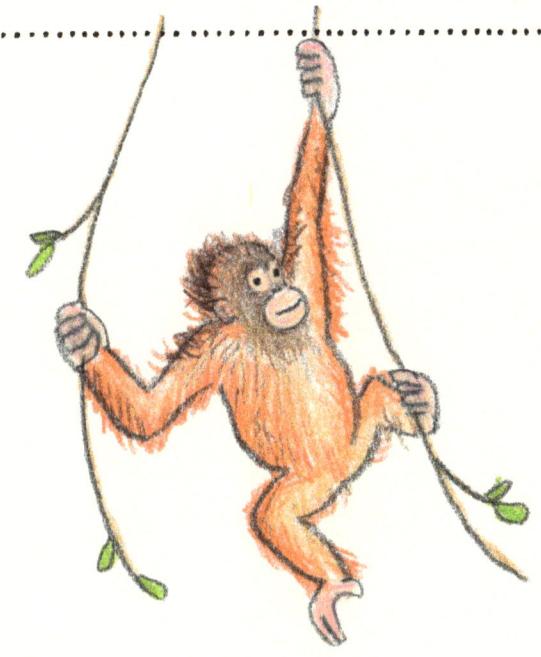

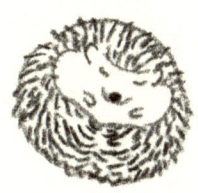

INDEX